THIRD EDITION

THE ACTIVE

LOOK IT UP!

Look it Up! with activities

PETER FORRESTAL
VIC GUEST · JO ESHUYS

NELSON
CENGAGE Learning

Australia • Brazil • Japan • Korea • Mexico • Singapore • Spain • United Kingdom • United States

NELSON
CENGAGE Learning

The Active Look It Up!
3rd Edition
Peter Forrestal
Jo Eshuys
Vic Guest

Publishing editor: Helen Sykes
Project editors: Katharine Day, Aynslie Harper
Editor: Sandra Balonyi
Text designer: Vonda Pestana
Cover designer: Vonda Pestana
Photo researcher: Corrina Tauschke
Indexer: Max McMaster
Production controller: Tanya Wasylewski
Reprint: Jess Lovell
Typeset by S4 Carlisle

Any URLs contained in this publication were checked for currency during the production process. Note, however, that the publisher cannot vouch for the ongoing currency of URLs.

For product information and technology assistance,
in Australia call **1300 790 853**;
in New Zealand call **0800 449 725**

For permission to use material from this text or product, please email
aust.permissions@cengage.com

National Library of Australia Cataloguing-in-Publication Data
Forrestal, Peter...[et al.].
The Active Look It Up!

3rd ed.
9780170183048 (pbk.)
For secondary school age

English language--Usage--Textbooks.
English language--Rhetoric--Textbooks.
English language--Usage--Juvenile literature.

428

Cengage Learning Australia
Level 7, 80 Dorcas Street
South Melbourne, Victoria Australia 3205

Cengage Learning New Zealand
Unit 4B Rosedale Office Park
331 Rosedale Road, Albany, North Shore 0632, NZ

For learning solutions, visit **cengage.com.au**

Printed in China by China Translation & Printing Services.
5 6 7 8 9 10 11 17 16 15 14 13

CONTENTS

Acknowledgements.. v

How to use this book... vi

1 LANGUAGE CONVENTIONS: SPELLING... 1

Improving your spelling.. 1

Understanding dictionaries.................................... 19

2 LANGUAGE CONVENTIONS: PUNCTUATION............................... 21

Apostrophes 21

Brackets.. 23

Capital letters... 23

Colons 25

Commas... 25

Dashes 27

Ellipsis points 27

Exclamation marks 28

Full stops 28

Hyphens 29

Italics 30

Question marks.. 31

Quotation marks.. 31

Semicolons 33

3 LANGUAGE CONVENTIONS: GRAMMAR 35

Paragraphs 35

Sentences... 36

Clauses 36

Phrases 36

Types of sentences... 37

Word order.. 39

Inflection 40

Content words 41

Structural words 52

Grammar and usage 57

4 LANGUAGE CONVENTIONS: USAGE 60

Usage conventions 60

5 LANGUAGE: REGISTER AND STYLE....................................... 76

Register 76

Style.. 77

Inclusive language 80

6 PUBLISHING CONVENTIONS 85

Numbers 85

Titles 88

Referencing 89

Bibliographies 90

Quoting other writers... 90

Formatting your written work 93

Good writing practice for any occasion.......................... 95

7 INTRODUCING TYPES OF TEXTS 99

Audience 99

Purpose 101

Choosing a written text type 101

Text types and essay writing 103

8 IMAGINATIVE TEXT TYPES 105

Descriptions 105

Recounts 106

Narratives 108

Drama scripting 110

Film and television scripting 113

Poetry 116

9 INFORMATION TEXT TYPES 118

Explanations 118

Procedures 120

Descriptions 121

Recounts 122

Reports 122

Film and television documentaries 124

Newspaper reports 125

Feature articles 128

Letters 130

Job applications 134

Résumés 138

10 ARGUMENT TEXT TYPES 140

Presenting an argument 140

Persuasion text types 143

Discussion text types 144

Editorials 145

Letters to the editor 148

Responses (or reviews) 151

11 ORAL TEXT TYPES 156

Types of oral texts 156

Giving a talk 156

Working in small groups 161

Debating 162

Interviews 166

12 VIEWING IMAGES: THE CONVENTIONS OF VISUAL GRAMMAR 168

Balance 168

Colour 168

Contextualised and decontextualised 169

Foreground and background 169

Framing, frame breaking and bleeding 170

Intertextuality 170

Layout 171

Line and shape 171

Offers and demands 171

Perspective 172

Portrait and landscape 172

The reading path 172

Salience 173

Social distance 173

Texture 173

Typography 173

Vanishing point 174

Vectors 174

Vertical and horizontal axes 174

Viewing angle 174

13 VISUAL TEXT TYPES 175

Cartoons 175

Advertisements 176

Websites 177

Films 179

Index 183

ACKNOWLEDGEMENTS

This book is dedicated to my very good friend, Janice Hawkins (1943–1982).

The third edition of this book has been possible because of the vision, sheer hard work and painstaking attention to detail of Helen Sykes and the team at Cengage. Its origins owe much to my wonderfully talented friend and colleague Jo-Anne Reid and to the work of Judith Rivalland and Sarah Fitzherbert. Along the way, Helen Sykes wrote 'Types of Text' and Joanna Gardiner played the pivotal role in the second edition. Thanks also to Judy Embrey and Beverley Pennell for their contributions to this third edition.

The publishers and editorial staff at Cengage over the years have given great support. I thank Eleanor Curtain for her patience and steadfast belief in this book through its long gestation period; Averill Chase and Jackie Tidey for their encouragement and advice; Angelo Calandra for his support and supervision during previous editions and the amazing Jane Moylan for her dazzling effort during the second edition.

Peter Forrestal

The authors and publishers would like gratefully to credit or acknowledge the following sources for permission to use copyright material.

Images and illustrations:

© Advertising Archives. Image Courtesy of The Advertising Archives: p. 177; Corbis Australia: p. 172 (right); Getty Images: p. 100 (theatre audience, using computer); Always Adam, by Sheldon Oberman, illustrated by Ted Lewin, Gollancz Children's Paperback London, 1995: p. 169 (top left & right); Mark Fergus Photography: p. 180; MIRAMAX/DIMENSION FILMS / THE KOBAL COLLECTION: p. 182; Ziba Came on a Boat, written by Liz Lofthouse, illustrated by Robert Ingpen, Penguin/Viking 2007. Reproduced with permission of Penguin Group (Australia): p. 169 (lower left & right); Photolibrary: pp. 100 (boy studying), 172 (left); Photos12.com/Collection Cinema Rumbalara Film (Australia) Pty Ltd: p. 181; © Sean Leahy. Available as free e-cards or signed prints at: http://www.leahy.com.au; also on Facebook at: http://www.facebook.com/leahycartoons: p. 176; © Shaun Tan, reproduced with permission: p. 178; Shutterstock: pp. 100 (texting, job interview, talking on phone, watching TV, talking, reading novel), 123; Copyright © 1983 Anthony Browne From GORILLA by Anthony Browne Reproduced by permission of Walker Books Australia on behalf of Walker Books Ltd, London SE115HJ: p. 170

Text:

The Macquarie Library. p.617 from The Concise Macquarie Dictionary 5th edition, p. 617, ISBN: 9781876429850. Reproduced with permission: p. 19; Extract from Looking for Alibrandi (Screenplay) by Melina Marchetta © Belle Ragazze Pty Ltd 2000. Reproduced by permission from Currency Press Pty Ltd, Sydney Australia: pp. 114-115; 'Fish of the day hooks the gourmets', Richard North, Independent, 1 April 1987: p. 126; 'A grim tale of humourless narks', Miranda Devine, Sydney Morning Herald, 30th September 2004 © Fairfax: p. 128; © MagpiesMagazine Pty Ltd: p. 132; Huxley, J 2002, 'Such sincere, sensitive exploitation', Sydney Morning Herald, 9 September 2002 © Fairfax: pp. 147-148; Kerry Bashford 2005, Lord of the Rings Part 1, NineMSN Movie Guide, viewed 14 January 2005: p. 154; Looking for Alibrandi, by Melina Marchetta copyright © 1992, Reproduced with Permission of Penguin Group (Australia): p. 159.

Every attempt has been made to trace and acknowledge copyright holders. Where the attempt has been unsuccessful, the publisher welcomes information that would redress the situation.

HOW TO USE THIS BOOK

The Active Look It Up! is a reference book about the English language and how to use it. You will refer to it regularly when you want to improve your skills as a writer, a reader, a viewer, a speaker and a listener. Spend some time looking through the table of contents and then browsing through the book to give you an idea of the kind of help that is available to you here.

This is not a book that you will read through from cover to cover. You will turn to particular sections of the book when you need them. If you are about to take part in a debate, you will turn to that section in the chapter on oral text types. If you have never participated in a formal debate before, you will find here everything you need to know. However, it is more likely that you have done some debating in the past, so you will use this section to revise what you know and to remind you of the best way to prepare for a debate. If you have a written assignment to produce a feature article or an editorial, you will turn to the appropriate sections in the chapters on written text types to make sure that you know exactly what is required.

One of the most common uses of *The Active Look It Up!* is to follow up on corrections that a teacher or a fellow student has made to your writing. Often when someone corrects your work, you can see immediately what is wrong: that you forgot the apostrophe, or that you used 'it's' when you meant 'its', or that you became so carried away by your story that you slipped from the past tense into the present. But sometimes you will realise that you're not quite sure of what is required. When does the apostrophe come after the 's', and why? Which words are always 'i before e'? Why has someone corrected your sentence when you wrote: 'Benjamin loaned me his pen'? You can find explanations for all of these language conventions – and many, many others – in *The Active Look It Up!* In most cases, you will check the table of contents first: go, for example, to the punctuation chapter and find the section on apostrophes. In some cases, the detailed index at the back of the book is the place to start; look up 'loan' in the index and it will direct you to the section in the usage chapter on the difference between 'loan' and 'lend'.

When you turn to a section for help, you will find that in many cases there is an activity that will enable you to test that you have fully understood the topic. Working through these activities will help you become a more confident and competent user of the language. You will also find them an excellent way of revising before tests such as NAPLAN.

You will find further support for the Australian Curriculum in English at www.nelsonenglishusage.com.au, where you will find a variety of resources organised according to the strands and sub-strands of the curriculum. Resources include self-correcting quizzes, crosswords and word finders, cartoons, background information, and weblinks to a range of online material. These resources will help students to consolidate what they have already learnt.

LANGUAGE CONVENTIONS: SPELLING

1

Spelling is important because:

- your reader may not understand what you have written if your spelling is inaccurate
- many people regard accurate spelling as a sign of someone who takes care with her or his writing
- if you are able to spell with ease, you will be free to concentrate on what you are saying in your writing.

Improving your spelling

Find patterns

Look closely for patterns within words. The letter sequences found in words in the English language are quite predictable. There are many common letter sequences, such as ation, eigh, ace, inter and dis. Some patterns, such as kwg, zqa, inbp, pct, csrp and jbf, are never found in English spelling.

Become familiar with the common patterns or possible letter sequences so that you can narrow down the choice of letters in words that you have difficulty spelling. Note the 'pp' in appeal, appear, applaud, appoint, apply and oppose; the similar endings of ambition, condition and ignition; and the common patterns in rebellion, rebellious and rebelliously.

ACTIVITY 1

Patterns

Create three words using each of the following patterns and write each word in a sentence.

1 ation _____ _____ _____
_____
_____
_____

2 eigh _____ _____ _____
_____
_____
_____

3 ough _____ _____ _____
_____
_____
_____

4 ace _____ _____ _____
_____
_____
_____

5 inter _____ _____ _____
_____
_____
_____

6 dis _____ _____ _____
_____
_____

7 ign _____ _____ _____
_____
_____

Think about the meaning

Think about the meaning of every word. In English, words based on the same meaning always have a common pattern in their spelling. For example:

sign, signal, signature, signify   assign, assignation   medicine, medicinal, medical

Words that sound the same but have different meanings tend to be spelt differently.

to, too, two   it's, its   their, there, they're   weather, wether, whether

passed, past   principal, principle   stationary, stationery

Think about the origin of the word

Knowing the origin of a word (its etymology) can help you to understand why it is spelt in a certain way.

The English language has a rich history. Over the centuries English has borrowed from almost every language on earth, and those foreign words – with their foreign spellings – have been incorporated into the language. Sometimes the foreign spelling remains for all time and sometimes we adapt it to make it sound more like other English words.

The most important influences have been the Norman Conquest, when the French invaded England and for some centuries French was the official language; the period when the classics were rediscovered and large numbers of Latin and Greek words (or parts of words) came into English (see page 15); and the period of the British Empire when English speakers spread around the globe, picking up new words for unfamiliar animals, plants, food and even concepts.

Knowing that many English words have come from other languages helps explain some of our stranger spellings. Here are just a few examples.

Language	Borrowed words
Aboriginal English	galah, coolabah, mallee
Malay	amok, orangutan, satay
Scandinavian	fjord, sauna, flounder
Czech	howitzer, robot, pistol
Dutch	aardvark, apartheid, frolic
Japanese	anime, haiku, manga
Persian	sherry, serendipity, pistachio
Portuguese	albatross, caramel, cashew
Chinese	bok choy, tea, silk

ISBN 9780170183048

Italian	arcade, corridor, virtue
French	attaché, connoisseur, liberty
Russian	cosmonaut, pavlova, vodka
Urdu	bungalow, khaki, roti
Spanish	chocolate, hammock, nacho

ACTIVITY 2

Foreign borrowings

1 Choose one language from anywhere in the world – perhaps one you are familiar with – and do some research to find out which words from that language are used in English.

You can begin your research with an Internet search, but do check the words you find in a good etymological dictionary (that is, one that includes the origin of words).

In some cases, you will find that a word came through several countries before it was picked up by English speakers. For example, many words from Latin came into English through other European languages, such as French, Italian, Spanish or Portuguese. The word 'chocolate' originally came from an Aztec language in Central Mexico, but it came to England by way of Spanish speakers.

Make sure that different members of the class are researching different languages. Present your research in poster form (computer generated if possible) and have a wall display so that you can share the results of your research.

2 Is there a word that you find particularly interesting? Find out all you can about it and write a brief story of the word and its origins.

A closer look at patterns in words

There are some age-old generalisations about English spelling that you might find interesting and useful. However, as there are many exceptions to all these rules, there is no substitute for memorising spellings and keeping a personal spelling list.

ie or *ei*

Remember the phrase 'i before e, except after c' when a word has an 'ee' sound.

> believe, shriek, siege, niece

Leaving aside names such as 'Sheila' and 'Keith', there are only five exceptions.

> codeine, caffeine, protein, seize, counterfeit

If a word does not have the 'ee' sound, it is generally spelt 'ei'.

> height, rein, feign, foreign

If the sound is 'ee' after c, use 'ei' in most cases.

> receive, deceit, perceive, receipt

Note the exceptions to these rules. Look at the spelling of the following words.

> sheikh, weird, neither, science, view, seize

ACTIVITY 3

ie or *ei*

1 Fill in the letters 'ie' or 'ei' in each of the following words.

a bel___f   **e** for___gn   **i** dec___ve   **m** pr___st

b h___ghten   **f** r___n   **j** p___ce   **n** p___r

c rec___pt   **g** caff___ne   **k** sh___ld   **o** bel___ver

d w___rd   **h** s___zure   **l** w___ghty

2 Did you get any of them wrong? If so, go back and look at the rules again to see if you can understand where you went wrong.

Write out any words you got wrong several times. It might be a good idea to write out some of the other words that follow the same pattern.

Irregular plurals

1   There used to be very complicated rules about whether nouns ending in –o were spelt –os or –oes when they were made plural. However, the modern trend is to spell these words –os, with only very few still always spelt –oes.

Although the –oes words are the exception these days, they include some very common words and you will be regarded as a poor speller if you get them wrong. Make sure to learn these –oes words:

   cargoes   echoes   heroes   potatoes   tomatoes

For many *other* words, either –os or –oes is acceptable. For example:

   torpedos *or* torpedoes

   volcanos *or* volcanoes

   buffalos *or* buffaloes

   mosquitos *or* mosquitoes

   halos *or* haloes

2   Nouns ending in –y change to –ies when they become plural, unless the letter before the 'y' is a vowel.

Singular noun	Plural noun	Singular noun	Plural noun
ally	allies	convoy	convoys
monkey	monkeys	valley	valleys
family	families	city	cities
guy	guys	bay	bays
army	armies		

3   A few very old nouns in English still form their plural the way they did before the Norman Conquest introduced a final –s as the usual way to make a word plural.

Singular noun	Plural noun
man	men
woman	women
child	children
foot	feet
tooth	teeth
goose	geese
mouse	mice
ox	oxen
brother	brethren (old fashioned but still used)

ISBN 9780170183048

4   Most nouns ending in –f become –ves when they are made plural. Nouns ending in –fe also become –ves when they are made plural.

Singular noun	Plural noun
half	halves
wolf	wolves
calf	calves
thief	thieves
dwarf	dwarves

Singular noun	Plural noun
elf	elves
loaf	loaves
life	lives
wife	wives
knife	knives

5   Some nouns that have been borrowed from other languages retain their original plural form. Sometimes the word can have two plurals: the form from the original language, and an English form with –s.

Singular noun	Plural noun
alumnus	alumni
analysis	analyses
appendix	appendices
bacterium	bacteria
beau	beaux
chateau	chateaux or chateaus
cherub	cherubs or cherubim
crisis	crises
criterion	criteria
diagnosis	diagnoses

Singular noun	Plural noun
erratum	errata
genius	geniuses or genii
hypothesis	hypotheses
index	indices
kibbutz	kibbutzim
oasis	oases
phenomenon	phenomena
syllabus	syllabi or syllabuses
synopsis	synopses
thesis	theses

ACTIVITY 4

Irregular plurals

Complete the following table.

Singular noun	Plural noun
echo	
life	
criterion	
goose	
boy	
lady	
crisis	
potato	
enemy	
foot	
dwarf	
tomato	
phenomenon	
hero	
oasis	

Adding a suffix

Spelling often becomes tricky when a suffix – or ending – is added to a word. Common suffixes include:

–able –ment –ible –ing –less –ful

Suffixes are joined to base words to create new words. For example:

dark *(base word)* + –ness *(suffix)* = darkness

Here are some *general* guidelines to follow when altering a word by adding a suffix.

1   When adding a suffix that begins with a vowel to a base word ending in –e, drop the 'e'.

dance + –ing = dancing

2   When adding a suffix to a word ending in –y, change 'y' to 'i'.

happy – happiness   pity – pitiless, pitiful

3   If you add –s to a word ending in –y, change 'y' to 'ie'.

hurry – hurries   marry – marries   tragedy – tragedies

4   There is no change in spelling when adding –ing to a word ending in –y.

cry – crying   multiply – multiplying

5   If a suffix begins with a consonant, most base words remain the same.

amaze + –ment = amazement

fruit + –less = fruitless

frightening + –ly = frighteningly

6   Words of one syllable that end with a single consonant preceded by a vowel double the consonant when adding a suffix.

swim – swimming   run – running

7   In words of more than one syllable, the final consonant is doubled if the final syllable is stressed and contains a short vowel.

forget – forgettable   begin – beginning   regret – regretted

8   If adding –able to a word ending in –e, you usually drop the 'e'.

note – notable   like – likable

9   Words ending in –l change to –ll when suffixes are added.

fulfil – fulfilling   model – modelled

Words that don't follow this pattern are those to which the suffixes –ise, –ity, –ism or –ic are added.

equal – equality   social – socialism, socialise

10   The suffix –full drops one 'l' when it is joined to a word.

thought – thoughtful   grace – graceful

All these rules look very daunting, especially as there are exceptions to some of them. However, you already know most of them – even if you can't always explain the rules.

6

ISBN 9780170183048

ACTIVITY 5

Adding a suffix

Complete this table.

Base word	Add suffix	New word
hope	–full	
yodel	–ing	
equal	–ed	
dial	–ing	
marvel	–ous	
create	–ing	
glory	–ous	
hungry	–ly	
comedy	–s	
use	–ing	
scurry	–ed	
pity	–ed	
hate	–ed	
hat	–ed	
hop	–ed	
hope	–ed	
bate	–ed	
bat	–ed	

Adding a prefix

A suffix is added to the end of a word. A prefix is added to the beginning.

1   When adding a prefix such as dis– or mis– to the beginning of a word that starts with s–, double the 's'.

      spell – misspell   satisfied – dissatisfied

2   This rule also applies to the negative prefix im– if added to a word beginning with 'm'; to ir– if added to a word beginning with 'r'; and to il– if added to a word beginning with 'l'.

      mortal – immortal   regular – irregular   legal – illegal

ACTIVITY 6

Adding a prefix

Complete this table by adding the prefixes to the adjectives.

Base word	Negative prefix	New word
logical	il–	
movable	im–	
similar	dis–	
reverent	ir–	
agree	dis–	
legitimate	il–	
moral	im–	
obey	dis–	

Memorise spellings

Work at improving your ability to spell by memorising words that you find difficult, especially those that do not follow the basic rules. Here are some useful strategies.

Look–say–cover–write–check

The look–say–cover–write–check method is one method which can help you memorise words that you want to learn to spell.

1   First, *look* up the word in a dictionary or compact speller. If you have no idea where to look for a particular word, your teacher or a friend might tell you the first three (or four) letters to help you locate it.
2   Look carefully at the word and memorise it. *Say* it aloud.
3   After you have memorised the word, *cover* it and *write* it, from memory, on your personal spelling list (see page 9).
4   Then, *check* that you have spelt the word accurately. If you have not, go through this procedure again.
5   Ask a friend, or your parents, to give you regular tests of the words on your personal spelling list. If you can spell a word accurately five times, you know it.

Sound out each syllable

Sound out each syllable (or sound unit) of a word. Deliberately emphasising the syllables that form a word can help to clarify its spelling.

gar-den / en-vi-ron-ment / com-pu-ter / ir-re-gu-lar / ac-com-mo-da-tion

Note any irregular features

Look carefully at the irregular features of any word you are learning to spell; for example, note the silent 'gh' in night, or the 'w' in who, or irregular plurals such as thieves and halves. Group together words with the same irregular features, such as the silent 'k' in knife, know, knee and kneel.

Alternatively, focus on the letter sequences that you have difficulty remembering, such as the 'cc' and 'mm' in accommodation, the 'dn' in Wednesday or the 'c' in the noun practice and the 's' in the verb practise.

ACTIVITY 7

Irregular features

Create three words using each of the following letter combinations and write each word in a sentence.

1 gh _____ _____ _____
_____
_____

2 ves _____ _____ _____
_____
_____

3 kn _____ _____ _____
_____
_____

4 wh _____ _____ _____
_____
_____

ISBN 9780170183048

Know your own strengths and weaknesses

What kind of speller are you? Some people are naturally good spellers; for others, spelling is hard work. You need to know which methods of learning spelling work for you. While the look–say–cover–write–check method works well for most people, there are other strategies that work for particular types of learners. Try some of these.

1   Close your eyes and visualise the word as you spell it aloud.

2   Write the word several times, highlighting any irregular features. Use highlighter pens of different colours. Write the word in different colours. Type the word in different fonts.

3   Group words with similar patterns together.

4   Set yourself a goal of learning a few words every day – and make sure that someone tests you. Revise the words you have learnt regularly.

5   Use the spell check on your computer.

6   Read what you have written aloud. You will pick up such things as missing or repeated words.

7   Re-read what you have written, looking especially for those little words that are most commonly misspelt, such as:

> it's / its
> to / two / too
> you're / your
> their / they're / there
> who's / whose
> theirs / there's

8   Don't be embarrassed about asking someone else to proofread your work – and pay close attention to the changes that are made.

Decide that spelling matters

You will hear people say that spelling doesn't really matter – that the reader knows what you mean. Whether we like it or not, spelling is one of the main criteria that others use when judging the quality of our writing. If you want others to take your writing seriously, you need to make every effort to get your spelling correct.

Keep a personal spelling list

1   The words you need to be able to spell accurately are those you use in your writing. Include words that you need to know or want to use in your writing; for example, subject-specific words such as parallel in Mathematics, tragedy in English, isthmus in Geography, photosynthesis in Science and soufflé in Food and Nutrition.

2   Keep a column for similar words in your personal spelling list or book. This may help you to focus attention on the predictable patterns or irregular features of the word you are learning. For example, you might include knot, knight and knuckle in the similar words column alongside know because they are spelt with a silent 'k'. You might also include knew, known, knowing and knowledge alongside know because these are all parts of the same family and have a similar meaning and spelling pattern.

   You have already read that spelling is related to meaning and not necessarily to sound. For this reason, you would not include new in your list of similar words alongside knew. Because their meanings are different, they are spelt differently.

Sample personal spelling list

Word	Key features	Similar words	Tests				
parallel	par<u>all</u>el	par<u>all</u>elogram par<u>all</u>eled					
ambition	ambit<u>ion</u>	condit<u>ion</u> ignit<u>ion</u>					
applaud	<u>app</u>laud	<u>app</u>lause <u>app</u>eal <u>app</u>ear					
knowledge	<u>kn</u>owledge	<u>kn</u>own <u>kn</u>ee <u>kn</u>ife					
signature	si<u>gn</u>ature	si<u>gn</u>al si<u>gn</u> assi<u>gn</u>					
thieves	th<u>ie</u><u>ves</u>	th<u>ie</u>f cal<u>ves</u> hal<u>ves</u>					
accommodation	a<u>cc</u>o<u>mm</u>odation	a<u>cc</u>o<u>mm</u>odate					
ignore	i<u>gnore</u>	i<u>gnor</u><u>ance</u>					
disappear	d<u>is</u>/<u>appear</u>	d<u>is</u>/<u>appear</u>ance d<u>is</u>/satisfaction					
disservice	d<u>is</u>/<u>service</u>	d<u>is</u>/satisfaction					
believe	bel<u>ie</u>ve	bel<u>ie</u>f r<u>el</u><u>ief</u>					
receive	rec<u>ei</u>ve	rec<u>ei</u>pt dec<u>ei</u>ve					

ACTIVITY 8

Create a personal spelling list

Create a list of words that you would like to be able to spell, taken from various subjects. Choose – three words per day for the next three weeks. Make sure that you know their meanings, and use your dictionary if necessary. Learn to spell them using the method that works best for you. At the end of the three weeks, ask a friend to test you on your words.

ISBN 9780170183048

If you are unable to spell any of your chosen words, try re-learning them using one of these methods.

- Use the look–say–cover–write–check method.
- Look at the word, close your eyes and picture it, then spell it aloud. Open your eyes and check that you spelt it correctly.
- Write the word out at least five or six times. Check to make sure that you are writing it correctly.
- Think about whether there are other words with similar patterns.
- See if there is any way of remembering the word. Some people find mnemonics helpful – for example:

my pal the princi*pal*

American and British spelling

The English language is changing all the time in several ways: new words are added; old words are used as different parts of speech or with changed meanings; and even accents – the way we pronounce words – change over time. Changes in spelling were common too for centuries, but since the invention of printing, the English spelling system has become standardised.

While people all around the world speak English quite differently, they all share a common written language. One of the few developments in spelling was the result of a determined campaign by an American man – Noah Webster – who was convinced that the spelling system needed to be simplified. Webster published a spelling book for American schools that sold millions of copies from the late eighteenth century onwards. Some of the spelling simplifications that Webster introduced into his speller became common practice in the US. Examples include the preference for –or rather than –our in words such as favour; the use of –er rather than –re in words such as theatre; the dropping of double letters in some cases (for example, trialed); and the use of –s– rather than –c– in words such as defense. The other changes that he suggested did not catch on.

While Webster's changes do simplify the spelling system, they affect only a small number of words and do very little to make English spelling any easier to learn. The British decided to ignore Webster's reforms. In Australia, we have traditionally followed British spelling practices. Rather than adopting the American spelling of words such as color and rigor, we tend to use colour and rigour, as the British do.

It is becoming increasingly common in print media such as newspapers and magazines, however, to use American spelling. This is partly due to the influence of American word-processing programs such as Microsoft Word. It is now quite acceptable, for example, to use American spellings for the words program and focused. Microsoft Word does allow you to set the language you are working in and the spelling system – for example, 'English (Australian)'. You may find it useful to adjust your default settings.

Australians have traditionally used –ise instead of –ize in words such as sympathise and realise, unlike American and British English, which prefer the –ize spelling. However, there are a few exceptions:

- baize
- capsize
- maize
- prize
- seize
- size

The most important thing is to be consistent.

ACTIVITY 9

American and Australian spellings

Complete this table.

American spelling	Australian spelling
behavior	
	centre
	colour
donut	
favorite	
	honour
humor	
marvelous	
neighbor	
omelet	
	pyjamas
skillful	
	theatre
traveler	

Spelling reform

Many people other than Webster have campaigned for spelling reform, arguing that a simpler and more regular spelling system would save students many hours of time and effort. The complexities of English spelling are the result of the rich history of the language. At least 80 per cent of English words are regular and easy to learn, but the rest can be challenging. Some problems are caused by the fact that pronunciation has changed, while spelling has remained the same. This is the case with words such as knife and know, where the k is now silent. There are words that had silent letters added to them in the eighteenth century by an earlier generation of spelling reformers – words such as doubt had a b added to acknowledge the connection with the Latin word from which it was derived. Other consequences of intended reform were the gh in words such as delight and tight, introduced in an attempt to make them consistent with words such as light. Many thousands of words were borrowed from other countries without any attempt to anglicise the spelling, including *perestroika* from Russia, *anime* and *tsunami* from Japan, *guru* and *pyjamas* from India, *coyote* from Mexico and *wallaroo* from an Australian Aboriginal language.

While reforming the irregular spelling of words in English might seem like a good idea, any reform would need to be based on ensuring that words were spelt the way they sounded. The problem with this is that there is huge diversity among English speakers around the world in the way words are pronounced. A truly regular spelling system would mean that we could no longer read texts written in other English-speaking countries. Eventually, we would also be unable to read texts written in the past.

Computer spell checks

Your computer's spell-check function can be a great help, especially if you have set it to English (Australian), but you can't rely on it entirely. If you can't spell at all, you won't even be able to make the right choice from the alternatives the spell check offers you. The spell check also has one serious limitation: it usually can't distinguish between words that sound the same but have different meanings (that is, **homophones**). For example, a spell check may not highlight the spelling error in this sentence:

It's nice to receive a complement.

ISBN 9780170183048

The spell check can't tell that you meant compliment (praise), not complement (something that fits together to make something complete).

The inability of a computer spell check to distinguish between homophones means that it might not pick up some of the most common spelling errors of all. These are little words such as:

to / two / too   it's / its   your / you're   their / they're / there
theirs / there's   who's / whose

Making mistakes in words such as these can give a reader a very poor impression of your writing. Check that you can distinguish between them by looking at pages 21–3.

Some common homophones

Homophones are words that sound the same but have different meanings – and different spellings. There are many hundreds of homophones in English. Remember that these are the words you are most likely to misspell because they can't be picked up by a computer spell check.

This list contains some of the most common ones.

allowed / aloud	farther / father	made / maid	sauce / source
altar / alter	feat / feet	mail / male	saw / soar / sore
assent / ascent	fir / fur	meat / meet	scene / seen
ate / eight	flea / flee	miner / minor	sew / so / sow
bare / bear	flour / flower	morning /	sight / site
be / bee	for / four / fore	mourning	some / sum
bean / been	formally /	none / nun	son / sun
berry / bury	formerly	ode / owed	stair / stare
berth / birth	fort / fought	one / won	stationary /
blew / blue	fourth / forth	or / ore / oar /	stationery
board / bored	gorilla / guerrilla	awe	steal / steel
boarder / border	grate / great	pair / pear / pare	tail / tale
brake / break	guest / guessed	passed / past	there / their /
buy / bye / by	hail / hale	pause / paws /	they're
cell / sell	hair / hare	pores / pours	threw / through
cent / scent / sent	hear / here	peace / piece	to / too / two
cereal / serial	heard / herd	peal / peel	waist / waste
chartered /	him / hymn	plain / plane	wait / weight
charted	hoarse / horse	pray / prey	ware / wear /
coarse / course	hole / whole	principal /	where / we're
complement /	idle / idol	principle	warn / worn
compliment	its / it's	profit / prophet	weak / week
counsellor /	key / quay	rain / reign / rein	weather /
councillor	knew / new	rap / wrap	whether /
creak / creek	knight / night	rapt / wrapped	wether
currant / current	knot / not	raw / roar	which / witch
dear / deer	know / no	right / rite / write	who's / whose
doe / dough	lead / led	ring / wring	won / one
dyeing / dying	lightening /	road / rode /	yore / you're /
earn / urn	lightning	rowed	your
ewe / yew / you	loan / lone	sail / sale	

ACTIVITY 10

Homophones (1)

Choose the correct homophones from the alternatives in brackets.

1 I don't know (weather / whether / wether) I'll be going to the farm this weekend. It depends on the (weather / whether / wether).

2 Those shoes (compliment / complement) your outfit. Thanks for the (compliment / complement).

3 The ship's captain (chartered / charted) the waters through the reef while the owners (chartered / charted) a plane to check the map.

4 Without (it's / its) goal scorer, the team struggled in the second half. '(It's / Its) crazy,' screamed the coach, 'that we can't put her back on the court.'

5 Place (they're / there / their) tent over (they're / there / their) next to ours as (they're / there / their) our friends.

6 Are you (allowed / aloud) to stay up a bit longer? I should like to read my story (allowed / aloud) to you.

7 I am (dying / dyeing) this curtain black. It will make a much better backdrop for the scene where the hero is (dying / dyeing).

8 I was introduced (formally / formerly) to the man who had (formally / formerly) been our mayor.

9 The dawn was near and the sky was (lightening / lightning), but the thunder and (lightening / lightning) were as wild as ever.

10 The (guerrilla / gorilla) fighters frightened a band of (guerrillas / gorillas) who were sleeping in the forest.

ACTIVITY 11

Homophones (2)

Choose the correct homophones from the alternatives in brackets.

1 The fish is cooked on a bed of (coarse / course) salt. It makes an excellent first (coarse / course).

2 A figure on horseback, the black (knight / night), loomed out of the shadows of the (knight / night).

3 I (sent / scent / cent) her a present of some expensive (sent / scent / cent).

4 He was standing there absolutely (stationary / stationery) behind the (stationary / stationery) cupboard.

5 The (principal / principle) insisted that the most important (principal / principle) in life was to always think of others first.

6 I will read you the (tail / tale) of the naughty little mouse whose (tail / tale) became caught in a mouse trap.

7 The first time Stanley had to dig a (whole / hole) in the desert, it took him almost the (whole / hole) day.

8 (You're / your / yore) required to put (you're / your / yore) clothes away neatly.

9 Our school (counsellor / councillor) has decided to stand for election as a (counsellor / councillor) at the next local government election.

10 The (profit / prophet) said, 'What will it (profit / prophet) you to gain the whole world if you lose your sense of self-respect?'

ISBN 9780170183048

How words are made

Understanding how words are made is an important strategy for improving your spelling. It also increases your vocabulary.

Latin and Greek roots

Many words in the English language are built from words borrowed from Latin or Greek. Knowing the meanings of these Latin and Greek words can give you clues to the meanings of many words used in English. Here are some of the most commonly used word roots and their meanings.

Word root	Origin	Meaning	Example
alter	Latin	other	alteration
annus	Latin	year	anniversary
anti	Greek	against	anti-clockwise
aqua	Latin	water	aquarium
audi	Latin	hear	audible
bene	Latin	well	benefactor
bio	Greek	life	biology
cap	Latin	head	captain
cent	Latin	hundred	century
circum	Latin	round	circumference
credo	Latin	believe	credible
deca	Greek	ten	decade
dent	Latin	tooth	dentist
femina	Latin	woman	feminine
graph	Latin	write	biography
kilo	Greek	thousand	kilometre
logo	Greek	word	geology
magna	Latin	great	magnify
man	Latin	hand	manual
micro	Greek	small	microphone
milli	Latin	thousand	milligram
mono	Greek	one	monologue
multi	Latin	many	multiple
pac	Latin	peace	pacify
port	Latin	carry	portable
pup	Latin	doll	puppet
semi	Latin	half	semi-automatic
solo	Latin	alone	solitary
tele	Greek	far	television
uni	Latin	one	universe

ISBN 9780170183048

ACTIVITY 12

Latin and Greek roots

1 Brainstorm some more words that have been made up from the Latin and Greek roots in the table on page 15. Then use a dictionary to check that you are right. You will need a dictionary large enough to contain etymological information (that is, one with information about the origins of words).

2 Make your own table of Latin and Greek roots, either on a large sheet of cardboard or on the computer. If you are working on cardboard, leave plenty of room to add further examples as you come across them. The advantage of having an electronic table is that it is easy to add more examples.

You might want to add a further column in which you write the meaning of the English word – for example, biology: the study of living things.

Prefixes

A prefix is a unit placed before a word that changes the meaning of the word. Prefixes have come into English from Old English, French, Greek and Latin. For example, the Latin *dis*, meaning 'not', changes like to dislike ('to not like'); and the Greek *bio*, meaning 'life', makes biography ('the story of a life'). If you add the prefix *auto*, meaning 'self', you have an autobiography ('the life story of one's own life').

Common prefixes

auto–	autobiography, automobile, automaton
bi–	bicycle, bisect, bilateral
dis–	dissatisfied, disservice, disappearance
ex–	exile, expel, exclude
extra–	extraordinary, extrasensory, extracurricular
fore–	forehead, foreshadow, foresight
il–	illegal, illiterate, illegible
im–	immortal, immoral, impossible
in–	inaccurate, indefinite, inexperienced
inter–	international, interaction, interwoven
ir–	irregular, irreligious, irresponsible
mal–	malpractice, malnutrition, malfunction
mis–	misguided, mistaken, misused
non–	non-smoker, non-alcoholic, non-event
over–	overact, override, overhear
post–	postcolonial, postgraduate, post-mortem
pre–	predict, preview, precede
re–	recapture, reappearance, reprint
trans–	transatlantic, translate, transport
sub–	submarine, subculture, subtract
super–	superhuman, superman, supermarket
tri–	tricycle, triplet, tripod
un–	unhappy, uncertain, undignified
under–	underachieve, underrate, underdone

ISBN 9780170183048

ACTIVITY 13

Prefixes

1 Choose five words that you do not know well from the table of prefixes. Look up their meanings in a dictionary and write sentences showing how they are used.

2 Make your own table of prefixes, either on a large sheet of cardboard or on the computer. You might want to add a further column in which you write the meanings of any words that you do not know well, with perhaps a sentence showing how each word can be used.

3 Make some more words from prefixes by adding the prefix in the left-hand column to the root word in the second column. The first one is done for you.

Prefix	Root word	New word
pre–	*diction*	*prediction*
super–	hero	
un–	likely	
post–	traumatic	
trans–	parent	
re–	create	
dis–	loyal	
fore–	cast	
inter–	regional	
sub–	way	

Suffixes

Suffixes are the endings that tell you about the grammar of English words. Some suffixes tell you what part of speech a word is, some change the meaning of a word and others show how words relate to each other.

Common noun suffixes

–acy	diplomacy, accuracy, delicacy
–age	storage, courage, language
–ance	reliance, brilliance, defiance
–ation	precipitation, negotiation, migration
–dom	kingdom, freedom, officialdom
–ée, –ee	fiancée, employee, awardee
–eer	engineer, auctioneer, profiteer
–ence	independence, audience, difference
–er	foreigner, jeweller, prisoner
–ery	gallery, pottery, grocery
–hood	neighbourhood, sisterhood, knighthood
–ian	magician, electrician, Parisian
–ice	cowardice, justice, service
–ism	criticism, idealism, communism
–ist	chemist, dentist, realist
–ition	imposition, ignition, fruition
–ity	hostility, fragility, civility
–ling	darling, duckling, underling
–logy	technology, geology, biology
–ment	employment, advertisement, development
–ness	happiness, darkness, weakness
–or	tailor, auditor, emperor

continued

–ory	lavatory, observatory, factory
–ship	friendship, ownership, championship
–ty	certainty, unity, enmity

Common verb suffixes

–en	lengthen, strengthen, weaken
–ify	intensify, satisfy, glorify
–ise	criticise, moralise, stabilise

Common adjective suffixes

–able	acceptable, believable, probable
–al	magical, educational, typical
–an, –ian	Indian, republican, Elizabethan
–ant	ignorant, abundant, flamboyant
–ar	angular, circular, spectacular
–arian	antiquarian, humanitarian, octogenarian
–ary	arbitrary, legendary, literary
–ate	affectionate, separate, delicate
–ent	absent, decent, different
–esque	picturesque, statuesque, grotesque
–fold	manifold, twofold, threefold
–ful	useful, dutiful, wonderful
–ible	edible, visible, horrible
–ic	poetic, manic, authentic
–ine	equine, canine, feline
–ious	cautious, precious, luscious
–ish	childish, squeamish, boyish
–ive	active, decisive, selective
–like	lifelike, childlike, warlike
–less	careless, hopeless, tasteless
–most	uppermost, foremost, utmost
–ory	contradictory, cursory, explanatory
–ous	enormous, infamous, mountainous
–y	angry, stony, worthy

Common adverb suffixes

–ly	softly, slowly, gently
–ward, –wards	afterwards, seaward, onward
–wise	otherwise, clockwise, moneywise

ACTIVITY 14

Suffixes

1 Choose five words that you do not know well from the table of suffixes. Look up their meanings in a dictionary and write sentences showing how they are used.

2 Make your own table of suffixes, either on a large sheet of cardboard or on the computer. You might want to add a further column in which you write the meaning of any words that you do not know well, with perhaps a sentence showing how the word can be used.

ISBN 9780170183048

Understanding dictionaries

Dictionaries, both printed and electronic, come in different sizes and some provide a great deal more information than others. People usually consult a dictionary to find out the meaning of a word or to check the spelling, but there are dictionaries that provide much more information than that. Some dictionaries include information about the way words are pronounced, their origins, the parts of speech of words, the forms of associated words (such as the spelling of plurals of nouns or the main parts of irregular verbs) and even advice as to how the word is used.

All dictionaries include a set of features for their entries and these features are explained at the beginning of the dictionary so readers can understand what information has been included in each entry. Checking the explanatory notes at the beginning of your printed dictionary or the 'Info' page of your electronic dictionary will enable you to use your dictionary more effectively.

Below is a page from *The Concise Macquarie Dictionary* with the features labelled.

Labels around the dictionary page: Guide word · Entry · Forms of the verb · Headword · Part of speech · Usage note · Pronunciation · Definition · Prefix · Origin of word · A range of different meanings listed · Suffix · Spelling of noun plural

idler wheel — 617 — **Iliad**

importance, or significance: *idle talk.* –*v.* (**idled, idling**) –*v.i.* **6.** to pass time in idleness. **7.** to move, loiter, or saunter idly. **8.** *Machinery* to operate, usually at minimum speed, while the transmission is disengaged. –*v.t.* **9.** to pass (time) in idleness. [ME, OE *idel* empty] –**idler**, *n.* –**idleness**, *n.* –**idly**, *adv.*

idler wheel /'aɪdlə wil/ *n.* a cogwheel placed between two other cogwheels in order to transfer the motion of one to the other without changing the direction of rotation.

idol /'aɪdl/ *n.* **1.** an image or other material object representing a deity to which religious worship is addressed. **2.** *Bible* a false god, as of a heathen people. **3.** any person or thing blindly adored or revered. **4.** a mere image or semblance of something, visible but without substance, as a phantom. **5.** a figment of the mind. **6.** a false conception or notion; fallacy. [ME, from OF, from L, from Gk: image, phantom, idol]

idolatry /aɪ'dɒlətri/ *n.* (*pl.* -**ries**) **1.** the worship of idols. **2.** blind adoration, reverence, or devotion. [ME, from OF, from LL, from Gk] –**idolater**, *n.* –**idolatrous**, *adj.*

idolise /'aɪdəlaɪz/ *v.t.* (-**lised, -lising**) to regard with blind adoration or devotion. Also, **idolize.** –**idolisation** /aɪdəlaɪ'zeɪʃən/, *n.* –**idoliser**, *n.*

Idriess /'idrəs/ *n.* **Ion Llewelyn**, 1889–1979, Australian novelist; author of *Lasseter's Last Ride* (1931) and *Flynn of the Inland* (1932).

ID10T error /aɪ di tɛn ti 'ɛrə/ *n. Computers Colloq.* (*humorous*) an IT problem created by the ignorance of the user rather than by faulty hardware or software. [a disguised form of the word *idiot* + ERROR]

idyll /'aɪdl, 'ɪdl/ *n.* **1.** a poem or prose composition consisting of a little picture, usually describing pastoral scenes or events or any charmingly simple episode, appealing incident, or the like. **2.** an episode or scene of idyllic charm. Also, *US*, **idyl.** [L, from Gk] –**idyllic** /aɪ'dɪlɪk/, *adj.*

-ie a hypocoristic suffix of nouns, the same as -**y²**, used colloquially: **1.** as an endearment, or affectionately, especially with and among children: *doggie*, a dog; *littlie*, a child. **2.** as a familiar abbreviation: *budgie*, a budgerigar; *conchie*, conscientious, or a conscientious objector; *mozzie*, a mosquito; *postie*, a postman. **3.** as a nominalisation: *greenie*, a conservationist; *stubbie*, a small, squat beer bottle. *Usage:* There are some words which fluctuate between an -*ie* ending and a -*y* ending, such as *cabbie*, *auntie*, or *bogie*. The -*ie* ending is to be preferred for shortened forms such as *pressie* for *present*, and for noun forms which need to be distinguished from homophonic adjectives, such as *chewie* (chewing gum) as opposed to *chewy* (tough).

i.e. /aɪ 'i/ *that is: apparel, i.e., clothing.* [L] *Usage:* The desire of some writers to reduce the amount of punctuation in abbreviations has produced some evidence of *ie* without stops.

Iemma /'jɛmə/ *n.* **Morris**, born 1961, Australian state Labor politician; premier of NSW 2005–08.

-ier variant of -**eer**, as in *brigadier*, *halberdier*, etc. [F, from L]

-ies a word element representing the plural formation of nouns and third person singular of verbs for words ending in -*y*, -*ie*, and sometimes -*ey*.

if /ɪf/ *conj.* **1.** in case that; granting or supposing that; on condition that. **2.** even though. **3.** whether. –*n.* **4.** a condition; a supposition. –*phr.* **5. if only**, (used to introduce a phrase expressing a wish, especially one that cannot now be fulfilled or is thought unlikely to be fulfilled): *if only I had known!*; *if only he would come!* [ME, from OE *gif*]

if-clause /'ɪf-klɔz/ *n. Gram.* → **conditional clause.**

-iferous See -**ferous.**

iftar /'ɪftɑ/ *n. Islam* a meal eaten after sunset during Ramadan. [Ar.]

-ify variant of -**fy**, used when the preceding stem or word element ends in a consonant, as in *intensify*. [-I- + -FY]

igloo /'ɪglu/ *n.* (*pl.* -**loos**) a dome-shaped Inuit hut, built of blocks of hard snow. [Inuit]

Ignatius of Loyola /ɪg,neɪʃəs əv lɔɪ'oulə/ *n.* **Saint** (*Iñigo López de Recalde*), 1491–1556, Spanish soldier and priest; founder of the Jesuit order.

igneous /'ɪgnɪəs/ *adj.* **1.** of or relating to fire. **2.** *Geol.* formed by the action of heat, as rocks. [L: of fire]

igneous rock /ɪgnɪəs 'rɒk/ *n.* rock formed from magma which has cooled and solidified either at the earth's surface (volcanic rock) or deep within the earth's crust (plutonic rock).

ignis fatuus /ˌɪgnɪs 'fætʃuəs/ *n.* (*pl.* **ignes fatui** /ˌɪgniz 'fætʃuaɪ/) **1.** a flitting phosphorescent light seen at night, chiefly over marshy ground, and supposed to be due to spontaneous combustion of gas from decomposed organic matter; will-o'-the-wisp; marsh light. **2.** something deluding or misleading. [L: foolish fire]

ignite /ɪg'naɪt/ *v.* (-**nited, -niting**) –*v.t.* **1.** to set on fire; kindle. –*v.i.* **2.** to take fire; begin to burn. [L] –**ignitable, ignitible**, *adj.* –**ignitability, ignitibility** /ɪg,naɪtə'bɪlətɪ/, *n.* *Usage:* For spelling variation see note at **collectable.**

ignition /ɪg'nɪʃən/ *n.* **1.** the act of igniting. **2.** the state of being ignited. **3.** (in an internal-combustion engine) the process which ignites the fuel in the cylinder.

ignition coil /ɪg'nɪʃən kɔɪl/ *n.* an induction coil used in an internal-combustion engine for converting the battery voltage to the high tension required by the sparking plugs.

ignoble /ɪg'noubəl/ *adj.* **1.** of low character, aims, etc.; mean; base. **2.** of low grade or quality; inferior. [L: unknown, of low birth] –**ignobility** /ɪgnou'bɪlətɪ/, **ignobleness**, *n.* –**ignobly**, *adv.*

ignominious /ɪgnə'mɪnɪəs/ *adj.* **1.** marked by or attended with ignominy; discreditable; humiliating: *an ignominious retreat.* **2.** covered with or deserving ignominy; contemptible. [L: ignominious], *adv.* –**ignominiousness**, *n.*

ignominy /'ɪgnəmənɪ/ *n.* (*pl.* -**nies**) **1.** disgrace; dishonour; public contempt. **2.** base quality or conduct; a cause of disgrace. [L: disgrace, dishonour]

ignoramus /ɪgnə'reɪməs, ɪgnə'rɑməs/ *n.* (-**muses**) an ignorant person. [L: we do not know, we disregard]

ignorant /'ɪgnərənt/ *adj.* **1.** destitute of knowledge; unlearned. **2.** uninformed; unaware. **3.** due to or showing lack of knowledge: *an ignorant statement.* [ME, from L: not knowing] –**ignorance**, *n.* –**ignorantly**, *adv.*

ignore /ɪg'nɔ/ *v.t.* (-**nored, -noring**) **1.** to refrain from noticing or recognising: *ignore his remarks.* **2.** *US Law* (of the grand jury) to reject (a bill of indictment) as without sufficient evidence. –*phr.* **3. treat with ignore**, *Aust. Colloq.* to disregard entirely. [L: not to know, disregard] –**ignorable**, *adj.* –**ignorer**, *n.*

Iguaçú Falls /ɪgwasu 'fɒlz/ *pl. n.* a waterfall of great volume on the Iguaçú River on the boundary between Brazil and Argentina. 64 m high; about 4 km wide. Also, **Iguassú Falls.**

iguana /ɪ'gwanə/ *n.* any of various large lizards of the family Iguanidae, especially *Iguana iguana*, of tropical America, often having spiny projections on the head and back. [Sp., from Carib (a South American language)]

iguanodon /ɪ'gwanədɒn, ɪgju'an-/ *n.* any member of the extinct bipedal dinosaurian genus *Iguanodon*, found as a fossil in Europe, Asia, and northern Africa, comprising reptiles from five to nine metres long, with denticulate teeth like those of the iguana. [IGUANA + Gk: tooth]

ikebana /ɪki'banə/ *n.* the art of Japanese flower arrangement in which flowers are displayed according to strict rules.

I-Kiribati /ɪ-'kɪrɪbæs/ *adj.* **1.** of or relating to Kiribati or its inhabitants. –*n.* **2.** the Polynesian language spoken on Kiribati.

il-¹ variant of **in-²**, (by assimilation) before *l*, as in *illation.*

il-² variant of **in-³**, (by assimilation) before *l*, as in *illogical.*

-il variant of -**ile**, as in *civil.*

ilang-ilang /ˌilæŋ-'ilæŋ/ *n.* → **ylang-ylang.**

-ile a suffix of adjectives expressing capability, susceptibility, liability, aptitude, etc., as in *agile, docile, ductile, fragile, prehensile, tensile, volatile.* Also, -**il.** [L]

Île de France /il də 'frõs/ *n.* a region and former province in northern France, including Paris and the region around it. Pop. 10 952 011 (1999); 12 011 km².

ileum /'ɪlɪəm/ *n. Anat.* the third and lowest division of the small intestine, continuous with the jejunum and ending at the caecum. [NL, from LL: groin, flank]

ilex /'aɪlɛks/ *n.* **1.** any tree or shrub of the genus *Ilex.* **2.** holly. [NL: the holly genus, L: the holm oak]

Iliad /'ɪlɪəd, 'ɪlɪæd/ *n.* **the**, a Greek epic poem describing the siege of Troy, ascribed to Homer. [L *Ilias*, from Gk, from *Ilion* Ilium, Troy] –**Iliadic**, *adj.*

How to use a dictionary

Spelling

If you are not sure of a spelling, look for the headword in your dictionary.

1   The guide words, which show the range of entries on that page, and the headwords, which are the word or words about which information is given, are in strict alphabetical order (a b c d e f g h i j k l m n o p q r s t u v w x y z). Ignore hyphens, apostrophes and spaces. For example, the following are in alphabetical order:

> drunkard   drupe   dry cell   dry-clean   dry dock   dryer

2   Use the guide words at the top of each page to find the general location of the word.

3   When you are close to your headword, scan by moving your eyes down the page.

4   Use the letters that you are sure about to track down the word. If you can't find it, you may have to think of other possible spellings.

Meaning

If you are not sure of the meaning of a word, look it up. Many words have more than one meaning, and each is numbered in the entry. You may need to read all the meanings to find the one you want. The most common meaning will be placed first.

Abbreviations

If you are not sure what an abbreviation stands for, check the list of abbreviations at the front (and/or back) of the dictionary.

ACTIVITY 15

Dictionary exercise

1   Arrange the following words in alphabetical order.
auxiliary
audience
ambulance
prosperous
applaud
ridicule
memorise
arbitrary
punctuation

2   Beside each word, write what you think it means; then check the meaning in a dictionary.

3   Write each word in a sentence.

4   Write five dictionary headwords from the dictionary page on page 19 and beside each one write:
   a its definition
   b its origins
   c its part of speech
   d how it is pronounced.

5   Find answers to these questions on the dictionary page on page 19.
   a What is the plural of 'ignis fatuus'?
   b What is the plural of 'igloo'?
   c 'I'll' is a contraction. What words are being shortened?
   d What example is given for the use of the suffix –ify?
   e What are the related adverb and noun forms of the adjective 'ignominious'?
   f What language does the word 'igneous' come from?
   g How can you tell that the word 'Iliad' is pronounced in two different ways?
   h From which South American language did the word 'iguana' come?

ISBN 9780170183048

LANGUAGE CONVENTIONS: PUNCTUATION 2

Punctuation helps people read what has been written. There is a major difference, for example, between 'Will you come over here?', a polite question, and 'Will you come over here!', a command.

Punctuation shows the reader how to sound out your writing: whether to pause for just a short time (indicated by a comma) or for a longer time (indicated by a full stop); or whether it is time for a change in tone of voice (indicated by a question mark or exclamation mark).

Apostrophes

The apostrophe (') has two main purposes. It can be used to show:

1 that a letter or letters have been left out of a word
  a when two words are shortened into one

> Don't go yet *for* Do not go yet
>
> You're late *for* You are late
>
> three o'clock *for* three of the clock
>
> They must've finished *for* They must have finished

These shortened forms are called contractions.
  b when words are written as they sound

> Hangin' five
>
> G'day from WA

2 ownership

> The teacher's books were left in the classroom.
>
> Jackie's car is a gas-guzzling Land Rover Discovery.
>
> Only members may use the members' entrance to the grounds.
>
> A message was emblazoned on the runners' backs: 'Stop at Mog's'.

You can test whether a word should have an apostrophe to show ownership or possession by asking yourself if you can substitute 'of' for the word ending in –s. Can you say 'the car of Jo-Anne' instead of 'Jo-Anne's car', or 'the books of the teacher' instead of 'the teacher's books', or 'the backs of the runners' instead of 'the runners' backs'?

When you want a singular word to show possession, add –'s (unless the word is a pronoun – see points 2 and 3 on page 22).

> The dog's leash is in the corner. (one dog)
>
> His sister's friend waited outside. (one sister)
>
> The company's office is located in Biram Street. (one company)

ISBN 9780170183048

When you want a plural word ending in –s to show possession, write the plural word and then add an apostrophe.

> The dogs' leashes are in the corner. (more than one dog)

> His sisters' friends were waiting for him. (more than one sister)

> The companies' offices are located in Ramsey Street. (more than one company)

When the plural form of a word does not end in –s, add –'s.

> The women's partners waited outside. (more than one woman)

> The men's basketball team usually loses its home matches. (more than one man)

Points to note

1 In most cases, if the singular word ends in –s, add –'s.

> James's room is on the third floor.

2 Possessive pronouns (such as 'his', 'hers', 'its', 'ours', 'yours' and 'theirs') do not have an apostrophe because they are already possessive.

> Is this laptop yours?   These books are theirs.

3 One common problem is the confusion between 'its' and 'it's'. 'Its' is always a possessive pronoun and 'it's' always means 'it is' or 'it has'.

> Its problems are underrated.   It's a common problem.

Similarly, make sure that you are clear about the difference between:

> whose *and* who's   your *and* you're   their *and* they're

In each case, the apostrophe indicates a contraction, not possession: 'who is' or 'who has', 'you are' and 'they are'.

4 Apostrophes are also used when writing the plural form of letters.

> Mind your p's and q's.

Remember, apostrophes are not used for words ending in –s unless they show ownership.

ACTIVITY 16

Contractions

1 Rewrite the following words using an apostrophe to shorten them and delete any unnecessary letters. Then write each word in a sentence.

do not	must have	what is	will not
you are	how is	cannot	must not
it is	I had	you had	he will
did not			

Ownership

2 Rewrite the following sentences, adding an apostrophe to show ownership. You may have to add –s.

a Claytons towel was left on the beach.

b I prefer to drive Huongs BMW.

ISBN 9780170183048

   c Only athletes may use the athletes toilets.
   d All the cyclists shirts carried the slogan, 'Freddys place for fractured bikes'.
   e The girls partners had to wait outside.
   f Marks tent is a mess. In fact, all the students tents are a mess.

Apostrophes

3 Rewrite the following sentences, adding apostrophes where needed.
   a Its hamburgers are the best in town and Im not the only one who feels this way about Hanjos place.
   b Its attitudes like yours that cause trouble for the clubs members because the swimmers needs wont be met if they cant eat.

Brackets

Additional information that is not essential to a sentence may be placed in brackets ( ), also known as **parentheses**. This might include an explanation, a comment or an example.

> Fling was incredibly friendly (after all, he was only a puppy) but he had a habit of nibbling everyone's ankles.

> The night I saw the ghost (I shiver now as I remember it) is something that I will never forget.

> Adele's love of small dogs (such as beagles, Jack Russells, poodles and kelpies) is well known.

Use brackets when you want to separate clearly the extra information from the rest of the sentence. Brackets should always be used to enclose explanations and comments, as in the first two examples. Commas or dashes can sometimes be used instead of brackets – for example, they could be used in the last example above (see also 'Commas', page 25, and 'Dashes', page 27).

> Adele's love of small dogs, such as beagles, Jack Russells, poodles and kelpies, is well known.

> Adele's love of small dogs – such as beagles, Jack Russells, poodles and kelpies – is well known.

It is often just a matter of personal preference. Dashes are more appropriate in less formal writing.

Capital letters

Capital letters are also called 'upper case' letters. Words can be written in capital (UPPER CASE) letters or small (lower case) letters, or they can be 'capitalised' (only the first letter of the word is written in upper case). The following types of words are capitalised.

1 The first word of a sentence

> Bring me that glass.

2 People's names and titles

> Zach

> Olivia

> Dr Saint Jorre

3 Proper nouns, including the names of particular organisations or groups

the Australian Stock Exchange

Murdoch University

Rockpool Restaurant

the Hoyts Cinema

the Koori people

4 Days of the week, months of the year and geographical names

Wednesday

August

Alice Springs

Cape Mentelle

5 The greeting in letters

Dear Ronald

Dear Mr Stein

Dear Ms Wasko

My Friends

6 The first word of the complimentary close in letters

Yours sincerely

Yours faithfully

7 Titles of books and films. There are two ways of doing this (use either, but be consistent).

a One way is to capitalise all the important words.

Harry Potter and the Order of the Phoenix

The Man from Snowy River

b Another way is to capitalise only the first word and any words that would normally take a capital

Harry Potter and the order of the phoenix

The man from Snowy River

8 Historical events or periods

the Middle Ages

the Depression

the First World War

ACTIVITY 17

Capital letters

Rewrite the passage below, using capital letters where necessary.

she pleaded with amie to leave perth for her health, 'it will be good to see the whales in hervey bay. they're the largest in the pacific ocean.' She fell silent for a minute, then asked, 'will I be able to listen to my cds of savage garden while we cross the nullarbor?'

ISBN 9780170183048

the next day they went to mcdonald's for breakfast and kfc for lunch: a real pigout! that night she got sick in the toyota and they had to stop at a service station near eucla to rest and clean out the car.

'i'm okay,' she whispered through clenched teeth, 'just don't tell david I was sick.'

Colons

A colon (:) signals that what follows will expand the first part of the sentence. A colon is used to:

1 separate a statement from one that explains or expands on it

> I was overjoyed: I had backed the winner of the Melbourne Cup, won $10000 with scratch and match, and finished my homework in time to watch *MasterChef*.

2 introduce a list

> I lent him four books: *Then* by Morris Gleitzman, *Black Jack Anderson* by Elaine Forrestal, *Dragon Moon* by Carole Wilkinson and *Sixth Grade Style Queen (Not!)* by Sherryl Clark.

3 introduce a quotation

> As the saying goes: 'A healthy mind, a healthy body'.

ACTIVITY 18

Colons

Rewrite the following sentences, adding colons if necessary.

1 Simone was overawed she had won the music award, came first in the athletics and was allowed to wear her nose ring.
2 Ringo was opposed by two giants Patterson from Year 10 and Killer Kelly, a Year 12 repeat.
3 Check the following the town itself, where the militia are reported to be and who fired the first shot.
4 I gave him three videos *Skeleton Key*, *A Lot Like Love* and *Napoleon Dynamite*.
5 You know what they say 'Absence makes the heart grow fonder'.
6 They also say 'Out of sight, out of mind'.

Commas

A comma (,) is used to:

1 separate items in a list or a series

> Issac had an affectionate, intelligent, unpredictable cat.

> Some winners of the Children's Book Council Book of the Year are Libby Gleeson, Shaun Tan, Sonya Hartnett and James Moloney.

2 separate phrases or clauses that add more information but are not essential to the sentence

> Brodie, an only child, was allowed to play with his friend Jonathon.

> Isabelle Thompson, the Wet Fish Manager, gave an interesting talk on conserving stocks of Blue Fin tuna.

> This company, which was formed in 1974 to acquire the operations of a gold mine in South Australia, has become one of the largest in the country.

Pairs of commas, used as in the examples above, are called 'parenthetical commas' because they do similar work to a pair of brackets (also called 'parentheses'). In most cases, it is better to use parenthetical commas because they keep the language flowing.

3 introduce direct speech

> Dan said, 'Now that I've had a cartoon published in the paper, they'll be sure to have a job for me as a cartoonist.'

4 separate the person being addressed from the rest of the sentence

> 'You'll be sorry in the morning, Kathryn Malcolmson, and don't say I didn't warn you!'

> 'Gina, please may I borrow your car today?' enquired her father.

5 separate different parts of a sentence
a when this is necessary to avoid misunderstanding

> The Collingwood team, said the sports writer, is really hopeless.

> While Lucy was cooking, the baby slept in the next room.

Try reading these sentences without the commas; they have a very different meaning.

b when two main clauses that have different subjects are linked by a conjunction such as 'and' or 'but'

> The Federal Government (subject A) has passed the new law, and the Treasurer (subject B) hopes that this will lead to an improvement in the value of the Australian dollar.

> The house (subject A) was advertised as 'a renovator's dream', but we (subject B) all know what that means.

c to separate numbers of five or more digits

> 10,392

> 2,428,547

In printed material, a space is often used instead of a comma for this purpose.

> 10 392

> 2 428 547

ACTIVITY 19

Commas

1 Rewrite the following sentences, adding commas.
a Chi is a warm affectionate intelligent person.
b Pietro screamed. The scriptwriter producer director and Pietro's partner stood open-mouthed.
c This shop which only opened yesterday is already a favourite with the seniors.
d My boyfriend standing between the two officers looked for the first time in his life rather embarrassed.
e Sam whispered 'I'm finally famous'.
f 'If you take me to the concert you never know what might happen' he said which annoyed me.
g 'Johan let go of my jumper.'
h 'You know what Tania Sherwood you're mad!'
i The girl claimed the owner ran away.
j While Juanita ate the cat purred.

ISBN 9780170183048

2 Rewrite the paragraph below, adding colons and commas in the appropriate places.

> Wong whispered 'We need to stick together.' My heart raced my breathing was quiet. The weapons guns knives grenades and booby-traps were ready. I was scared I knew we could die. Wong the only soldier among us looked calm. The enemy said Wong was gutless but as we moved silently through the mud water and reeds we knew they were wrong.

Dashes

Dashes (–) should be used carefully and sparingly, otherwise your writing can become hard to read. A dash can be used:

1. to show a change of thought

    'Come here immediately – and stop sulking.'

    'You'll never believe what I heard about Georgina – not that I want to gossip about her behind her back.'

2. to show that a speaker has been interrupted

    'The trouble with you kids is that you won't listen to – '

    'Aw, come off it, Mum,' said Alexander. 'We've heard it all before.'

3. in place of a colon, before a list

    She looked in disbelief at the contents of the shopping bag – a Mars bar, a packet of chewing gum, a can of Coke, two doughnuts and a can of cat food.

4. to separate additional information from the rest of the sentence in exactly the way that brackets do

    When studying, you should take breaks – five minutes every half hour is ideal – otherwise your concentration will lapse.

    Every spring, she waits for the vegetables to come out in her garden – carrots, beetroot, parsnips, cabbages, leeks, zucchinis and radishes – then digs them all out and starts again.

Ellipsis points

Ellipsis points (…) are three full stops.

1. Ellipsis points are used to indicate that something has been left out of a quotation.

    Winston Churchill is remembered for the rousing speech he made: 'We shall go on to the end … We shall fight on the seas and oceans … We shall fight on the beaches, we shall fight on the landing grounds, we shall fight in the fields and in the streets, we shall fight in the hills; we shall never surrender …'

    The ellipsis points in the middle of the text show that some words have been left out. The ellipsis points at the end indicate that this was not the end of the quotation; more was said that has not been included here.

2. Ellipsis points can also be used in dialogue and sometimes in fictional narrative, to indicate incompleteness or indecision.

    It was the start of a new summer and I had no idea then what it would bring …

    No … no … I didn't mean that.

Exclamation marks

An exclamation mark (!) is used instead of a full stop:

1   after orders

> Watch your step!

> Come over here!

2   after exclamations

> That's ridiculous!

> Hear, hear!

> Hey!

> No way!

3   to show irony or sarcasm

> With friends like you, who needs enemies!

Exclamation marks are usually found in dialogue as they indicate the tone of voice of the speaker.

Full stops

A full stop (.) is used:

1   to end a sentence

> The young beagle barked at the nervous visitor.

2   after an abbreviation

> The Rev. A. Stubbs arrived in Larnook Cres. at 5 p.m.

The most common error with full stops is to forget to put them at the end of sentences.

Points to note

1   An abbreviation is a shortened form that does not end with the final letter of the word – for example, Rev. for Reverend, Cres. for Crescent.

2   A contraction is a shortened form that ends in the final letter of the word – for example, Mr for Mister, Dr for Doctor, Rd for Road, Dept for Department. Full stops are not required after contractions.

3   Abbreviations may be written without full stops when they consist of more than one capital letter – for example, RSVP, NSW, ACT, NT, WA, YMCA, RSPCA, ACTU, PhD.

4   An acronym is a pronounceable word formed from the initial letters of a descriptive phrase. Acronyms are written in block capitals.

> AIDS: Acquired Immune Deficiency Syndrome

> EFTPOS: Electronic Funds Transfer at Point of Sale

If they are considered to have passed into common usage, they may be written in lower case.

> Anzac (originally ANZAC): Australian and New Zealand Army Corps

> laser: light amplification (by) stimulated emission (of) radiation

> radar: radio detection and ranging

> scuba: self-contained underwater breathing apparatus

Acronyms are written without full stops.

5   Symbols or units of measurement do not take full stops.

> km (kilometre)   g (gram)   ha (hectare)   A (ampere)   Hz (hertz)

ISBN 9780170183048

ACTIVITY 20

Full stops

Rewrite the following sentences, putting in full stops where they are needed.

1 Kylie has returned to Sydney for another concert from the moment the show opens the audience is swept away by the spectacle the singer first appears floating over the stage, elegant in a dramatic black and gold costume there is a huge screen that bombards the audience with colourful visuals the star is backed by a talented and athletic dance troupe

2 The film *Twilight* opened to huge box office returns thousands of avid fans of Stephenie Meyer's series of books waited with anticipation they were not disappointed the director has taken care not to change the plot too much as a result the film is rather slow at first but there was plenty to keep the audience enthralled the male lead, Robert Pattinson, is already known to fans for his role in the *Harry Potter* films but this performance will make him a big star

Hyphens

1 Hyphens (-) are used to join two words when this is necessary to make the meaning clear.

> a little-known cricketer *vs* a little known cricketer

> more-useful inventions *vs* more useful inventions

> re-form *vs* reform; re-cover *vs* recover; re-treat *vs* retreat

2 Hyphens are also used to join several words together to make compound words that create a new meaning.

> brother-in-law

> vice-president

> one-twelfth

> long-suffering

> twenty-two

> blue-grey

> even-handed

> well-mannered

Note, however, that two words that are hyphenated to create a compound adjective preceding a noun are not hyphenated when they occur elsewhere.

> a well-known writer *but* the writer was well known

> a good-natured child *but* the child was good natured

3 Complex words, made up of a root word plus a prefix (extra/ordinary, mis/take) generally do not take a hyphen, unless:

a the prefix is followed by a capital letter

> anti-American

> pro-Jewish

> post-Impressionist

b a vowel is doubled

re-establish

de-emphasise

The hyphen makes it easier to know how to pronounce these words. However, in the case of 'coordinate' and 'cooperate', it is now common usage to leave out the hyphen.

c a date is added to the prefix

post-1944

pre-1788

d the prefix is 'ex', 'non' or 'self'

ex-army officer

non-profit organisation

self-taught winemaker

4 Hyphens are also used if you have to divide a word at the end of a line. Where possible, try not to divide words. When you have to, think of your readers and break words according to syllables and sound – for example, com-puter rather than comp-uter; ami-able rather than am-iable. Never divide a word of only one syllable.

There are a few hard and fast rules about the use of hyphens. Generally, hyphens should be used only if they clarify meaning. Check in a dictionary if you are unsure.

Italics

The italic font is used in a way that is very similar to the use of punctuation marks. In handwriting, underlining can be used to indicate italic font.

Italics are used to:

1 emphasise a particular word in a sentence

I told you that I wanted to wear the *blue* tie, not the red one.

I want to make it clear that this assignment *must* be handed in by Monday – without fail!

2 draw attention to an unusual word or to a word that is being used in an unusual way, including archaisms (old, disused words), neologisms (newly invented words) and dialect words

Few Australians appreciate being called *skippies*.

3 draw attention to a word that is being discussed. Quotations marks can also be used for this purpose

Few writers still make a distinction in meaning between *uninterested* and *disinterested*.

4 indicate a foreign word. There is disagreement about which words should be given this treatment, depending on the extent to which it is felt that the word has been adopted into English

The chef brought in the *pièce de résistance* – a beautifully decorated pavlova.

Most people would agree that chef has been accepted as an English word and does not need to be italicised in that sentence. The fact that the French accents are still thought to be needed in pièce de résistance is a good indication that italic font is appropriate.

5 indicate the titles of books, films, and radio and television programs

I like to watch *Home and Away* every night.

6 indicate the names of ships, trains and other forms of transport

The story of *Apollo 11* will never be forgotten.

ISBN 9780170183048

7   indicate stage directions in play or film scripts

> Bill (*laughing*): I told you so!

8   indicate the Latin names (genus and species) of plants and animals

> The Australian floral emblem is the Golden Wattle, *acacia pycnantha*.

Question marks

1   A question mark (?) is used to show that a question is being asked.

> Who will represent the poor and the underprivileged?

2   Question marks are placed immediately after the question. In the event of a nuclear war, what chance will there be for the human race?

> 'What's that you're carrying, Eccles?' enquired Bluebottle.

> Did you prevent the puppy from tearing the place apart? How?

> What kind of tea would you like: English Breakfast? Earl Grey? peppermint? chamomile?

3   If there is any other punctuation, the question mark always comes first.

> 'Did you buy the rum balls?' he asked anxiously.

4   Sometimes the wording of a question and a statement can be the same. The reader only knows the difference because of the punctuation. The listener knows the difference because of the pitch of the speaker's voice.

> He did that!

> He did that?

5   Question marks are also used to express doubt.

> In 1998 (?), Arsenal won the League and Cup double.

> Patrick White was the first (?) Australian to win the Nobel Prize for literature.

6   Question marks are not used for indirect questions or requests.

> Nishan asked Bronte whether she was going to the party. (indirect question)

> Would you please pass the butter. (request)

An indirect question is one that is reported rather than quoted. If the example above were a direct question, it would read:

> 'Are you going to the party, Bronte?' asked Nishan.

Quotation marks

Quotation marks (' '), also called quotes, speech marks and inverted commas, are used to show:

1   the actual words of a speaker (direct speech)

2   a quotation

3   the special use of a word or phrase.

You may use either double or single quotation marks in your writing. Publishers generally use single quotation marks for printed material but double quotes are recommended for handwritten material.

Double quotes are used within single quotes and single quotes are used within double quotes:

> Claire said to her friend Ana, 'When I first came here, I couldn't spell "Giddegannup".
> Now I dream of owning half the valley.'

1 Direct speech

1 The quotation marks are placed at the beginning and end of each person's speech.

> 'I ain't got my guitar', Paolo said.

2 There is a new paragraph for each new speaker.

3 When a speech lasts for several paragraphs, quotation marks are put at the beginning of each paragraph, but only at the end of the last one.

> 'Four score and seven years ago our fathers brought forth on this continent a new nation, conceived in liberty, and dedicated to the proposition that all men are created equal.
>
> 'Now we are engaged in a great civil war, testing whether that nation, or any nation so conceived and so dedicated, can long endure. We are met on a great battle field of the war. We have come to dedicate a portion of that field, as a final resting place for those who here gave their lives that that nation might live. It is altogether fitting and proper that we should do this.
>
> 'But in a larger sense, we cannot dedicate – we cannot consecrate – we cannot hallow this ground.'

4 If direct speech is interrupted by words such as 'she said', the first word of the second part only takes a capital letter if it is the beginning of a new sentence.

> 'It's dark,' Jerry Lee said. 'Won't hardly nobody even see you in a weak little light like this one.'
>
> 'Oh, for goodness' sakes,' said Olive, 'if the boy don't want to –'

These examples are from Katherine Paterson's novel *Come Sing, Jimmy Jo*. In the first, 'Won't' has a capital letter because it is the beginning of a new sentence. In the second, 'if' does not have a capital because it is a continuation of the sentence beginning 'Oh, for goodness' sakes'.

Direct speech in scripts for plays and films, and television and radio does not require quotation marks as long as the name of the speaker is in the margin or above. See page 111 for an example.

2 Short quotations

When quoting someone else, place their words in quotation marks.

> As Dennis says in *Monty Python and the Holy Grail*: 'Come and see the violence inherent in the system. Help, help, I'm being repressed!'
>
> Remember what Niland Stuart once said: 'The greatest compliment you can pay a book is to steal it.'

Page 90 gives information on how to set out longer quotations.

3 Indicating 'special' words or phrases

Quotation marks are used to enclose:

1 words or phrases that are being referred to or quoted

> The words 'imply' and 'infer' are often confused.

2 words or phrases that are considered slang, technical language or nicknames

> The American visitor was amused when his Australian friend said that he felt a little 'crook' with a cold.
>
> In basketball this is known as a 'double dribble'.

ISBN 9780170183048

Josh Keylock is sometimes called 'Digger' by his sister.

The quotation marks are only needed the first time these terms are mentioned.

3   titles of poems, songs, short stories, articles, essays, lectures, radio programs and episodes of television programs

'The Man from Snowy River' by Banjo Paterson has been made into a film.

My favourite episode of *The Simpsons* was 'Last Exit to Springfield'.

ACTIVITY 21

Direct speech

1 Rewrite the following statements, adding quotation marks.
  a What's she like after the accident? Henri asked. Can she walk?
  b I'm not keen on bungee jumping, Shane grunted, let's go scuba diving. I'm not going to jump off some bridge.
  c Where are you? she whispered.
  Over here, he mumbled.
  Why did you leave us? she asked.
  I can't stand being near her any more, he replied, it hurts too much.
  Oh!
2 Why is there a full stop after 'asked', followed by a capital letter in Question 1, but a comma and no capital after 'grunted' in Question 2?

Short quotations

3 Rewrite the following statements, adding quotation marks.
  a Lennox once said: You have only so many heartbeats in your life. Why use up those precious beats by exercising?
  b According to Willis: Our world is made up of the thinkers, the doers and the followers. Which one are you?
  c Who said: Beware of Greeks bearing gifts?
  d What is meant by: Don't get caught between a rock and a hard place?
  e Rewrite the following passage, inserting quotation marks where necessary. You may need to begin a new paragraph for a new speaker.

  You're not the person I once knew, Kerry sneered. Sophie ignored his remark. You used to be so glamorous, he continued venomously, and you were friendly! What about you? she suddenly blurted. Where were you when Jamie drowned? Where were you when everyone said it was my fault? Where were you when they took me away for years and years? Shh … He leant forward. I'm sorry. I'm sorry … I missed you.

4 Continue the dialogue in Question 3e, using quotation marks.

Semicolons

A semicolon (;) indicates a pause that is longer than a comma but shorter than a full stop. In most cases, a semicolon could be replaced by a full stop, but this would not highlight the connection between the two statements. Semicolons are used:

1   to emphasise the link between clauses that could have been separate sentences

Bridie Allen was the selectors' first choice; she was quiet, intelligent and determined to succeed.

ISBN 9780170183048

George Orwell tried to write a novel without using any semicolons; in spite of his best endeavours, he failed.

He spoke to Carolina with exaggerated politeness; his purpose was to insult her.

2   when items on a list need to be clearly separated

Those invited to the dinner party were Ben Vittino, video game designer; Oliver Burns, the popular actor; Freya Wheatley, the famous pianist; the well-known writer Elliot Codrington; Amelie Boulden, social worker for the Leukaemia Foundation; and Imogen Mugford, the Olympic gymnast.

3   when a clause begins with words such as 'that is', 'however', 'for instance', 'indeed', 'moreover', 'therefore', 'in fact', 'besides' and 'consequently'

Tia claimed that her brother was a misogynist; that is, a person who hates women.

We want to go trekking in Nepal later this year; however, we have made no definite plans.

ACTIVITY 22

Semicolons

Rewrite the following sentences, inserting semicolons.
1 When the surf's up, he's happy when it's down, he's down.
2 If you learn how to do this correctly, you'll have no problems if you learn it incorrectly, you'll never get it right.
3 This whale can be so unpredictable in a flash it surged out of the water with a huge violent spray.
4 The winning song was a mixture of rock and techno a video filled with action and colour a record company that was prepared to take a risk a radio station that gave it lots of air time and an audience that screamed the house down.
5 We will have to walk back to the river that is, if you want to reach Darwin tonight.
6 I just love everything about it for example, the way you can float down the mountain at dusk.
7 He trained so hard for that triathlon, he neglected everything else consequently he lost both his girlfriend and his job moreover, he didn't win.

ACTIVITY 23

Revising punctuation

Rewrite the following statements, adding punctuation. Compare your work with that of a partner. You could punctuate quite differently but still be correct.
1   I tore off my tee-shirt and walked down to the river Suzie was there washing some clothes
2   Hello she said
3   Gday
4   How are you feeling
5   Okay
6   Hungry
7   Yeah Im starvn
8   Im not surprised you havent eaten anything since the day before yesterday
9   Havent I have I been out that long
10 Come on Ill fix you something you like snags

ISBN 9780170183048

LANGUAGE CONVENTIONS: GRAMMAR

3

In the past, grammar was seen as a set of rules that tells us the correct way to say something. A more helpful view of grammar is to see it as one of the systems of language – a system that explains the way we combine words to make meaning. Grammar can be defined as both the way words are formed and structured (known as **morphology**), and the way words combine to form phrases, clauses and sentences (known as **syntax**). Understanding grammar may help us to make choices about the words we use in our writing and the order in which we use them. Knowing grammatical terms can also be an advantage when talking about how language works.

Those who speak English as a first language are, from a very young age, experts in English grammar. They know the language system and how to use it. There is unlikely to be any argument over which of the following sentences are grammatically correct and which are not.

1   James gave his brother a French stamp from his collection.
2   James a stamp French his brother from collection his gave.
3   The wind is extremely fierce today.
4   The wind are extremely today fierce.
5   The ruggin was trulling a nort into the custy diz.
6   The distance between Sydney and Melbourne is ten kilometres.

Sentences 2 and 4 do not conform to the basic structure of English sentences. Sentence 5 does, even though it contains five nonsense words; it is a grammatically correct sentence even though we do not understand it. The last sentence follows the English language system (in other words, it is grammatically correct), even though the information it gives is incorrect.

Paragraphs

Just as you can string together a series of words and make no sense if they are not in the correct grammatical order, you can string together a series of sentences to make what appears to be a paragraph but it can be meaningless if it lacks cohesion. Every paragraph needs a unified idea, often expressed in the first sentence (the topic sentence or paragraph opener). Sentences within the paragraph are tied or linked together by a number of grammatical features.

Cohesive ties or links are created by text connectives. These include adverbs such as 'however' and 'nevertheless', as well as adverbials of time such as 'first', 'second', 'to begin with' and 'finally'. Pronouns also operate as text connectives: instead of repeating nouns, we substitute pronouns, which refer back to those nouns, creating links. Word associations (sometimes called 'lexical chains') also make links: a paragraph about loyalty, for example, may use – as well as the word 'loyalty' itself – the related adjective 'loyal', its antonym 'disloyal', related nouns such as 'faithfulness' and 'devotion', and nouns that have an opposite meaning such as 'treachery'. Ellipsis (the leaving out of words or phrases) is also used for cohesion (to avoid unnecessary and awkward repetition); for example, 'The boys and girls lined up outside the classroom, (the boys and girls) filed into class and (the boys and girls) waited for the teacher to arrive'.

Sentences

One way of describing a sentence is as a 'chunk' of writing. We organise our writing into chunks because this makes it easier to understand. Good readers read chunks rather than individual words, and we speak in chunks rather than in single words. Native speakers of English pick up a great deal about English sentence structure from a very early age. They would immediately be able to tell which of the following is a complete sentence:

> Joel kicked

> Joel kicked a

> Joel kicked a football.

Sentences always begin with a capital letter and end with a full stop, a question mark or an exclamation mark. Complete sentences have a subject and a predicate. The **subject** describes who or what did the action, and always contains a noun or pronoun. The **predicate** tells what action was performed.

In the sentence above, 'Joel' is the subject, and 'kicked a football' is the predicate. In this case we can further divide the predicate into the verb ('kicked') and its object ('a football'). An object always contains a noun (or pronoun).

Some grammarians describe the noun or pronoun in the subject as the participant (telling us who or what participates in the action), and the verb as a process (telling us what happens). Many sentences also include the circumstances surrounding the action, called the adverbial.

The words that make up a sentence are categorised into parts of speech according to their function in the sentence; that is, they are nouns, verbs, adjectives or adverbs (see 'Content words' on page 41); or pronouns, conjunctions, prepositions or determiners (see 'Structural words' on page 52).

Clauses

Sentences are made up of one or more clauses. A clause is a unit of words that contains a subject and a verb.

> The first mangoes of the season are auctioned for charity. (Subject: the first mangoes of the season; verb: are auctioned)

> Joel kicked a football in his backyard. (Subject: Joel; verb: kicked)

Subordinate clauses are clauses that depend on main clauses and cannot stand on their own as sentences.

> We discovered *why he didn't want to come to the party*. (noun clause)

> I visited the town *where Hannah was born*. (adjectival clause)

> Amelia fished *while her mother read a book in the shade*. (adverbial clause)

Adverbial clauses make connections between ideas; for example: to provide a reason (I'm late *because the dog ate my homework*); to state a purpose (I thought up an excuse *so that I would not get into trouble*); to express a condition (I will lend you my homework *if you let me borrow your iPad*); to make a concession (I agreed *even though Mum had told me never to lend my iPad to anyone*); to express time (I waited *while he played a game*).

Phrases

A phrase is a group of words that act together as a unit of meaning in a sentence. Phrases can do the work of nouns, adjectives and adverbs.

> The man *in the top hat* works for a circus.

'In the top hat' is a phrase that does the work of an adjective; it describes the noun 'man'. It is an adjectival phrase. It could be replaced by an adjective: The *top-hatted* man works for a circus.

> Please place your lunches *in the basket*.

ISBN 9780170183048

'In the basket' is a phrase that does the work of an adverb; it is modifying the verb 'place'. It is an adverbial phrase. It could be replaced by an adverb: Please place your lunches *there*.

> *Eating mangoes* can be rather messy.

'Eating mangoes' is a phrase that does the work of a noun; it is the subject of the verb 'can be'. It is a noun phrase. It could be replaced by a noun: *Spaghetti* can be rather messy.

Phrases do not have a subject and a predicate and so cannot stand alone.

There are other groups of words that make a unit of meaning, although they do not have a subject or a verb. These are clusters, or groups, of words.

> the majority of eucalyptus trees in Australia (a noun cluster or noun group)
>
> had been walking (a verb cluster or verb group)
>
> long, lazy, fun-filled (an adjective cluster or adjective group)
>
> extremely quietly (an adverb cluster or adverb group)

Types of sentences

1   A **simple sentence** is a main clause with no other clauses linked to it.

> The beach was crowded on the first Saturday of summer.

2   A **compound sentence** has two (or more) main clauses. These are usually linked by a coordinating conjunction such as 'and', 'but' or 'or'.

> The beach was crowded on the first Saturday of summer but was totally deserted the next day.

3   A **complex sentence** has a main clause that contains at least one subordinate clause within it.

> We discovered the boy while he was lighting the fire.

4   A **compound-complex sentence** has at least two main clauses and at least one subordinate clause.

> The beach was crowded on the first Saturday of summer but was totally deserted when it rained the next day.

Sentences can have many patterns, including the following.

[Subject]	[Predicate]		
The young girl	welcomed the visiting musician.		
	[Verb]	[Object]	

[Subject]		[Predicate]	
Shannon	gave	the football	to his brother.
	[Verb]	[Object]	[Indirect object]

[Subject]		[Predicate]	
Lawnmowers		are	noisy.
		[Linking verb]	[Adjective]

[Subject]	[Predicate]
Boys	cry.
	[Verb]

Complete sentences are not essential in all types of communication. They are expected in expository writing, fiction (except in dialogue) and in formal speeches, but not in conversation, advertising and writing of a private nature such as journal or diary entries, lists or notes. Incomplete sentences are called fragmentary or truncated sentences.

ISBN 9780170183048

ACTIVITY 24

Sentences

1 Rewrite the following paragraph, filling in the blanks.

Sentences have a _____ and a _____. The _____ describes who or what did something and always contains a _____ or pronoun. The _____ tells us what action was performed and therefore contains a _____.

2 Rewrite the following sentences. Underline the subject and circle the predicate.
- **a** Maria stepped gingerly onto the ice.
- **b** Cassie tripped.
- **c** He felt an unruly anger pounding within him.
- **d** The whale surfaced, piercing me with its eye.
- **e** 'Come here', she screamed.

3 Rewrite the following sentences. Underline the verb and circle its object.
- **a** The tearful child looked at the officer.
- **b** Chui lobbed the ball.
- **c** Robert rose from his seat and began to circle the courtroom.
- **d** The ball, kicked hard by Loretta, arced high in the air.
- **e** He froze in the shade.

Phrases and clauses

4 Explain the difference between a phrase and a clause.

5 Identify the following types of phrases in the sentences: noun, adjectival or adverbial
- **a** I was watching the girl in the red dress.
- **b** You will find them in the garden.
- **c** Watching television is boring.
- **d** After dinner we watched the new DVD.
- **e** To err is human.
- **f** Wearing a new red dress, the girl felt very confident.

6 Create three different types of phrases of your own, identifying each type.

7 The following sentences have more than one clause. Rewrite them, underlining and identifying the clauses.
- **a** Brutus barked when he heard the footsteps.
- **b** We went to the grave where the ghost was buried.
- **c** Shako swam while Spiro sat and gazed into the sky.
- **d** 'If you come with me', she said, 'I'll show you how to turn yourself inside out.'
- **e** 'Hello, do you live around here, or are you part of the furniture?' he asked her quietly.

8 Match each main clause from Column A with the best subordinate clause from Column B

Column A	Column B
a We did the shopping	so we missed the opening.
b The car stopped	until her dog is found.
c She won't leave the grounds	while we stared at it.
d We were late	before it hit the koala.
e The cake disintegrated	because the centre was air-conditioned.

ISBN 9780170183048

Types of sentences

9 Write out the following sentences and identify whether they are simple, compound or complex.
- **a** D-day had come and after we checked our gear we boarded the Apaches.
- **b** A single shot rang out as the pilot desperately clawed skywards.
- **c** The aircraft was crammed with our equipment.
- **d** The day dawned while we dared to speak only in whispers.
- **e** The landing looked peaceful but that proved to be deceptive.
- **f** 'Stop!'

Word order

The meaning of a sentence is influenced partly by word order and partly by the choice of individual words. Look at the following examples.

1   Moving one word to different positions in a sentence can produce quite different meanings.

> Luke only saw Amy last week.
>
> Luke saw only Amy last week.
>
> Luke saw Amy only last week.
>
> Only Luke saw Amy last week.

2   The words ferocious, hit, the, criminal, policeman, cheerful and the can be rearranged into (at least) four different equally grammatical statements.

> The ferocious criminal hit the cheerful policeman.
>
> The cheerful criminal hit the ferocious policeman.
>
> The cheerful policeman hit the ferocious criminal.
>
> The ferocious policeman hit the cheerful criminal.

      The changes in word order have resulted in four sentences with quite different meanings. It is the order of the words, rather than the words themselves, that makes the meaning.

3   Changing the word order also changes the meaning in the following sentences.

> Alex is a diabetic.
>
> Is Alex a diabetic?
>
> Last week, Juan played the cello his mum bought.
>
> Juan played the cello his mum bought last week.
>
> Swimming between the jetties, we saw Isabella and Chloe.
>
> We saw Isabella and Chloe swimming between the jetties.
>
> Jessica called her friend handsome.
>
> Jessica called her handsome friend.

      Word order is very important in English as it is the main way of showing the relationship between the words in a sentence. In many other languages the relationship between words can be shown by inflections added to words (for example, an ending to a noun might indicate whether it is a subject or an object), whereas in English it is word order that tells us what is what.

Inflection

Inflection is a change made to a base word to show a grammatical relationship. Unlike many other languages, English has only a few inflections – word order is much more important than inflections in showing the grammatical relationships.

1   Most nouns inflect to become plural with the addition of –s or –es; for example, teachers is the inflected form of the base word teacher; bushes of bush; and babies of baby.

2   Nouns also inflect to become possessive with the addition of 's or just the apostrophe.

>   Elaine's cat

>   ten companies' reports

3   Verbs inflect to show changes in time. The base form of a verb (work, call or pull) is the one you will find in the dictionary (this form is called the infinitive). This is inflected by adding –s or –es for the present tense and –ed for the past tense; hence works, calls, pulls, worked, called and pulled.

We learn to inflect very early in our lives. Mistakes children make when they say 'Dan goed to school' or 'He bringed the toys' occur because they are using regular inflections with some of the many irregular verbs in the English language.

ACTIVITY 25

Word order

1   Rearrange the following sentences into as many different meanings as possible by shifting only one word.
   a   Boys ate only the girl's cooking last month.
   b   The dolphins usually swim towards us at dusk.

2   Rearrange the following sentences into as many different meanings as possible by shifting several words.
   a   The exhausted fireman gripped the old man firmly.
   b   The smiling girl offered to help the frightened boy.

3   Rearrange the following sentences to change their meanings.
   a   Juanita was working too hard.
   b   Tachia lost the football her dad bought last month.
   c   Racing around the back we called out to Nick and his mate.
   d   Jonno called his girlfriend gorgeous.

Inflection

4   Change the following nouns to plural.

>   woman   bee   ox   pass   ball   judge   screech   bacterium   lunch

5   Change the following nouns to make them possessive. Add another word to show what they possess.

>   Adam   girls   Kas   argument   dog   owner   wave   Stacey

6   Change the following verbs into the past- and present-tense forms used with the third-person singular pronoun 'he' or 'she'. The first one is done for you.

>   walk   *walks*   *walked*

>   whisper   belong   arise   seem   ride   jump   cast   sing

ISBN 9780170183048

Content words

Nouns, verbs, adjectives and adverbs are called **content** or **lexical words** because they have meaning even when they stand alone. In sentences, they are the words that provide most of the meaning. They are words whose meanings we might look up in a dictionary.

We can recognise whether a content word is a noun, verb, adjective or adverb from:

- the word order
- the way the word is inflected
- the signal words that accompany it.

Nouns

In traditional grammar, a noun is a 'word that names a person, place or thing'. This definition is now considered to be somewhat limited. Consider the following examples.

> Mia saw the changes.
>
> Aran changes the saw.

The word 'changes' is a noun in the first example and a verb in the second, and the word 'saw' is a verb in the first example and a noun in the second. We recognise a noun less by its definition than by its function in a sentence.

Recognising nouns

Several things will help you to recognise nouns when they are used in sentences.

1   Inflection (to show plural or possession).
2   Characteristic endings (or suffixes) such as –ion, –er, –ness, –ity, –ty, –ure, –ist, –ment, –hood, –ster, and –ship usually signify that the word is a noun.
3   Structure words, such as the definite article ('the') and the indefinite articles ('a' and 'an'), signal that a noun will follow. These may clear up ambiguity, as in the following example.

> Baby swallows fly.

Structure words clarify meaning and tell us which words are nouns and which are verbs.

> The baby swallows a fly.
>
> The baby swallows fly.

4   Word order: the fact that nouns can be either the subject (the thing that does something) or the object (the thing to which something is done) of a sentence, and are often found at the beginnings and ends of sentences, will help you to recognise nouns if you use this information with the other clues you have.

> The dog (subject) chased the ball (object).

Categories of nouns

1   **Proper nouns** name particular people, places and things and always begin with capital letters.

> *Adele* lives in *Wembley* and her birthday is in *August*.

2   **Common nouns** refer to people, places or things that we can see, hear, taste, touch or smell, and to things that are part of our physical world.

> The *cat* climbed out the *window*, chased after the *birds*, *dragonflies* and *lizards* and finally caught a little *snake*.

3   **Collective nouns** refer to groups of individuals.

> committee   army   audience   choir   team   orchestra   crowd

4   Proper nouns, common nouns and collective nouns are all concrete nouns: words describing people, animals, places or objects that we can see and touch. **Abstract nouns** refer to things we cannot experience in a physical sense; that is, to states of being (such as happiness, joy and thirst) and qualities (such as courage, dedication and pride).

ACTIVITY 26

Nouns

1   Classify each of the following nouns into one of the four types of nouns: proper, common, collective or abstract.

Pierre	Mt Kosciusko	happiness	audience	greed
ship	loyalty	convoy	birthday	
sadness	diligence	choir	warmth	

2   For each of the common nouns below, write a proper noun. The first one is done for you.

Common noun	Proper noun
country	Japan
explorer	
ship	
mountain	
hospital	
car	
clothes	
band	

3   Write out and identify the types of nouns in the following passage.

> Jo lives in Melbourne while Maria and Alexis live in Perth. All drive supercharged Commodores at fearful speeds across the Nullarbor. The police, army and SES have all tried to catch them in their bright yellow machines. But like ghosts in the night, they manage to slip through. When parked side by side they inevitably draw onlookers. Last year a snake slid out from under Jo's car and scattered the crowd. Happiness, joy and frivolity were not the words to describe their response.

4   Write a paragraph. Ensure you include and identify (in brackets) the four different types of nouns. Begin with:

'The skateboard had a mind of its own …'

5   For each of the following nouns, write three more precise ones. The first one is done for you.

Common noun (general)	Common noun (specific)
animal	lion, cougar, mouse
furniture	
city	
emotion	
disease	
athlete	
food	
plant	
performer	

ISBN 9780170183048

6 Replace the following pairs of words with a single noun. The first one is done for you.

Description	Single noun
cruel leader	*despot*
planned attack	
tall man	
rough person	
strong wind	
old person	
young person	
unpaid worker	

7 Create a collective noun that you feel fits the following common nouns. Use your imagination to create some interesting collective nouns. The first one is done for you.

a *murder* of crows

a _____ of bees   a _____ of soldiers

a _____ of elephants   a _____ of dancers

a _____ of children   a _____ of artists

a _____ of whales   a _____ of toenails

Verbs

A verb is a word that expresses an action or a state of being.

Juanita *hit* David.

David *screamed*.

Verbs have five main forms:

1   The base form (or infinitive)

play (or to play), grab, behave, tell, make

2   The present tense

He plays, grabs, behaves, tells, makes

3   The past tense

She played, grabbed, behaved, told, made

4   The present participle

(He is) playing, grabbing, behaving, telling, making

5   The past participle

(She has) played, grabbed, behaved, told, made

Transitive and intransitive verbs

1   **Transitive verbs** have a subject (which does something) and an object (the person or thing to which something is done).

[Subject]	[Transitive verb]	[Object]
The cat	chased	the dog.
[The doer]	[The action]	[The receiver]

[Subject]	[Transitive verb]	[Object]
Swarup	owned	a bird.
[The doer]	[The action]	[The receiver]

Transitive verbs can be used in either the active or the passive voice.

> The cat chased the dog. (active voice)

> The dog was chased by the cat. (passive voice)

In the passive voice, the subject of the active verb becomes the object of the passive verb. The object of the active verb is moved to the beginning of the sentence and becomes the subject of the passive verb. The active verb form (chased) changes to the passive form (was chased).

Note: Try to use the active voice as much as possible in your writing because it is more direct and more forceful. However, there is certainly a place for the passive voice, particularly in informational writing.

2   **Intransitive verbs** are verbs that cannot take an object. When you use an intransitive verb, you do not need any more words after the verb to complete the sentence.

[Subject]	[Intransitive verb]
The principal	laughed.
[The doer]	[The action]

[Subject]	[Intransitive verb]
The bus	stopped.
[The doer]	[The action]

Types of verbs

1   **Action verbs**: The majority of verbs are action verbs – run, jump, play, sing, wander, shout and so on. These are 'doing' words.

2   **Linking** or **relating verbs** do not express action, but simply link the subject to a word or group of words which define it (the 'complement'). The complement may be a noun, pronoun or adjective.

Munch	is	a dog.
[Subject]	[Linking verb]	[Complement]

Munch	is	a small, gentle, tricolour dog.
[Subject]	[Linking verb]	[Complement]

The dog	is	his.
[Subject]	[Linking verb]	[Complement]

The roast chicken	smells	delicious.
[Subject]	[Linking verb]	[Complement]

3   Some grammarians classify certain other types of verbs that in traditional grammar are included as action verbs. These include verbs of thinking, saying and sensing.

4   **Auxiliary verbs** are a small group of verbs that accompany other verbs when those verbs are written in certain tenses.

> He *has* explained the matter to me.

> As I walked past the house, the two boys *were* talking outside.

The main auxiliary verbs are 'to be', 'to have' and 'to do'. They take the following forms.

• 'To be' is the base form or the infinitive. This table shows the present- and past-tense forms.

Pronoun	Present tense	Past tense
I	am	was
you	are	were
he, she, it	is	was
we	are	were
you	are	were
they	are	were

ISBN 9780170183048

The present participle is being ('I am being'; 'you were being').

The past participle is been ('I have been'; 'you had been').

- 'To have' is the base form or the infinitive. This table shows the present- and past-tense forms.

Pronoun	Present tense	Past tense
I	have	had
you	have	had
he, she, it	has	had
we	have	had
you	have	had
they	have	had

The present participle is having ('I am having'; 'You were having').

The past participle is had ('I have had'; 'You had had').

- 'To do' is the base form or the infinitive. This table shows the present- and past-tense forms.

Pronoun	Present tense	Past tense
I	do	did
you	do	did
he, she, it	does	did
we	do	did
you	do	did
they	do	did

The present participle is doing ('I am doing'; 'You were doing').

The past participle is done ('I have done'; 'You had done').

The future tense is formed using the auxiliary verb will ('I will go to the pictures tomorrow; they will come with me'). English does not always use the future tense to express an idea of future time. We can say, for example, 'I am going to go to the pictures tomorrow'.

Modal auxiliary verbs are forms that show how obliged the subject is to perform the action of the verb. The following are modal verbs.

will, would   shall, should   may, might   can, could   must

Consider the subtle differences suggested by the following examples:

I will do my homework.

I can do my homework

I might do my homework.

I must do my homework.

The choice of modal verb determines whether a sentence is expressing a sense of permission, obligation or ability, or a degree of probability. Modality can also be expressed by the use of adverbs (perhaps, probably, never), adjectives (possible, likely) and nouns (the possibility, the certainty).

Moods

A verb may be in the indicative, imperative or subjunctive mood.

1   The **indicative mood** is used for all statements, questions and exclamations.

Ali can go to the shop.

Will you go to the shop?

Must you do that!

2   The **imperative mood** is used for commands.

Come here!   Don't do that!

3 The **subjunctive mood** is used to express a wish, a possibility or a doubt. It is not used much in English these days.

> I wish I were able to help.

> If I were you, I'd leave right now.

Recognising verbs

Several things may help you to recognise verbs when they are used in sentences: inflection, signal words, word order, and prefixes and suffixes.

1 Inflection

Verbs inflect to show changes in time. The base form of regular verbs (such as climb, shout and march) is inflected by:

- –s or –es for the present tense (climbs, shouts, marches)
- –ed for the past tense (climbed, shouted, marched)
- –ing for the present participle (climbing, shouting, marching)
- –ed for the past participle (climbed, shouted, marched).

2 Signal words – auxiliaries

Some verb tenses are formed with auxiliary verbs such as 'to be' and 'to have' (see page 44).

> Sas and Olivia were going to Western Australia for a holiday.

When you see an auxiliary verb in a sentence, it can indicate that the next word is a verb. In the example above, the auxiliary verb 'were' is followed by the verb 'going'.

Of course, not all verb tenses are formed with auxiliaries (Sas and Olivia went to Western Australia), and the auxiliary verbs are also main verbs in their own right (Sas and Olivia were in Western Australia), so you need to be careful.

3 Word order

Because verbs form the link between subject and object, word order provides an obvious clue to the verbs in a sentence.

> Rover ate his bone.

'Rover' is the subject and 'his bone' is the object, so the word that links the two, 'ate', is the verb.

4 Verb prefixes and suffixes

Apart from the regular inflections that show the parts of a verb (such as –ed to show the past tense), there are some prefixes and suffixes which are common to many verbs. Knowing these should help you to recognise verbs.

Prefixes

de–	meaning 'down', 'away'	depend, descend, depart, defend, deduct
re–	meaning 'back'	recall, repay
pre–	meaning 'before'	predict, prevent
dis–	meaning 'apart', 'away'	distinguish, dismiss, dispose, disappear
mis–	meaning 'badly'	mislead, misbehave

Suffixes

–ise		practise, advise, devise
–ify		glorify, qualify, verify
–ate		celebrate, decorate, hesitate
–en		lighten, widen, fasten

ISBN 9780170183048

ACTIVITY 27

Verbs

1 Write out the sentences below, underlining the verbs. Insert brackets around each verb.
   a She was trying to be extraordinary.
   b The dancer collapsed.
   c The coach leapt onto the stage.
   d He is a powerful, gentle protector.
   e All the crew were having a whale of a time.
   f I'm eating the watermelon.
   g I'm starving!
   h The car wheels screeched.
   i He smelt like a sewer but what a runner.

2 Rewrite the following sentences, changing present-tense verbs to past tense and past-tense verbs to present tense. Indicate, in brackets, which tense you have chosen.
   a She runs well.
   b David is going to school.
   c He climbed that wall yesterday.
   d I am climbing the same wall.
   e We are all running in the same race tomorrow.
   f They descended into the gorge slowly.

3 Rewrite the following sentences and underline the verbs.
   a To predict the future is a dream.
   b Can you distinguish between ice-cream and yoghurt?
   c Never glorify violence in films.
   d We must fumigate the whole house.
   e To our dismay, it rained after all.

4 Underline the modal auxiliaries in the following sentences.
   a You should apologise.
   b I might come with you.
   c The children may leave early today.
   d Could you help me with the washing up?
   e May I borrow your bike?

Noun–verb agreement

1   A singular noun takes a singular verb and a plural noun takes a plural verb.

   The dog was barking at the postman. (singular subject and verb)

   The dogs were barking at the postman. (plural subject and verb)

2   Compound subjects are plural and so take plural verbs.

   Alice and her mother live in St Kilda.

   The pies and sausage rolls were eaten before Glynda arrived home.

In the following sentences the singular is used because only one person is involved in each case.

   Here lies a brave Australian, a scholar and a wonderful husband.

   The leading goalscorer and club secretary is Phivo Georgiou.

3   When expressions such as 'in addition to', 'as well as' and 'besides' are used with a singular subject, the verb remains singular.

> Our teacher, as well as his wife and sons, is going to the opera with us tonight.

> That bunch of bananas, as well as the apples and peaches, is more than enough for me.

4   A collective noun is always singular when it refers to a group as a unit, but is plural when it refers to the members of the group individually.

> The choir is singing with the orchestra.

> Our class are having their teeth examined by the school dentist.

5   Most nouns that are plural in form but singular in meaning take singular verbs.

> Mathematics is my favourite subject.

> The television news starts at seven o'clock.

6   After a compound subject joined by 'or', 'nor', 'either ... or' or 'neither ... nor', the verb agrees with the nearer part of the subject.

> Either Arsenal or Spurs is certain to play in the Cup Final.

> Neither the players nor the captain has notified the manager.

> Neither the captain nor the players have notified the manager.

7   When a sentence begins with 'there' or 'here', the verb agrees with the subject that follows it.

> There was an interruption while the police cleared the pig from the oval.

> There were several interruptions while the Speaker tried to restore order.

> Here are some hints to save you from embarrassment.

> Here is a hint to save you from embarrassment.

8   The verb agrees with its subject, not its complement.

> Our first thought was for the sheep, goats and horses.

> The sheep, goats and horses were our first thought.

> My main involvement has been with the Year 8 and Year 9 groups.

> The Year 8 and Year 9 groups have been my main involvement.

ACTIVITY 28

Verbs

1 Rewrite the following passage, filling in the blanks using the words in orange. Some words will be used more than once.

verb   singular   subject   plural   number

> When a sentence has a _____ it must have a _____
> verb. If a sentence has a plural subject, it must have a _____
> verb. In other words, a _____ must agree with its subject in
> _____ as well as in person. A collective noun, such as 'the
> orchestra', usually takes a _____ verb. However, if we refer to the
> members of the orchestra then we must use a _____ verb.

ISBN 9780170183048

2 Rewrite the following sentences, selecting the correct noun–verb agreement.
  a The orchestra is/are well trained.
  b The brass section is/are all over 15.
  c Pietro was/were aiming at me.
  d Was/were Holden the best seller?
  e The team was/were bussed to the ground.
  f Our coach, as well as his assistant and the secretary, is/are going to the final.
  g Draughts is/are my favourite board game.
  h Either Emma or Esther is/are playing with our team.
  i Here is/are a bunch of flowers for your room.
  j The worst experience in my life, and the most frightening, was/were when I was only five.
  k Was/were any one of the athletes suitable?
  l Was/were either of the athletes suitable?
  m Good news travel/travels fast.
  n Our class is/are having its photo taken tomorrow.

3 Change the following nouns into verbs and write them in sentences.

  excitement   assessment   performance   adviser   encouragement
  admiration   description   approval   procedure   attendance

4 Rewrite the following sentences, replacing the verbs with stronger, more effective ones. The first one is done for you.
  a Zoe *thought for a long time.*   *Zoe pondered.*
  b Exhausted, she *walked on shaky legs* along the alley.
  c Chi *fell heavily* onto the concrete.
  d Full of anger, Robyn *spoke at the top of her voice.*
  e The swamp *was filled* with the sound of mosquitoes.
  f 'And,' she added with eyes that *were bright*, 'I could drive the Merc!'

Adjectives

Adjectives express qualities or properties of nouns or pronouns. Traditionally, they were called 'describing words' and were said to modify (or qualify) nouns. Here are some examples of adjectives.

  big   friendly   black   restless   magical
  grumpy   famous   national   active

The following grammatical signals will help you to recognise adjectives.

1 Word order may indicate whether a word is an adjective or not. In English, adjectives most commonly appear before nouns and after linking or relating verbs.
  a Before a noun, adjectives are modifying words.

    The friendly dog ran down to the beach.

    Estelle wrote in the black book.

  b After a linking or relating verb, adjectives modify the noun by acting as the complement.

    The dog is friendly. (friendly dog)

    Jaz wrote in the book, which is black. (black book)

2 Adjectives in turn can be modified by adverbs such as very, too, extremely, thoroughly and quite. These are called **intensifiers** because they change the force or intensity of the words that follow them.

    Emily had a thoroughly enjoyable holiday with Hannah and Christopher.

    You can work out other intensifiers by substituting other words for 'thoroughly'.

3 Adjectives can take three forms: absolute, comparative or superlative.

   a Absolute adjectives

       He chose a large apple.

   b Comparative adjectives, where two people or things are compared

       He chose the larger of the two apples.

   c Superlative adjectives, where more than two people or things are compared

       He chose the largest apple in the shop.

Most adjectives can be made into their comparative or superlative forms by adding –er or –est, or by using 'more' for the comparative and 'most' for the superlative.

       He was a courageous player.

       He was a more courageous player than his brother.

       He was the most courageous player in the team.

There are several adjectives that are irregular in the way they form the comparative and superlative. They include good, bad, many, much, little and far.

Absolute	Comparative	Superlative
good	better	best
bad	worse	worst
many	more	most
much	more	most
little	less	least
far	further or farther	furthest or farthest

Adjectives that do not take the comparative or superlative are those that have an absolute meaning, such as unique, real, right, empty, perfect, dead and equal.

4 Adjectives can be recognised by the following common suffixes.

–able	miserable, reasonable, probable
–ful	fearful, awful, careful
–ible	terrible, possible, sensible
–ic	terrific, athletic, electric
–ish	foolish, selfish, childish
–ive	positive, negative, defective
–less	helpless, careless, useless
–ous	courageous, curious, tremendous

5 Many adjectives form adverbs when –ly is added to them – for example, miserable becomes miserably.

       Zoe always felt miserable (adjective) when her father came home late.

       William batted miserably (adverb) last weekend.

There are exceptions, such as 'old' and 'tall', to which –ly cannot be added.

ISBN 9780170183048

ACTIVITY 29

Adjectives

1 Write out the following sentences and underline the adjectives.
   a The disastrous journey ended at noon.
   b The sailor was courteous to the barking officer.
   c It was a hopeful sigh of relief.
   d 'Big, bad and ugly – that's how I would describe him.'
   e The remote possibility of a shark in his bath never entered his tiny brain.
   f 'I realised he could be friendly, even amiable, but generous? Never.'

2 Explain the terms 'absolute', 'comparative' and 'superlative' when used to refer to adjectives.

3 Write out the following sentences, underlining the adjectives and identifying, in brackets, whether the adjective is in the absolute, comparative or superlative form.
   a He was a qualified technician.
   b She is a more qualified technician than he.
   c The boss is the most qualified technician in the firm.
   d We had bad weather for our camping trip.
   e They had even worse weather for their ski trip.
   f The weather at Buller last year was the worst ever.

4 Write out and complete the table.

Absolute	Comparative	Superlative
bad		
	further	
		most beautiful
	smaller	
big		
gigantic		
		least
much		
	more miserable	
equal		
	happier	

5 Write out the following adjectives and match each one to its correct meaning.

Adjective	Meaning
attractive	erroneous, incorrect, wrong
lazy	luscious, gourmet, delicious
mistaken	dangerous, threatening, unsafe
scrumptious	nonsensical, foolish, silly
abhorrent	deceitful, fraudulent, false
imposing	idle, slack, indolent
absurd	stately, majestic, towering
perilous	beautiful, handsome, becoming

Adverbs

Adverbs modify verbs (and, sometimes, adjectives and other adverbs).

He *often* walked *outside*.

He walked *quickly*.

The most common adverbs indicate time, place and manner.

1   **Adverbs of time** include immediately, never, occasionally, often, sometimes, soon, then, today, tomorrow, usually and yesterday.

2   **Adverbs of place** include above, away, below, down, far, here, in, outside, there, up and within.

3   **Adverbs of manner** include badly, bravely, fast, happily, heavily, merrily, quickly, quietly, rapidly, slowly, speedily, suddenly and well.

Recognising adverbs

Adverbs cannot be recognised by examining word order or inflection or by looking for signal words. They do not occupy any particular position in a sentence, and may be preceded by the same signal words and share many of the same inflections as adjectives. Many adverbs do end in –ly, but so do some adjectives.

1   The best way to recognise an adverb is to observe its function of modifying a verb.

2   Many adverbs can also be preceded by adverbs of degree. 'Often', for example, can be modified in the following ways.

often   more often   most often   less often   least often   very often

ACTIVITY 30

Adverbs

1   Give two examples each of adverbs of time, place and manner.

2   Change the adjectives in the table into adverbs.

Adjective	Adverb	Adjective	Adverb
boastful		strange	
young		brave	
annual		pure	
careful		loyal	
casual		honest	
sweet		hungry	
tight		dark	
painful		sarcastic	
ironic		tearful	
happy		weary	

3   Choose five of the adverbs you have created and write them in sentences.

Structural words

Structural words are important not for their meaning but because they signify a particular relationship between the content words in a sentence. The most important structural words in English are:

*   pronouns
*   conjunctions
*   prepositions
*   determiners.

You are unlikely to ever have to look these words up in a dictionary. Even if you do, the dictionary meanings of words such as 'the', 'up', 'their', or 'or' are probably not very helpful. These words are important not for their meanings but because of their function in a sentence and because of the way they link the content or lexical words.

ISBN 9780170183048

Pronouns

All pronouns are words that take the place of nouns in sentences. There are many types of pronouns. Some pronouns have a few of the characteristics of content words, but they are a finite group and are probably best thought of as belonging with structural words. For example, we add new nouns to the language all the time, but it is many centuries since we have added new pronouns to the language.

1   Personal pronouns

	Subject	Object	Possessive adjective	Possessive pronoun
First person singular	I	me	my	mine
Second person singular	you	you	your	yours
Third person singular	he	him	his	his
	she	her	her	hers
	it	it	its	its
First person plural	we	us	our	ours
Second person plural	you	you	your	yours
Third person plural	they	them	their	theirs

2   Reflexive pronouns

The reflexive pronouns are myself, yourself, herself, himself, itself, ourselves, yourselves and themselves. They reflect a preceding noun or pronoun in the sentence.

> Brett talked to himself.

> We watched by ourselves.

3   Relative pronouns

Relative pronouns connect clauses with other clauses or sentences. The reflective pronouns are who, whom, whose, which and that.

> Helen, whose father was the coach, hoped that her team would win the basketball final.

> The training, which Basil had done in secret, proved valuable when he played squash against his wife.

> Justin and Romeo worked hard to help their friend, who had been out fishing the day before instead of finishing his preparation.

In these cases, the relative pronoun is the first word of a new clause and connects it to the rest of the sentence. Each relative pronoun relates back to the preceding noun. In the first example, 'whose' relates back to 'Helen'; in the second example, 'which' relates back to 'training'; and in the final example, 'who' relates back to 'friend'.

Clauses beginning with relative pronouns are often embedded within another clause (usually the main clause): 'whose father was the coach' is embedded in the main clause 'Helen hoped', and 'which Basil had done in secret' is embedded in the main clause, 'The training proved valuable'.

4   Demonstrative pronouns

Demonstrative pronouns (that, this, these and those) are used to direct attention to particular things.

> This is Vashti's.

> These were grown on our own trees.

'This' and 'these' refer to things that are near and 'that' and 'those' refer to more distant things.

5   Interrogative pronouns

Interrogative pronouns (who, whom, whose, which and what) are used for asking questions.

> Who owns that iPod?   Whose is this?   What do you think will happen?

ACTIVITY 31

Pronouns

1 Rewrite the following charts, completing them with as many pronouns as possible.

a Personal pronouns

Person	Singular	Plural
First person – the person speaking		we
Second person – the person being spoken to	you	
Third person – the person being spoken about	he	

b Possessive pronouns

Person	Singular	Plural
First person – the person speaking		ours
Second person – the person being spoken to		
Third person – the person being spoken about	his	

c Reflexive pronouns

Person	Singular	Plural
First person – the person speaking	myself	
Second person – the person being spoken to		
Third person – the person being spoken about		

2 Rewrite the following passage using pronouns where appropriate.

Cory and Nathan had an idea. Cory and Nathan knew that the shop went right through to the back street. Cory and Nathan's idea was to get the medicine and then escape out the back. But when Cory reached the back door Cory realised the door was locked. When Cory turned round Cory could see by the agony on Nathan's face that Nathan had been shot. 'Hit?' Nathan nodded.

Looking back on that day, Nathan could not explain Cory's strength. Cory had picked up a huge block of concrete and attacked the door. The door disintegrated.

Carrying Nathan, Cory covered three blocks, avoiding the gang and the gang's automatic weapons. Cory lowered Nathan into Cory and Nathan's van and slammed the door.

Two hours later Cory and Nathan were safe.

3 Rewrite the following sentences, completing them by inserting relative pronouns.

a The athlete _____ won the race was shocked.

b I could see _____ was out of place.

c He emailed the guitarist _____ he met in Sydney.

d The doctor could only administer drugs to those victims _____ need was greatest.

e The kitten, _____ Amy had hidden in the cupboard, was gone!

f We sailed down the river _____ runs through Paris.

4 Complete the following sentences using demonstrative pronouns.

a _____ ball is mine.

b Did you know _____?

c If that's your preference, I'll wrap _____ up and put _____ back.

ISBN 9780170183048

5 Complete the following sentences using interrogative pronouns.
  a 'Sally, _____ are you doing tomorrow?'
  b '_____ will you go with if I can't go?'
  c 'By the way, _____ did you say telephoned earlier?'

Conjunctions

Conjunctions connect words, phrases or clauses. Conjunctions can be either coordinating or subordinating.

1   **Coordinating conjunctions** connect words, phrases or sentences that have equal status. The following examples show how they are used.

> fish and chips

> whiting or herring

> Walking fast and breathing heavily, he soon caught up with his quarry.

> Elizabeth went to the concert and she decided to stay for supper.

The coordinating conjunctions are and, as well as, but, either … or, neither … nor, nor, not, or, rather than, so, sooner than and yet.

2   **Subordinating conjunctions** connect subordinate clauses to main clauses. In each case, the main clause can stand alone but the subordinate clause cannot.

> Malcolm fought hard until the end of the game, although his side was well beaten.

> After the author had finished reading a chapter from her novel, the class asked her questions.

Subordinating conjunctions include after, although, as, because, before, for, if, since, unless, until, when, where, whether and while.

Prepositions

Prepositions show how two parts of a sentence are related in space and time.

> Ernie's cellar was below the floorboards.

> The granny flat is beyond that clump of trees.

> Kristy stayed at the dance until midnight.

Words that can function as prepositions include the following.

about	at	by	into	round	until
above	before	down	near	since	up
across	behind	during	of	then	upon
after	below	except	off	through	with
against	beneath	following	on	throughout	within
along	beside	for	opposite	to	without
among	between	from	out	towards	
around	beyond	in	over	under	

Prepositions relate nouns to other words in the sentence and so are always found with nouns (or pronouns) in what is known as a **prepositional phrase**.

> opposite him   before lunch   around the post

A pronoun used after a preposition is an object, not a subject.

> Between you and me, I don't trust him. (*not* Between you and I ...)

ACTIVITY 32

Conjunctions

1 Rewrite the following sentences, adding conjunctions wherever possible. Compare your answers with those of a partner.

> The car overheated. Matti stopped the engine. He and his mother got out. There was nothing they could do. They phoned home. They walked back to town. A big surprise awaited them.

2 Write a brief story using several conjunctions to make it flow. Underline your conjunctions. Begin with:

'I was starving …'

Prepositions

3 Create your own paragraph using the following prepositions.

about	across	against	beneath	beyond	during
into	through	towards	underneath	without	

Determiners

Determiners are the little words that hold a sentence together. The most important determiners are the definite and indefinite articles.

1 The definite article ('the') makes a particular reference.

> She searched for the hammer. (a particular hammer)

> Lucas is the chef at Boone's Restaurant. (a particular chef)

2 The indefinite article ('a', 'an') makes a more general reference.

> She searched for a hammer. (any hammer)

> Lucas is a chef. (a chef in general)

3 There are other little words that in traditional grammar were sometimes classified as adjectives, although they have nothing in common with descriptive adjectives. Most modern grammarians call them determiners. They are words such as some, few, that, this, those, these, each, every, either and neither.

> I'd like some apples, please.

> I'll take these grapes, thanks.

> Every shopper wins a prize today.

Note: Some words – such as this, that, these and those – can be determiners or pronouns, depending on how they are used.

> I'll take these grapes, thanks. (a determiner, or – in traditional grammar – an adjective)

> I'll take these, thanks. (a pronoun)

ISBN 9780170183048

ACTIVITY 33

Write the indefinite article 'a' or 'an' in each of the spaces below.

1 _____ dainty cup
2 _____ ingenious solution
3 _____ avid fan
4 _____ serious problem
5 _____ inexpensive gift
6 _____ arduous climb

Grammar and usage

Some common grammatical problems

between you and I

This is incorrect. Use 'between you and me'.

> The final choice was between you and me.

A preposition such as 'between' must be followed by the form of the pronoun that is used in the object (not the subject) position.

> 'me' not 'I'

> 'him and her' not 'he and she'

> 'them and us' not 'they and we'

This is an example of a mistake occurring because people try too hard. There was a time when the answer to the question: 'Who's there?' was supposed to be: 'It is I', not 'It is me'. This was always nonsense. It was based on the model of Latin grammar – which was thought to be superior – and never did reflect actual English use. However, as a result people got the idea that 'I' was the more proper choice.

but or *and* as sentence openers

There is nothing wrong with beginning a sentence with 'but' or 'and'. But this should not be overdone. Often these words emphasise the link between one sentence and the next.

> Don't forget to buy pumpkin muffins. And, whatever you do, don't leave them in the car when you get home.

dangling phrases or hanging participles

These occur when a group of words that is used to open a sentence does not accurately refer to what follows, for example:

> Flying low over the reef, a giant shark was sighted near the lagoon.

> On answering the phone, the message gave me a real shock.

> A talented singer, Eliza's concerts were always booked out.

Less confusing versions would be:

> As we were flying low over the reef, we saw a giant shark near the lagoon.

> When I answered the phone, the message gave me a real shock.

> As she was a talented singer, Eliza's concerts were always booked out.

everybody, everyone, everything

Because 'everybody', 'everyone' and 'everything' are singular, they are followed by a singular verb.

> Everybody has an equal chance.   Everything looks perfect today.

This may cause problems if the singular verb is to be followed by a singular pronoun.

> Everyone was trying his hardest.   Everyone was trying his or her hardest.

Both of these examples are correct. The first, however, is sexist and the second is clumsy. Most people accept what has been common in speech for some time – using plural pronouns.

> Everyone was trying their hardest.   Everyone believes their own ideas are best.

However, try to avoid the plural 'their' after the singular 'everyone' in formal written contexts.

none ... is or none ... are

Traditionally, 'none' was always regarded as singular and was followed by a singular verb (such as 'is', 'was' or 'has'). These days, when you use 'none' to mean 'no one' or 'not one', it should still be treated as singular.

> None but the brave dares follow in her footsteps.

However, when 'none' means 'not any', it is acceptable to follow it with a plural verb (such as 'are', 'were', 'have'), although the singular is also correct.

> Though some of these economic policies found their way into the Labor Party platform, none of them were (was) acted upon.

prepositions at the end of sentences

As long as it sounds right, there is no reason why a sentence should not end in a preposition, but there are times when a preposition can sound clumsy at the end of a sentence.

> What did you bring that book that I didn't want to be read to from up for?

When it sounds clumsy, the sentence should be reorganised.

> That is the song he composed.

is better than

> That is the song he is the composer of.

Because there is a widespread belief that sentences should not end with a preposition, there are times when, even though it sounds natural, a sentence should be changed to avoid distracting some readers.

> She makes a good job of anything in which she is interested.

However, this is another 'rule' that was never based on actual language use. It was invented in the eighteenth century by scholars who were attempting to 'improve' English based on the model of Latin grammar, which was thought to be superior. When it sounds natural, a sentence may end in a preposition.

> That's something I won't put up with.

run-on sentences

A common mistake is running on sentences – that is, not separating two or more sentences using a full stop or semicolon, or joining them with a conjunction. There are two complete sentences in the following example, but it is not clear where the break should be – after 'city' or after 'museum' – and this confuses the meaning.

> The traffic was thick in the city near the museum we were unable to find parking.

To correct this, you need to write one of the following.

> The traffic was thick in the city. Near the museum we were unable to find parking.

> The traffic was thick in the city; near the museum we were unable to find parking.

ISBN 9780170183048

The traffic was thick in the city, and near the museum we were unable to find parking.

The traffic was thick in the city near the museum. We were unable to find parking.

Another common error is the comma splice in which two sentences are joined by a comma rather than separated by a full stop or semicolon.

She worked impatiently, when her daughter came she relaxed.

To correct this, you need to replace the comma with a full stop or a semicolon.

split infinitives

The infinitive is the form of a verb starting with 'to'; for example: 'to follow', 'to eat', 'to remember'. A split infinitive occurs when an adverb is placed between 'to' and the other part of the verb.

His aim is to continually interrupt the speaker.

Traditionally, there has been opposition to splitting infinitives. In the above case, the verb is 'to interrupt', not 'interrupt'. As a result, usage guides and grammar books used to insist on one of the following.

His aim is to interrupt the speaker continually.

His aim is continually to interrupt the speaker.

George Bernard Shaw said in a letter to *The Times* in 1907: 'There is a busybody on your staff who devotes a lot of time to chasing split infinitives. Every good literary craftsman splits his infinitives when the sense demands it. I call for the immediate dismissal of this pedant. It is of no consequence whether he decides to go quickly, or quickly to go, or to quickly go. The important thing is that he should go at once.'

This is one of the false 'rules' of English that never had any basis in the way in which the language was used. Native speakers know whether it sounds right or not to have an adverb between the 'to' and the verb. Sometimes it is necessary to split infinitives so that a sentence is not ambiguous or because not splitting the infinitive would produce a different meaning.

To finally win the battle, the General had to make a difficult decision.

verbless sentences

Verbless sentences (also called 'truncated sentences' or 'sentence fragments') are acceptable when handled effectively.

Does this mean he should resign? Not really.

The big time at last for McCarthy? Not so. (Barry Oakley, *A Salute to the Great McCarthy*).

Ineffective use of verbless sentences can often be corrected by linking the adjoining sentences with a comma, as in the following example.

He had not shown up well in the past. Being inclined to laziness.

He had not shown up well in the past, being inclined to laziness.

ACTIVITY 34

Find five pieces of writing you have done for school in the last few weeks, some of them written for subjects other than English. Work with a partner and proofread your writing, looking for:
- run-on sentences
- verbless sentences.

In cases of run-on sentences, discuss the different options for improving your writing. Do you need a full stop, or would a semicolon be better? Should you rephrase the sentence, adding a conjunction? In cases of verbless sentences, consider whether or not a verb needs to be added to make the sentence complete and effective.

4 LANGUAGE CONVENTIONS: USAGE

Usage conventions

The study of usage is the study of the way in which language is used by speakers and writers of English. There is huge variety. You know that people from different parts of the English-speaking world use language differently. You can tell the difference between an Australian and a New Zealand accent, and you know that American speakers prefer to say 'sidewalk' whereas Australian speakers usually say 'footpath'. You know that teenagers in our society speak differently from their elders. You know, too, that your own use of language differs depending on your audience, context and purpose. You do not use language the same way when delivering a formal speech at the school assembly as you do when chatting with your friends, and the language you use when texting is very different from the way you would write a job application.

You are also aware that language constantly changes. No one dictates these changes: there is no authority which says that a certain word is old-fashioned and will rarely be used in the future, or that a form of expression that has been used for centuries should evolve into something slightly different. The changes often happen gradually, so there can be uncertainty about what is appropriate in a particular situation.

Using words correctly

Just as you want to be sure that your spelling, grammar and punctuation are correct when you are writing something important, you will want to know that you are following the usage conventions that are appropriate to your context. How do you know what the 'correct' usage is? There is no unquestioned authority, although there are lots of guide books to usage. Nowadays the best of these are based on huge computer databases that record how English speakers actually use the language. We have consulted a range of such sources to provide you with the notes below. We have selected a range of common usage questions and provided up-to-date advice on what is considered appropriate in Standard Australian English.

a or *an*

The general rule is that you use 'an' when the word following begins with a vowel (**a**, **e**, **i**, **o** or **u**); for example: an apple, an egg, an oil-stained t-shirt, an ostrich, an umbrella. You use 'a' when the word begins with a consonant; for example: a banana, a much-loved book, a lion. However, the rule depends on sounds, not on spelling. Exceptions to the rule include vowels that have a 'y' sound (a union, a ukelele) or a 'w' sound (a once-famous name), and words with a silent 'h' (an heir, an honour). There is dispute over some words beginning with 'h' (such as habitual, hallucination, heroic, historical, hotel, hypothesis and hysterical). Most people who pronounce the 'h' in these words use 'a', and those who use a silent 'h' use 'an'. Either 'a' or 'an' is acceptable.

The grammatical term for 'a' or 'an' is the **indefinite article**. 'The' is called the **definite article**.

advice or *advise*

In Australian and British English, 'advice' is the noun and 'advise' is the verb.

> You have given me some good advice.

> I will advise him to change subjects.

ISBN 9780170183048

Unlike 'practice' and 'practise' and 'licence' and 'license', this pair of words is pronounced differently, so there is no excuse for making a mistake.

affect or effect

'Affect' is usually a verb meaning 'to influence'.

> Music affects me in strange ways.

The main use of 'effect' is as a noun meaning 'result'.

> Music has a strange effect on me.

Much less commonly, 'effect' is used as a verb meaning 'to bring about' or 'cause'.

> The vet has effected a complete cure.

all right or alright

In the past, 'alright' was considered incorrect in sentences such as 'Do you feel alright?' Widespread use has made this quite acceptable, mainly because it is similar to words such as 'already', 'although' and 'always'. You may use either 'all right' or 'alright' to mean 'satisfactory' or 'OK', and 'all right' to mean 'all correct' as in:

> Min got her mathematics all right.

We make a similar distinction between 'already' and 'all ready'.

> He is here already.

> Are you all ready to go?

Some people will tell you that 'alright' is an incorrect spelling, because a book called *Fowler's Dictionary of Modern Usage* said so in 1926, even though at that time many writers were already spelling the word that way.

although or though

In most cases these are equally acceptable and interchangeable.

> Though she had sent an apology, he was offended that she did not come to his party.

> Although she had sent an apology, he was offended that she did not come to his party.

However, 'though' can be used in places where 'although' does not fit, especially in colloquial sentences such as:

> I wouldn't hold my breath though.

altogether or all together

'Altogether' means 'completely', 'quite' or 'on the whole', as in:

> That is altogether disgusting.

> I am altogether fed up.

'All together' means 'everybody at once', as in:

> We went all together to see the film.

among or amongst

'Among' is the more common form, used about five times more often than 'amongst' in Australian English. 'Amongst' is old-fashioned but sometimes sounds better before words beginning with a vowel. Use whichever sounds better to you.

between or among

Traditionally, 'between' was used for two things or people and 'among' for more than two things or people.

> They divided the property between Jennifer and Erin.

> The prize money was shared among the twelve members of the winning team.

However, it is now common to use either 'between' or 'among' for more than two things or people.

> It was a one-day competition between Australia, England and New Zealand.

'Among' is still only used for more than two things or people. We do not say:

> They divided the property among Jennifer and Erin.

Because language change is a slow process, using 'between' for two or more things or people is still considered incorrect by some people, despite the fact that such usage is very common.

around or round

These may be used interchangeably.

> Mark sailed his yacht around the buoy.

> Mark sailed his yacht round the buoy.

better or best

When you are comparing two things, you say that one is better than the other. If you are comparing more than two things, you say that one is the best.

> Cameron believed that the West Coast Eagles were better than Carlton.

> William thought that the Australian cricket team was the best in the world.

bought or brought

'Bought' and 'brought' are the past tenses of completely different verbs and should not be confused. 'Bought' is the past tense of 'to buy', as in:

> Rory bought a muffin from the tuckshop.

'Brought' is the past tense of 'to bring', as in:

> Rory brought a muffin to school for lunch.

'Bought' and 'brought' are quite often confused in informal speech.

but at the end of a sentence

In some Australian communities you will hear speakers adding 'but' at the end of a sentence, as in:

> I won't do it, but.

This should be avoided in formal speech and in writing. Likewise, 'though' is acceptable in speech:

> I won't do it, though.

but, however or yet

'But' and 'however' mean the same and can be used interchangeably. In general, 'but' has more force than 'however', as in the following examples.

> Adam wanted to fly to Perth but there was an aircraft refuellers' strike.

> Adam wanted to fly to Perth. However, there was an aircraft refuellers' strike.

Note that 'however' should follow a semicolon or a full stop. 'Nevertheless' can also be a useful alternative to 'but'; it, too, should follow a semicolon or a full stop.

Use 'yet' to imply a continuation rather than a definite contrast, as in the following example.

> There was an aircraft refuellers' strike, yet Adam was still able to travel to Perth.

can or may

'Can' and 'may' have different meanings.

'Can' means 'is able' or 'has the ability to'. 'May' means 'has permission' or 'is allowed'.

ISBN 9780170183048

Claire can ski really well.

'You may go to the movies, Calum,' said his mother, 'as long as Bianca goes with you.'

You might hear an adult correcting a child who asks:

Can I have another ice-cream?

by answering:

You can, but whether you may is another question.

Despite this reminder, most Australian speakers use 'can' instead of 'may' in informal speech, as 'may' is thought to sound stilted or too formal.

Can he have another chance?

May he have another chance?

'May' is also used to suggest a sense of possibility.

Climate change may lead to the flooding of some islands in the Pacific.

cannot, can't or can not

'Cannot' is the usual negative form of 'can', meaning 'is not able' or 'does not have the ability to'.

I cannot get to Perth because of the refuellers' strike.

'Can't' is a contraction of the word 'cannot'. Contractions are used in speech and in informal writing. 'Can not' is only used when it is necessary to place a special emphasis on 'not'.

You can not behave in that outrageous way in this classroom.

can't hardly or couldn't hardly

Use 'can hardly' or 'could hardly' instead.

I can hardly believe what you've told me.

centre around or centre on

'Centre on' or 'centre in' is logical as something cannot be both central and around.

After Easter, the attention of many Australian sports fanatics centres on various codes of football.

The local dairy industry is centred in Harvey.

comprise

This word traditionally means 'to include', 'to consist of', 'to be composed of', 'to constitute', 'to form' or 'to be made up of'. 'Comprise' is often used clumsily when the alternatives would be clearer.

This company comprises four departments.

This company has / is made up of / consists of four departments.

You will also hear people say:

This company is comprised of four departments.

Four departments comprise this company.

This company comprises of four departments.

There is disagreement about whether these uses of the word – especially the last example – are acceptable. As suggested above, 'comprise' can be clumsy and it might be wise to avoid it.

continual or continuous

The distinction in meaning between these words is fading, and both can now be used to mean 'nonstop', a meaning which was once only that of 'continuous'.

'Continual' still keeps the meaning of 'recurring frequently; going on and on but with breaks in between'.

Reading has been Merelyn's continual passion since she was a child.

Native animals are threatened by the continual onslaught of suburban development.

'Continuous' means 'going on without breaks, happening all the time, unceasing or without remission'.

The heartbeat is continuous until death.

contrast

Use 'in contrast with', not 'in contrast to'.

could of or could have

'Could of' is a misunderstanding. The contracted form of 'could have' is 'could've', which sounds like 'could of'. 'Could of' is heard quite often in Australian speech, but it should be avoided in formal situations.

(See also 'would of or would have' on page 74.)

could or might

'Could' or 'might' are often interchangeable.

They could have forgotten the time.

They might have forgotten the time.

In questions, 'could' is used in Australian English more commonly than 'might'. When 'might' is used, it has a sense of tentativeness, as if the speaker is not sure whether the request will be granted.

Could I borrow your pen?

Might I borrow your pen?

criteria

Historically, this is the plural form of 'criterion'. 'Criterion' was borrowed from Greek, which is the reason for the strange plural form.

There are three main criteria.

The main criterion for selection is the ability to write clearly.

'Criteria' is frequently used as if it is the singular form, as in:

The main criteria for selection is the ability to write clearly.

Although this use is common in Australian English, it should be avoided as many people still regard it as incorrect. The word 'criteria' is overused and can often be replaced with words such as 'qualities', 'standards', 'principles', 'tests' or 'rules'.

different from, different to or different than

Traditionally, 'different from' was the preferred form, but now both 'different from' and 'different to' are acceptable.

Coca-Cola is quite different from Pepsi.

Coca-Cola is quite different to Pepsi.

Although 'different than' is used in speech and in American English, it is discouraged in writing in Australia and the UK.

ISBN 9780170183048

disinterested or uninterested

These words have been used in the past to indicate quite different meanings. 'Disinterested' was used to mean 'impartial', 'unbiased' or 'free from prejudice'; while 'uninterested' means 'not interested', 'indifferent' or 'apathetic'.

> As she had nothing to gain from the result of the meeting, Hannah was a disinterested observer.

> As he had always found cricket boring, Christopher was an uninterested spectator at the test match.

This was a very useful distinction. However, in the majority of current uses of 'disinterested' the word is used to mean 'not interested' – the old meaning has been lost. Furthermore, 'disinterested' is used more often than 'uninterested', which seems to be falling out of fashion. This use is so widespread that Pam Peters in *The Cambridge Guide to Australian English* advises writers and speakers to use other synonyms (such as 'unbiased' or 'indifferent') if they want to be sure to make their meaning clear.

e.g.

'e.g.' is an abbreviation of the Latin *exempli gratia*, meaning 'for example'. A full stop is used after each initial. 'e.g.' is not followed by a comma. Abbreviations such as this are appropriate in note form, but in passages of formal writing, use 'for example' or 'for instance' rather than 'e.g.'.

enquiry or inquiry, enquire or inquire

These words are interchangeable, although 'inquiry' is by far the more common spelling in Australia. Oddly 'enquiry' seems to be the preferred form on public signs.

> Enquiry desk

While some people make a distinction between the two, most Australian users reserve 'enquiry' for an official context. It is safe to always use the 'inquiry' and 'inquire' spellings.

etc.

'etc.' is an abbreviation for the Latin *et cetera*, meaning 'and the rest'. It is interesting that we pronounce it in full as 'et cetera' (with a soft 'c'), whereas with other Latin abbreviations – such as 'e.g.' and 'i.e.' – we pronounce the initials of the abbreviated words but not the words themselves. 'etc.' is the most common Latin abbreviation in English. It should be followed by a full stop.

While different guides have slightly different views, the most common advice is that 'etc.' should be avoided in formal writing. It can be replaced by phrases such as 'and so on' and 'and so forth'. It is not a good idea to overuse it in any context, as it can suggest that the speaker or writer is being lazy and leaving it up to the listener or reader to supply the other example(s).

fewer or less

'Fewer' means 'a smaller number of' and 'less' means 'a smaller quantity of'.

> There were fewer than ten tickets left for the concert.

> There were fewer tables than people.

> Daisy made less apricot jam than last year.

> There was less land than was needed to satisfy the demand for housing.

Today, there is more tolerance of 'less' as a replacement for 'fewer', especially in speech. 'Fewer' is seen by most Australian users as conveying a more formal tone.

first or firstly

Either may be used. An old rule held that we should say 'first', 'secondly', 'thirdly', but common practice in Australia has been 'firstly', 'secondly', or even 'first', 'second'.

former and *latter*

These can be used as pronouns to refer to two people or things that have been previously mentioned. 'The former' is the first mentioned and 'the latter' the second.

> Elaine and her husband have two pets, a cat and a dog. The former is an Abyssinian called Razzy and the latter a beagle called Munch.

As with all pronouns, the referents or antecedents (the words that 'former' and latter' refer to) should not be placed too far away, so that the meaning is clear.

got or *gotten*

The past participle of the verb 'to get' is 'got' in Australia. In the US both 'got' and 'gotten' are used.

> Although they had gotten to the Superbowl with the more impressive record, the Buffalo Bills were beaten 19–20 by the New York Giants.

Younger Australians sometimes use 'gotten' in the way Americans do, but in places where it means 'become'.

> He had gotten angry.

This use should be avoided in formal writing.

i.e.

'i.e.' is from the Latin *id est*, meaning 'that is'. A full stop is used after each initial. 'i.e.' is not followed by a comma. Abbreviations such as this are appropriate in note form, but in passages of formal writing, use 'that is' or 'namely' rather than 'i.e.'.

imply or *infer*

These words are often confused, although they have quite different meanings. To 'imply' is to hint at rather than to actually say something.

> Although he did not explain the consequences, Dion implied that selling the house would be an unwise move.

To 'infer' is to work out or conclude from what has been said.

> From her remarks, I inferred that Emilia had agreed to sell all the avocado plants.

it's or *its*

'It's' is a contraction standing for 'it is' or 'it has'. The form with the apostrophe is only used in this sense. 'Its' is a possessive adjective but, although it is showing ownership, it does not have an apostrophe.

> It's a sunny day today.

> The cat was licking its paw.

lend or *loan*

'Loan' is a noun.

> Dan gave me a loan of his guitar.

'Lend' is a verb.

> Luke decided to lend his surfboard to his sister for the afternoon.

In informal Australian speech 'loan' is frequently used as a verb, although this is still discouraged in formal writing.

> Will you loan Amy a dollar?

The use of 'lend' as a noun can also be heard in speech but is avoided in formal speech and in writing.

> He gave me a lend of his aunt's novel.

ISBN 9780170183048

licence or *license*

In Australian and British English, 'licence' is the noun and 'license' is the verb.

> Do you have your driver's licence with you?

> You must license your vehicle with the local authorities if you move interstate.

ACTIVITY 35

Usage conventions

1 Rewrite the following sentences, placing the correct words in the blanks.

a (bought/brought) I _____ home a dog which I _____ from the pet shop.

b (affect/effect) The _____ of the music on my feelings will _____ the way I behave towards even my best friends. Do you know how to _____ this change?

c (licence/license) When do you expect to get your instructor's _____?

d (licence/license) Can I see your driver's _____, please, sir?

e (bought/brought) He's _____ me some fresh vegetables from his garden.

f (affect/effect) What will be the _____s of the economic downturn?

g (affect/effect) He was badly _____ed by his friend's illness.

h (advice/advise) Do you have any _____ for me as I start my new job?

i (it's/its) _____ obvious that he paid too much for his new car. _____ in quite bad condition. _____ tyres need replacing immediately.

2 Rewrite the following sentences more formally.

a My brother's quite different than me.

b He would of liked to have come today.

c They had gotten there quite early.

d He reads lots of graphic novels, Japanese manga, etc.

e The main criteria for success is hard work.

f The graphic novel has come of age; e.g. look at the sophistication of Tan's *The Arrival*.

lie or *lay*

These are really confusing. There are three separate verbs with different meanings.

1 'Lie' means 'to tell an untruth'.

2 'Lie' means 'to recline' or 'to move into a horizontal position'.

3 'Lay' means 'to put down'.

This table shows the main parts of the three verbs.

The verb	Its meaning	The past tense	The past participle	The present participle
lie	tell an untruth	lied	lied	lying
lie	recline	lay	lain	lying
lay	put down	laid	laid	laying

> Imogen lies all the time about her homework. She lied (past tense) yesterday when she said the dog ate her homework. She has lied (past participle) before. She was lying (present participle) last week when she said that her little sister had torn it up.

> Mai lies down on her bed for a rest. She lay (past tense) down for a rest yesterday. She had lain (past participle) down because she had a headache. She was lying (present participle) down when I dropped in to see her.

> Giovanni laid (past tense) some pavers yesterday, having first laid (past participle) a bedding of sand. By laying (present participle) the bricks himself, he will save money.

like or as

'Like' is a preposition that introduces a noun or a pronoun.

> She looks like her mother.

> He looks like a sumo wrestler.

'As' is a conjunction that links one clause to another.

> She looked beautiful, as she always did.

'Like' is increasingly used, especially in speech, as a conjunction.

> This lemonade tastes lemony, like it should.

This is still best avoided in formal writing, although the evidence for 'like' being frequently used as a conjunction by Australians is very strong. Sentences such as the following are common.

> They don't make movies like they used to.

> They don't give staff an annual bonus, like they do in other similar companies.

Traditional advice would be to replace 'like' with 'as' in these two examples, but it could be argued that in the first example at least such a change would slightly change the meaning. This is a good example of changing usage.

literally

'Literally' has become an overused word with the result that its original meaning has been seriously weakened. It means 'really' or 'actually'; the origin of the word is 'according to the letter'. The opposite of 'literally' was 'metaphorically' or 'figuratively'. The correct use of the word is as follows.

> There are literally millions of people around the world without enough food.

An example of the common use, which weakens the word, follows.

> Literally millions of kids rushed into the playground when the fight started.

Statements such as the following are absurd, although quite common.

> It was literally raining cats and dogs.

> He was literally green with envy.

loose or lose

These words have nothing to do with each other and are pronounced quite differently, but 'loose' is often written where 'lose' is intended.

> Did you lose your hat? I'm not surprised. The elastic is quite loose.

media

'Media' usually refers to the mass communications industries: radio, television and newspapers. 'Media' is a plural noun (the singular is 'medium'), but is often treated as a singular noun. You can therefore write either of the following.

> The media in Australia have always supported worthy charities.

> The media in Australia has always supported worthy charities.

The singular 'medium' is sometimes the word that should be used.

> The medium of television is very different from the medium of radio.

nice

Many people believe that 'nice' is overused and that it should be replaced by more precise adjectives such as pretty, attractive, pleasant, agreeable, delightful, kind, friendly and warm. Nice is a good example of a word

ISBN 9780170183048

whose meaning has weakened by overuse. Its original and more precise meanings included 'subtle', 'sensitive', 'deft' and 'fastidious'.

Avoid sentences such as:

> That nice girl from No. 96 took Bonnie and Will on a nice walk.

one

There are many problems with using the pronoun 'one' and it is probably best avoided. It often sounds pompous and it is difficult to know which pronoun to use to refer to it. This is illustrated in the following sentences.

> One ought to state one's beliefs.
>
> One ought to state her or his beliefs.
>
> One ought to state his beliefs.
>
> One ought to state their beliefs.

The first two examples sound clumsy, and this gets worse with a sentence such as:

> One ought to state one's beliefs, shouldn't one?

The third example is sexist and the fourth is a problem because the singular pronoun 'one' shouldn't be followed by a plural pronoun such as 'their'. One option is:

> People ought to state their beliefs.

Just occasionally, 'one' can be useful if you do not want to use a more precise pronoun such as 'I' or 'you'. Consider the different implications of:

> What can one say to that?
>
> What can I say to that?
>
> What can you say to that?

passed or past

'Passed' is both the past tense and the past participle of the verb 'to pass'.

> I passed him at the gate yesterday.
>
> I had passed him there last week as well.

'Past' has all kinds of uses, but it has no relation to the verb 'pass'.

> Knowing about the past can help us avoid mistakes in the future.
>
> We walked past the oval.

phenomena

'Phenomena' is the plural form of the noun 'phenomenon'. The word was borrowed from Greek, which is the reason for the strange plural form. Many users think 'phenomena' is the singular form and you will commonly hear sentences such as:

> Childhood obesity is a worrying recent phenomena.

Strictly speaking, 'phenomenon' should be used in this sentence.

> Childhood obesity is a worrying recent phenomenon.

It is a good idea to use 'phenomenon' as the singular and 'phenomena' as the plural.

practice or practise

In Australian and British English, 'practice' is the noun and 'practise' is the verb.

> I have tennis practice at five.
>
> I like to practise my tennis as often as possible.

ACTIVITY 36

Usage conventions

1 Rewrite the following sentences placing the correct words in the blanks.

a (practice/practise) The _____ was called off so we will have to _____ tomorrow.

b (past/passed) As she went _____ me she _____ me the ball.

c (practice/practise) _____ makes perfect.

d (lie/lay) Would you _____ the table for me? I want to _____ down for a while before dinner.

e (lie/lay) The hens have to _____ some more eggs this morning.

f (lose/loose) If you _____ your library card, you will have to pay for a replacement.

2 Rewrite the following sentences so that they are more acceptable in a formal context.

a There were literally hundreds of relatives squashed into our kitchen on Christmas day.

b I'll be there as soon as possible after the meeting, i.e. soon after five.

c She's an outstanding phenomena: one of the great athletes of her age.

d I was terrified; I literally turned to stone.

e I've been reading about the early Australian explorers: Burke and Wills, etc.

prophecy or prophesy

In Australian and British English, 'prophecy' is the noun and 'prophesy' is the verb.

> The scientists' prophecy about climate change is alarming.

> They prophesy that many Pacific islands will be flooded.

As with the pair 'advice' and 'advise' – but unlike the pairs 'practice' and 'practise', or 'licence' and 'license' – these are pronounced differently, making it easier to choose the right one.

quiet or quite

These are not homophones because they are pronounced differently. 'Quiet' can be either a noun or an adjective, and it has to do with an absence of noise. 'Quite' is an adverb that modifies adjectives and other adverbs.

> I like peace and quiet.

> It was a quiet night.

> You are quite right.

recurrence

'Reoccurrence' is sometimes used in conversation, but 'recurrence' is correct and should be used in writing.

shall or will

At one stage 'shall' was thought to be the appropriate form with first-person pronouns, and school grammar books showed the future tense as follows.

> I shall go   we shall go
> you will go   you will go
> he/she/it will go   they will go

This never did reflect the quite complex ways these two little words were used in language. These days, 'shall' is usually replaced by 'will', especially when used to express the future tense.

> I will go to the beach.

> We will have a barbecue dinner when we get home.

ISBN 9780170183048

There are some cases when 'shall' is still used. For example:

1 to express determination

> We shall prevail.
>
> I shall play in the Grand Final in spite of this injury.
>
> You shall succeed.
>
> They shall never surrender.

2 when a question is being asked

> Shall I invite Becky to the picnic?

'Will' is usually used when making a request, not when asking a question.

> Mike, will you collect the mail please?

3 in legal statements

> The landlord shall give notice of any visit to the tenant in writing.

should of or should have

'Should of' is a misunderstanding. The contracted form of 'should have' is 'should've', which sounds like 'should of'. 'Should of' is heard quite often in Australian speech but should be avoided in formal situations.

should or would

As with 'shall' and 'will', it was once thought that 'should' should be used with first-person pronouns and 'would' with second- and third-person pronouns, but that rule has not been followed in Australian English for many years. 'Would' is the preferred usage, except when someone wants to appear particularly polite.

> I should be honoured to have your company.

'Should' is still used to:

1 express a sense of obligation

> Children should be seen and not heard.

2 mean 'ought to'

> I should have remembered his ability to make Christmas cakes.

the reason is because, the reason why

These expressions sound clumsy because they are examples of tautology (saying the same thing twice). 'The reason is' has a similar meaning to 'because' or 'why'. For example, we can say either of the following.

> He did it because he was tired.
>
> The reason he did it was that he was tired.

You should avoid the following.

> The reason she walks is because it is healthier.

Instead, use either of the following.

> The reason she walks is that it is healthier.
>
> She walks because it is healthier.

they're, their or there

'They're' is a contraction; it can only be used when it means 'they are'. 'Their' is a possessive adjective and is also used to show ownership, although it is never used with an apostrophe: their dog, their car. Use 'there' in all other cases.

there's or theirs

'There's' is a contraction and is only used to mean 'there is' or 'there has'.

'Theirs' is a possessive pronoun.

> Whose books are these? I think they are theirs.

until or till

These may be used interchangeably. 'Until' is more commonly used at the beginning of sentences and in more formal writing.

> Until the report is tabled by the Treasurer, I cannot comment on it.

'Till' should not be written as 'til or 'till because it is not an abbreviation of 'until'.

two, too and to

Most people know the difference between these three forms, but they are often written incorrectly. 'Two' is the number. 'Too' means 'also'. Use 'to' in all other cases.

try and or try to

Use 'try to'. Although 'try and' is used and has become acceptable in speech in Australia, it is grammatically incorrect and should not be used, especially in writing. In the following sentence, you could replace 'try' with any of the verbs in brackets. They would sound correct if followed by 'to', but not if they were followed by 'and'.

> We will try (attempt / strive / endeavour / aim) to win the premiership.

unique

This is another word whose meaning has been weakened by overuse. It once meant 'one of a kind'. For example:

> Uluru is a unique rock formation.

However, it has been increasingly used to mean 'rare' or 'unusual' or 'remarkable', and you will now hear people qualifying the word in a way that is not possible if it is strictly referring to one of a kind.

> Our Christmas sale is the most unique opportunity to snap up the latest fashions.

People who like their writing to be precise will keep to the strict, older meaning of 'unique', but the battle to resist the change in the meaning of the word has been lost.

while or whilst

'While' is more common in Australia nowadays. 'Whilst' is still used, especially before words beginning with vowels, but it is now considered old-fashioned.

who, which, that

'Who' is a relative pronoun used for people.

> Dan is an up-and-coming musician who writes his own songs.

'Which' is a relative pronoun used for things.

> These are olives, which are grown in the hot, dry countries of the world.

'That' is a relative pronoun used mainly for things. But, in some cases, it can be used for people.

> Munch was the dog that won the hearts of the nation.

> It was the under-20s team that won the game.

'That' and 'which' are not always interchangeable. Look at the following examples and note that the meanings of these sentences are different.

ISBN 9780170183048

a   Blowfish, which are poisonous, should not be eaten.

b   Blowfish that are poisonous should not be eaten.

c   Blowfish which are poisonous should not be eaten.

Note: You cannot say:

Blowfish, that are poisonous, should not be eaten.

Sentence **a** warns that all blowfish are poisonous and so should not be eaten, while sentences **b** and **c** say that the poisonous blowfish should not be eaten, suggesting that not all blowfish are poisonous. In sentence **a**, 'which' introduces a clause that is not essential to the sentence but adds extra information. The commas are essential. The sentence could just as easily be written as follows.

Blowfish should not be eaten because they are poisonous.

If you can place a clause (in this case, 'which are poisonous') in brackets to separate it from the rest of the sentence (see 'Commas' on page 25), you should use 'which'. This rule also applies to any clause you can place after a comma.

I like olives, which have a distinctive flavour.

Why not visit Sydney, which is a glorious harbour city?

'That' introduces a clause which is an essential part of the sentence because it actually defines the subject. In sentence **b**, it is not just blowfish in general that we are referring to, but those particular blowfish which are poisonous. When the clause you are using defines the subject in this way, making it a particular animal or object, you can use 'that' (or 'which' without a comma before it).

Here are more examples.

I like olives that have a distinctive flavour.

In this case, it is not all olives I like – only those with a distinctive flavour. In the previous example, where 'which' is preceded by a comma, the assumption is that all olives have a distinctive flavour.

The Yarra is the river that flows through Melbourne.

The Yarra is the river which flows through Melbourne.

Both of these are acceptable. In this case, it is not just any river, but the particular river that flows through Melbourne.

'That' should also be used in the following cases.

1   After superlatives

Razzy was the greatest cat that ever lived.

2   After ordinal numbers (first, second, third …)

The Honda Getz was the second new car that he had owned.

3   After 'all', 'any', 'everything', 'little', 'much', 'nothing', 'some' and 'something'

Adam did everything that he could for his younger sister.

4   Where both people and things are referred to

It was the drivers and their vintage cars that were the highlight of the parade.

who or *whom*

'Who' and 'whom' are either relative or interrogative pronouns, depending on how they are being used.

'Who' is the form that should be used when the pronoun is the subject of a verb and 'whom' is the form that should be used when the pronoun is the object of a verb.

Emily was a quiet, intelligent student who always did her homework.

It was always McKenzie whom her mother chose to do the shopping after school.

In the first sentence, 'who' stands for 'Emily' and is the subject of the verb 'did'. The object of the verb 'did' is 'her homework'.

In the second sentence, 'whom' stands for 'McKenzie' and is the object of the verb 'chose'. The subject of this verb is 'her mother'.

In practice, it has become acceptable to use 'who' instead of 'whom' in speech and even in writing.

> It was always McKenzie who her mother chose to do the shopping after school.

> I should like to introduce the person who I met at the concert.

In these sentences, the correct grammatical form is 'whom' as the words are in the object position, but the 'who' form is often seen now, even in writing.

However, 'whom' is generally used after a preposition (for example: about whom, between whom, for whom, in whom, of whom, opposite whom, to whom, with whom).

> Sally was the person from whom I received the gift.

'Who' is much more common than 'whom' when it is the first word in an interrogative question.

> Who did you see?

> Who do you think I visited yesterday?

In both cases, 'whom' should have been used, to be strictly grammatically correct, because in both cases the word ('whom') is the object of a verb.

In deciding which form to use, take the context into account. Think about the difference in tone between

> To whom were you speaking?

and

> Who were you speaking to?

It is an advantage if you understand the grammar of the sentence and know whether the word is being used as the subject or object. You can then make a decision based on what seems better in the context.

who's or whose

'Who's' is a contraction and only used to mean 'who is' or 'who has'. 'Whose' is either a relative pronoun or an interrogative pronoun.

> Whose books are these?

> The students whose books were left in the library can collect them at lunch time.

would of or would have

'Would of' is a misunderstanding. The contracted form of 'would have' is 'would've', which sounds like 'would of'. 'Would of' is heard quite often in Australian speech but should be avoided in formal situations.

you're or your

'You're' is a contraction and should only be used to mean 'you are'. 'Your' is a possessive adjective but, although it expresses ownership, it never has an apostrophe.

> You're due to leave in ten minutes.

> Is your bag packed?

ISBN 9780170183048

ACTIVITY 37

Usage conventions

1 Write out the following sentences placing the correct words in the blanks.
  a (quite/quiet) Please be _____ as some of the patients are _____ ill.
  b (their/they're/there) I've asked them to bring _____ musical instruments. You can put your guitar over _____.
  c (too/to/two) I expect Josh will bring a guitar _____.
  d (who's/whose) _____ guitar case is this?
  e (you're/your) _____ in danger of losing one of _____ best friends.
2 Rewrite these sentences so that they are appropriate for a formal context.
  a The reason why I failed my exams is because my teacher didn't like me.
  b I would of done much better if she'd been nicer to me.
  c I should of told my mum.
  d I'll try and do better next term.
  e Perhaps the reason you failed is because you didn't try.

5 LANGUAGE: REGISTER AND STYLE

Register

The term **register** is used to describe the type of language we use in different situations. We naturally adjust the way we speak depending on the context, and it is important that we learn to similarly adjust the way we write. If, for example, you were named Young Australian of the Year and were asked to make a speech before the Prime Minister and assembled dignitaries, you would use a very formal register. When you were telling your mates about the occasion afterwards, your language would be quite different: the register would be casual and informal. Most of our use of language is somewhere between the two, in what we can call the 'standard' register. The 'standard' register is the language that educated adults use in most of their everyday transactions, such as meetings at work or contact with customers or suppliers.

The written language has a similar range of registers. At the most formal end are documents such as legal contracts and academic papers. Among the most informal are such texts as personal emails or text messages. The essays and reports that you write for school are not at the most formal end of the spectrum, but they do require formal language. The different registers reflect a different relationship between writer and reader. Very formal documents imply a distant and impersonal relationship; informal documents assume that there is a close and friendly relationship between writer and reader.

The relationship between speaker and listener, and writer and reader, is sometimes called tenor.

The characteristics of formal language

1 Contractions (can't, didn't, it's, and so on) are avoided.
2 Sentences and paragraphs may be quite long and there is frequent use of compound or compound-complex sentences.
3 The first- and second-person pronouns are avoided and passive constructions may be used. Instead of saying: 'You must lodge a tax return annually', a formal style might say: 'Tax payers are required to lodge a return annually'.
4 There is a tendency to use noun clusters or nominalisation: 'the school canteen healthy foods proposal' is used instead of 'the proposal to encourage healthy foods in school canteens'.
5 Expressions such as 'provide an explanation' are used in preference to 'explain'.
6 Longer and less familiar words are preferred to simpler ones. Here are some examples.

approximately	about	institute	start, set up
implement	carry out	detrimental	harmful
assist	help	obtain	get
inaugurate	start, begin	eminently	highly
communicate	tell, inform	obviate	avoid, prevent
initially	first, at first	endeavour	try
desist	stop	predominantly	chiefly, mainly

ISBN 9780170183048

eventuate	happen, result	utilise	use
substantial	big, large	feasible	possible
facilitate	help	virtually	almost

7 Colloquial words and slang (see below) are not used.

Note: While formal language will always be necessary in some contexts, there has been a successful move in Australia since 1992 to encourage 'plain English', especially in documents where government or organisations such as insurance companies are communicating with the public.

Colloquial language

Colloquial or conversational language is informal language used in everyday speech. Colloquial language includes contractions (can't, didn't, it's, and so on). The many phrasal verbs in English are particularly common in colloquial language: 'get up' instead of 'arise'; 'slow down' instead of 'decelerate'; 'put up with' instead of 'tolerate'. Our word choice is also different when we are speaking or writing colloquially. Talking together in the staffroom, your teachers refer to you as the 'kids'. Talking to each other, you say that you are going to 'maths' and 'PE'. In the annual school report, where a formal register is required, you are referred to as the 'students' and your subjects are 'mathematics' and 'physical education'.

Idioms are another form of colloquialism. An idiom is a word or phrase that is specific to a particular culture or geographic area. For example, well-known Australian idioms are phrases such as 'fair dinkum' or 'Go, you good thing!'

Slang

Another form of colloquial language is slang. Slang words or expressions are words that are adopted by certain groups, such as an age cohort (for example, teenagers) or a group who work together. 'Sheila', 'chick', 'bird', 'broad' and 'babe' have all been slang terms for 'woman'. Each of these belongs to a certain cultural context and some are more acceptable and current than others.

Jargon

This refers to the technical or special language used by a particular group or profession. Teachers, doctors, mechanics, engineers, musicians, salespeople and public servants each use a particular jargon. While jargon is often needed to explain something complicated or specialised, it can be alienating if it is used with people who do not belong to the specific group. Effective use of language involves carefully considering your audience. Look at the following examples of jargon.

computer jargon:	service provider, cut and paste, printer driver functionality
educational jargon:	core learning outcomes, common curriculum elements, criteria sheets
medical jargon:	triage, electrocardiograph, immunosuppressive, febrile

Style

Some of the language choices we make are to do with questions of style. Stylistic choices are difficult because they are often not governed by clear rules. Sounding out your writing is one of the best strategies. Does it sound right? The best way of testing what you have written is to read it aloud. If it sounds awkward or clumsy, then you need to think about revising it.

Following are some stylistic choices that should be avoided.

Archaic language

Archaisms are outdated words and phrases that can sound odd or even pompous in modern contexts. The archaisms listed below are generally better replaced with more current expressions, unless your purpose is to create an old-fashioned tone in your writing.

unbeknownst	unknown
hitherto	until this point
aforementioned	previously mentioned
suffice to say	in short
ergo	therefore

Clichés

This term comes from the French word meaning 'to stereotype'. A cliché is an overused phrase; for example: burning with desire, hard as nails or crystal clear. Many are metaphors or similes which no doubt sounded very original the first few times they were used, but have been so overused that they have become tired and readers or listeners no longer respond to them. Some clichés are proverbs or well-known sayings; for example: It takes two to tango or Too many cooks spoil the broth. While clichés can express truths, they are usually better replaced with fresh, more original phrases.

Foreign words and phrases

Some people pepper their sentences with foreign words and phrases to show off. Only use them if there is no English equivalent. They should be italicised if not in common use.

'get' and 'got'

Many words have been written about the importance of avoiding these two innocent little words. Certainly, in good writing more precise terms are preferable: words such as fetch, receive, gain or bring. But there are many instances when 'get' and 'got' are essential, especially when followed by those little words that in other uses work as prepositions: get up, get by, get on, get with. These are phrasal verbs and are very common in English. The little words ('up', 'by', and so on) are in these cases called particles because they are not doing the usual work of prepositions: they are in fact part of the verb. You will find some guides that will tell you to avoid phrasal verbs – for example, to use 'arise' instead of 'get up' – but, as always, it depends on context, audience and purpose. We could not survive ordinary conversation without them.

Mixed metaphors

Metaphors and other comparisons can enrich your writing, but it's important to avoid the unintended comic effects of using different and contradictory metaphors in the same sentence.

Someone is sure to upset your applecart if you put all your eggs into the one basket.

We'll stand shoulder to shoulder as we're both in the same boat.

You can look forward to a stiff climb in the middle of the year, but by the last term it should be plain sailing.

Once you've set your hand to the plough you should keep the ball rolling.

ISBN 9780170183048

Nominalisation

Nominalisation is the process of replacing verbs with nouns or noun groups. It is a common feature of academic writing and has the effect of taking the emphasis off the action and focusing it instead on the concept or idea. For example, 'The committee recognised his lifetime achievement by granting him the award' emphasises the action, while 'The recognition of his lifetime achievement by the committee …' places the emphasis on the concept of recognition. A text that uses frequent nominalisations is much more abstract and formal, but it can also be very dense in meaning.

Here are two examples.

> Human beings contribute to global warming. They must change the way they behave.
>
> The contribution of human beings to global warming demands a change in behaviour.

> People need to change their behaviour. This is urgent.
>
> The necessity for people to change their behaviour is urgent.

Redundancy

Redundant words are those that add nothing to the meaning of a sentence and would be better left out. Words such as definitely, virtually, very, actually, rather, absolutely and real may be redundant in some sentences and make them clumsy.

> I am definitely sure that Lee will become an absolutely brilliant athlete.

'Sure' and 'definitely sure' mean the same thing. 'Absolutely brilliant' means no more than just 'brilliant'. 'Definitely' is correctly used in the following example, however.

> 'Are you sure he came back?' she asked. 'Definitely', he said.

Redundant words are acceptable in speech where they are used for emphasis. They are not acceptable in writing. (See also 'Tautology', below.)

Tautology

'Tautology' means saying the same thing in different words, or trying to strengthen your writing by adding unnecessary words. Here are some examples.

ascend up	completely empty	true facts	new initiatives	stone dead
quite unique	two equal halves	a positive step	in the right direction	free gift

A wit once defined tautology as 'repeating the same thing twice'.

ACTIVITY 38

Tautology

1 Rewrite the following sentences, deleting the unnecessary words.
   a That was a very false and untrue statement you made.
   b Lie perfectly still and motionless until the convoy passes.
   c A rugby game consists of two halves while an AFL game consists of four quarters.
   d As the blizzard blew we descended down the mountain.
   e The survey aimed to find out a truly accurate result.
   f The reason why I did that is because I respect you.

Clichés

2 Replace the clichés in these sentences with more original expressions.
- **a** He was as sick as a dog.
- **b** He has a memory like an elephant.
- **c** The cowboy bit the dust.
- **d** I'm feeling as flat as a pancake.
- **e** Ever since he turned fifteen, he's been growing like a weed.
- **f** I have an axe to grind with you.
- **g** It's a dog eat dog world.
- **h** He's in the doghouse again.
- **i** That's chicken feed.
- **j** The smells from the kitchen make my mouth water.

Verbosity

'Verbosity' means 'wordiness' – too many words when fewer, and perhaps simpler, words would be more effective. Speakers and writers are sometimes verbose to make themselves or their subject-matter sound more important. Students writing essays might hope that verbosity will hide a lack of information. Here are two examples of verbosity.

> You have a continuing tendency towards prevarication. (You lie all the time.)

> It is no doubt within my capacity to undertake such an enterprise. (I could do it.)

Inclusive language

Language can be used to exclude or discriminate against people on account of their sex, race, culture, age or disabilities. Inclusive language treats everyone equally. This section looks at the problems of sexist and racist language and offers suggestions to enable you to use inclusive language at all times.

Non-sexist language

The term 'sexism' originally referred to discrimination against women. It is now applied to any stereotyping of males and females on the basis of gender. There are four major problems caused by the use of sexist language: invisibility, dependence, trivialisation and stereotyping.

Invisibility

The problem

The opening words of the original version of Australia's national anthem offer a striking example of how language can make women invisible: 'Australia's sons, let us rejoice for we are young and free ...'. This has been replaced by the more acceptable 'Australians all ...', which includes women in its rallying call.

Some of the major ways in which women have traditionally been made invisible in language are listed below.

1 The English language does not have a pronoun to represent both 'he' and 'she' (or 'his' and 'her'). 'He' has been used to represent both sexes.

> A student should check his work carefully before he hands it in.

2 When referring to 'the human race' the word 'man' has been used.

> Man's search for the meaning of life is never-ending.

3 Words such as 'businessmen' and 'salesmen' tend to exclude women, although these groups include both men and women.

ISBN 9780170183048

Possible solutions

1 Instead of using the male pronoun 'he', to represent both sexes

a leave out the pronoun if this does not alter the meaning. Instead of

> You can judge an employee's position by his salary.

take out 'his'

> You can judge an employee's position by salary.

b change to the plural. Instead of

> A secretary should keep her desk tidy.

you could make this sentence plural so that it becomes

> Secretaries should keep their desks tidy.

c replace the masculine pronoun with 'one', 'you', 'he or she' or 'his or her'. Change

> The buyer of a new car should check his insurance cover.

to one of the following

> When buying a new car, you should check your insurance cover.

or

> The buyer of a new car should check his or her insurance cover.

d reword or rephrase a sentence to eliminate gender pronouns. Change

> You can tell a man's income by the make of car he owns.

to one of the following

> The make of a car is a good indicator of its owner's income.

or

> Your income is revealed by the make of car you drive.

If the above alternatives appear clumsy, you can alternate between female and male pronouns.

> A newborn baby must always have her head supported. Wrap your baby securely in his blanket.

2 Avoid the use of terms that exclude women.

Gender-marked terms	Possible substitutes
man, mankind	humans, human beings, humanity, the human race, people, civilisation
to man (*verb*)	to staff, attend, drive, operate, use, work
'Man' as a prefix	
man-made	artificial, constructed, fabricated, synthetic
manpower	labour, personnel, staff, workforce
'Man' as a suffix	
businessman	business executive, owner, manager, entrepreneur
fireman	firefighter
policeman	police officer, detective, police cadet, police (*plural*)
salesman	sales representative, salesperson, sales clerk
sportsman	athlete, competitor, player, sportsperson
workman	worker, employee
Frenchman, Frenchmen	a French person, the French

Dependence

The problem

Women are often referred to in relation to men.

> Jon Cook and his wife Chris
>
> Mrs Graham Keylock
>
> Mrs Beet, wife of Carlton Manager Barrie Beet

Possible solutions

1   Women and men should be given parallel treatment.

No	Yes
Jon Montenegro and Katherine	Jon Montenegro and Katherine Bennetts
Katherine and Montenegro	Katherine and Jon
Ms Bennetts and Montenegro	Ms Bennetts and Mr Montenegro

2   Women should not be identified in terms of their marital relationships unless similar references are made to men.

No	Yes
Jon Cook and his wife Chris	Jon and Chris Cook; Mr Jon Cook and Mrs Chris Cook
Mrs Graham Keylock	Mrs Carmela Keylock; Ms Carmela Keylock; Carmela Keylock
Mrs Beet, wife of Carlton Manager, Barrie Beet	Mr Barrie Beet, the Carlton Manager and Mrs Lee Beet; Lee and Barrie Beet; Mr and Mrs Beet; Mrs Lee Beet and Mr Barrie Beet

Trivialisation

The problem

Some of the ways in which women's actions and activities are trivialised include

1   describing women by physical attributes and men by their intellectual attributes or professional position

2   using expressions that belittle women, such as the little woman, the ball and chain and the weaker sex.

Possible solutions

1   Use parallel language to give the sexes equal treatment.

No	Yes
Rob Listro is a talented engineer and his wife Margaret is a striking redhead.	The Listros are an attractive couple. Rob is a handsome blond and Margaret is a striking redhead. The Listros are a capable couple. Margaret is a freelance food consultant and Rob is a partner in an engineering firm.

2   Use 'man'/'woman', 'girl'/'boy', 'lady'/'gentleman' as parallel terms. Do not refer to workers as 'girls'/'boys', as these terms are patronising and inappropriate for adult workers.

3   Alternate the order in which men and women are mentioned.

> women and men   he and she   her and him   males and females

4   Avoid diminutives or words that imply 'smallness', either literal or metaphorical, to describe women. Sweet young thing, cute or lovely young lady may be considered offensive and demeaning when applied to adult women.

ISBN 9780170183048

Stereotyping

The problem

1 Women are often shown in stereotyped ways
    a as having feminine strengths and weaknesses
    b as filling womanly roles: mother, housewife, wife.
2 Instead of referring to women as 'doctors' or 'lawyers', they are sometimes referred to as 'women doctors' or 'lady lawyers', as though it were odd or unusual for women to engage in these occupations.
3 Feminine suffixes such as –ess (authoress), –ette (usherette) and –trix (aviatrix) imply that a woman is to be considered firstly as a female and secondly as a person of talent.

Possible solutions

1 Members of both sexes should be shown with human strengths and weaknesses, not with characteristics seen traditionally as masculine or feminine. Characteristics that have been praised in males – such as boldness, initiative and assertiveness – should also be acknowledged in females; similarly, characteristics that have been praised in females – such as gentleness, compassion and sensitivity – should be acknowledged in males.
2 Women and men, girls and boys should be shown as having the same abilities, interests and ambitions.
3 Sex-specific words should not be used.

No	Yes
lady lawyer	lawyer, e.g. The lawyer made her summation to the jury.
woman doctor	doctor
male nurse	nurse, e.g. The nurse was late for his shift.
cleaning lady	cleaner
matron	director of nursing
actress	actor
aviatrix	aviator (or pilot)
comedienne	comedian
heiress	heir
manageress	manager
waitress	waiter

ACTIVITY 39

Inclusive language

Rewrite the following sentences so they are non-sexist. At the end of each sentence identify, in brackets, whether your change was due to invisibility, dependence, trivialisation or stereotyping.

1 A doctor should update his knowledge annually.
2 A receptionist should check her email daily.
3 No man is an island.
4 Come and meet Mrs Crawford, wife of the famous aviator Peter Crawford.
5 Stop behaving like an old woman and get on with the job.
6 Meet Gillian; she is a woman pilot.
7 Maria is an usherette but prefers her old job as an air hostess.
8 Wanted: an attractive young lady to be a waitress at a businessman's lunch.
9 The male nurse was very friendly with the patients.
10 Man has caused so much pollution.

Non-racist language

Be even-handed

People of all races and ethnic backgrounds should be treated in an even-handed way. The ethnic background of people is too often mentioned in negative reports ('Lebanese committing crime'), but not in positive reports ('Australian rugby league star Hazem El Masri'). As reference is not made to gangs of Anglo-Celtic youths, it should not be made to gangs of Sudanese youths or those of any other nationalities. Do not refer to a person's race or nationality unless it is relevant.

No	Yes
Cleopatra is played by the Aboriginal actor Miranda Stevens.	Cleopatra is played by actor Miranda Stevens.
a man of German appearance	a man 165 cm tall with blond hair, blue eyes and fair skin
alien, ethnic, migrant	Avoid using these words as nouns. They are inappropriate for those who have lived in Australia for some time.

Avoid racial stereotypes

Stereotypes are oversimplified, fixed views about groups. Just as it is unreasonable to suggest that all accountants are boring, it is unreasonable to say that all the Irish 'have the gift of the gab'; that all Jamaicans have good rhythm; that all Japanese work hard; or that all Australians are suntanned, adopt 'She'll be right, mate!' as their motto and drink lots of beer. These stereotypes are the basis for racist jokes and are quite unfair to individuals and groups alike.

No	Yes
Catarina had a typical Latin temperament – fiery and fun-loving.	Catarina was a fun-loving person with a fiery temperament.
Soo had the excellent business mind characteristic of the Chinese.	Soo had an excellent business mind.

ACTIVITY 40

Non-racist language

Rewrite the sentences that use racist language. Indicate in brackets the reason for your changes.

1 The Aboriginal athlete won the gold medal.
2 The Vietnamese youths were hanging around the corner shop.
3 Like all Asians, Chui studies every day and is very good with computers.
4 Sean is a typical Irishman: he loves drinking and hates working.
5 The Aboriginals are very good with horses.

ISBN 9780170183048

PUBLISHING CONVENTIONS

Just as punctuation helps people make sense of what they read, so the conventions used in publishing help comprehension and make reading easier. And just as the rules for punctuation have changed over time, so have publishing conventions.

Many organisations and publications have their own house style, where they specify preferences for certain conventions. In some cases, there are no fixed rules and you can follow your personal preferences, as long as your choices are consistent. The acknowledged authority for Australian publishing conventions is the *Style manual for authors, editors and printers*. While the notes below will cover most of your needs, if you have a question that is not answered here, the *Style manual* is the place to go.

Numbers
Words or figures?

Numbers can be represented by words (six, five thousand, tenth) or by figures or numerals (6, 5000, 10th). Which to use depends on the type of text. In a text such as a narrative or a description, you are more likely to find words, while a procedural text or scientific report is more likely to use figures. However, there are some general rules.

1   Avoid using figures to start a sentence. If it is necessary to start a sentence with a number, it should be written in words.

> One hundred and sixty-six sheep were slaughtered that week.

> Sixty per cent of his flock was sent to the abattoir.

It may be better to restructure the sentence.

> There were 166 sheep slaughtered that week.

> The abattoir received 60 per cent of his flock.

2   Avoid using figures at the end of sentences. Use words instead, if possible.

> The final tally was three hundred and forty-two.

However, if two or more numbers appear at the end of a sentence, it is not necessary to express the final figure in words.

> The tally was increased from 342 to 392.

> My three assessment marks were 42, 44 and 49.

3   Sentences that might otherwise begin with dates, currency or measurements should be reorganised to avoid beginning with figures. Rewrite

> 1929 was the beginning of the Great Depression.

as

> The Great Depression began in 1929.

Rewrite

> $500 000 will buy you a modest house.

as

> A modest house can be bought for $500 000.

4   Similarly, if a number at the beginning of a sentence is followed by other numbers in the same passage, it may be easier to recast the sentence. Rewrite

> Six hundred and twenty-one applications were received; of these 531 were well-qualified.

as

> Of the 621 applications received, 531 were well-qualified.

5   Most style guides and editors have a rule specifying that, in written text, small numbers should be written in words and big numbers in figures, but there is no agreement about what is meant by 'big' and 'small'. Some guides say that you should use words up to the number ten, and then figures; some specify up to twenty; many say that you use words for numbers up to one hundred but figures after that: 101, 102 and so on. So it is a matter of personal preference. Again, the nature of the text needs to be considered. If it is a text that uses very few numbers, words are more likely to be appropriate. Figures will always be used, for example, in tables.

6   Words are used for large numbers that indicate approximation.

> about four hundred
>
> a crowd of twenty thousand
>
> nearly ten million

7   Where there is a list of quantities, the numbers should be written in figures.

> The convoy included 15 motor bikes, 21 four-wheel-drive vehicles, 6 utilities, 10 cars towing caravans and 5 trucks.

8   Where two sets of numbers occur together, one should be written in numbers and one in figures.

> Of the 30 students in the class, 6 had one brother, 8 had one sister, 7 had a brother and a sister, 3 had two sisters, 2 had two brothers, 2 had a brother and two sisters and 2 had no siblings.

9   Where two numbers occur together, one should be written in numbers and the other in figures.

> two 18-carat diamond rings
>
> 5 four-wheel-drive vehicles

ISBN 9780170183048

The setting out of numbers

1   In numbers of five or more figures (a number greater than 9999), a comma was traditionally used to indicate thousands (after each three figures).

    23,001   301,500   5,001,175

This caused confusion with the European habit of using a comma as the decimal marker, so this use is now confined strictly to handwriting. In print, a space is used to separate the groups of numbers.

    23 001   301 500   5 001 175

2   In numbers of four figures or fewer, there is no need to use a comma or a space.

    222   3201   1015

3   We easily recognise round numbers up to 10 million whether they are written in words or numbers.

    four hundred   six thousand   eight million
    400   6 000   8 000 000

However, large, complex numbers can be confusing in the middle of a passage of text, whether they are written in words or figures. It is often better to use a combination of words and figures. Write:

    2.5 million

rather than

    2 500 000

or

    two million five hundred thousand.

4   With numbers less than one, use a zero before the decimal point. Write:

    0.03

not

    .03

Measurement

1   When numbers are used with a symbol of measurement, figures should always be used.

    $10.95

    90°

    31.57S

    21 g

    42 km

2   Even when the measurement unit is written in full, figures are the more common choice.

    90 degrees

    42 kilometres

3   However, in a general text such as a narrative or description in which numbers do not play an important part, words may be more appropriate.

    He still had forty kilometres to travel.

    I had twenty dollars to spend.

ACTIVITY 41

Numbers

1 Rewrite the following sentences, correcting the way the numbers have been written.

  a There were 20 000 people at the rock concert.

  b For dinner, we had five chickens, twenty rolls, six tubs of ice-cream, four loaves of bread and ten kilos of sausages.

  c When I logged on there were one hundred and twenty-two emails still unread.

  d 1914 saw the outbreak of World War I.

  e Did you really buy five ten dollar scratchies?

  f 500 times I've told you not to go near there!

  g The final score was 5 goals to two.

  h You will need two tablespoons of oil, three cupfuls of rice and one and a half teaspoons of cumin.

  i Give me two metres of that curtain fabric, please.

  j His final score was 98.

2 Now work with a partner. Look at your rewritten sentences and in each case explain why you made the changes.

Titles

If you want to refer to the title of a book, a film, a song or any other such work in your writing, you need to make this clear to your readers. There are agreed publishing conventions for indicating titles.

Italics

Italics (or underlining in handwriting) is used for the titles of:

- books

     Elaine's first novel, *The Watching Lake*, was published by Puffin.

- journals, periodicals and newspapers

     The Australian is the country's only national newspaper.

- plays and long poems

     The School of Arts was performed in Brisbane to celebrate Queensland's sesquicentenary.

- films, DVDs and videos

     Gone with the Wind starred Vivien Leigh and Clark Gable.

- television and radio programs

     Neighbours is even more popular in the UK than in Australia.

- musical works

     While she was on exchange in Italy, Kath saw the opera *Aida* in Milan.

- art works

     She also saw Botticelli's *Birth of Venus* at the Uffizi Gallery in Florence.

ISBN 9780170183048

Quotation marks

Single quotation marks (double quotation marks in handwriting) are used for the titles of:

- book chapters

    Read the chapter 'The early settlers' for homework tonight.

- short stories and poems

    The ABC Book of Australian Poetry: A treasury of poems for young people compiled by Libby Hathorn includes 'One Return' by Nicolette Stasko.

    Make sure you read Thalia Kalkipsakis's story 'Tick-Tock Time Machine'. It's in her collection of stories called *Head Spinners*.

- songs

    The 2011 Eurovision Song Contest was won for the first time ever by Azerbaijan with a love song called 'Running Scared'.

- journal, periodical and newspaper articles

    He wrote an article, 'Averting a malaria disaster', for *The Lancet*.

- television and radio series episodes

    My favourite episode from *Buffy* was 'Once More with Feeling'.

Note: Quotation marks are also referred to as 'speech marks' and 'inverted commas'.

ACTIVITY 42

Titles

Rewrite the following sentences, punctuating the titles correctly.
1 Take out your copies of Australian History since 1900. Read the chapter called The Vietnam War.
2 Josh Whedon, creator of Buffy the Vampire Slayer, lists Dopplegangland as one of his favourite episodes.
3 Judith Wright's poem Bora Ring is published in her collection A Human Pattern.
4 The Opera Company has announced a new season of the ever-popular opera La Bohème.
5 The most famous painting in the Louvre is the Mona Lisa.
6 Baz Luhrmann's expensive film Australia opened to mixed reviews.
7 John Marsden's well-known series Tomorrow, When the War Began was originally conceived as a trilogy.
8 Have you read this article in the Courier Mail?

Referencing

You must acknowledge your source whenever you

- quote someone else's exact words
- use an idea or information directly based on another writer's work
- summarise something written by another person.

Failing to acknowledge your source is plagiarism. Plagiarism is when you claim to have written or created a piece of work that someone else originated. It is regarded as cheating and can have serious consequences, including the loss of all marks for the work you have submitted. Plagiarism can occur even if you change some of the wording: if you are borrowing someone else's ideas, you must acknowledge the debt. Sources that need to be acknowledged include books and articles, websites, even interviews – anything from which you have borrowed ideas or copied wording.

There are various ways of acknowledging sources. Many educational institutions, including schools, have their own system. The rules for setting out the information about the sources are usually very precise and need to be followed. The purpose of these rules is to encourage writers to set out their sources in a consistent way that will make it easy for readers to find the source if they wish to.

If you consult a range of authorities about referencing, you will find variations in such things as

- the use of punctuation and capital letters
- the order in which the information is given
- the use of italics and abbreviations.

Always find out first if your educational institution has a preferred style. You can find detailed help on the website for this book (www.nelsonenglishusage.com.au).

Bibliographies

A bibliography is a list of all the works you have consulted in preparing your work. It is important that you keep careful records as you do your research, so that you can compile your bibliography.

A bibliography is usually placed at the end of the work and is arranged alphabetically according to author. As with footnotes and reference lists, different institutions specify different ways of setting out a bibliography. If you do some research on the Internet, you will find a variety of methods. You can find detailed information about setting out a bibliography on the website for this book.

Quoting other writers

If you are using something that someone else has written, you must show this clearly to your readers. Unless you indicate that you are quoting another person's words, you are cheating.

Short quotes

If you are using a short quote, place what has been said in quotation marks. The quotation is often introduced with either a comma or a colon.

> I believe that if civilisation as we know it is to survive, then the way we celebrate the first of April must be changed. As Niland Stuart (1998) said, 'Civilisation is only skin deep, and on the first of April the skin is often pretty thin'. We must listen to such wisdom or pay the consequences.

Longer quotes

Longer passages (more than about three sentences or about thirty words) should be set off from the body of your writing by being indented. You do not need to use quotation marks. Longer quotes are often introduced by a colon and may be printed in a slightly smaller font than the body of the text. It is usual to leave a line before and after the indented material. See the examples on the following page.

ISBN 9780170183048

The press release contained the following background information.

> The committee was first convened on the 20th September 2006 with instructions to submit their report by the end of the year. The chairperson, Sunita Khalij, announced that submissions would be heard from members of the general public as well as from industry professionals. It was assumed that the report would make recommendations that would have significant impact on the next budget.

The document was distributed to all journalists who attended the press conference.

One of Dickens' most memorable passages is the opening page of *Great Expectations* when the narrator, the orphaned Pip, reflects on his impression of his dead parents.

> As I never saw my father or my mother, and never saw any likeness of either of them (for their days were long before the days of photographs), my first fancies regarding what they were like were unreasonably derived from their tombstones. The shape of the letters on my father's gave me an odd idea that he was a square, stout, dark man with curly black hair. From the character and turn of the inscription, 'Also Georgiana Wife of the Above', I drew a childish conclusion that my mother was freckled and sickly.

Pip goes on to talk about the five brothers he had also never known, all of whom had died as babies, and his fancy, based on their tiny tombstones, that 'they had all been born on their backs with their hands in their trousers pockets'.

Quoting lines of poetry

Lines of poetry should show line divisions, even when they are placed in quotation marks in the body of the text. The line division is shown by a slash (/). It is important to quote exactly what is printed, including the correct punctuation, and capital letters.

ISBN 9780170183048

> As Hamlet says, 'tis an unweeded garden, / that grows to seed'. It is possible at this moment that he is entirely disillusioned.

Otherwise, poetry should be treated in exactly the same way as other quoted material. For a short quote, use quotation marks.

> One overwhelmed commentator after another applauds the lyricism of the scene; what is worth adding perhaps is that the self-enclosed passion of the lovers is presented with beautiful comic edge from Juliet's first words on. 'Ay me!' she says, and Romeo falls enthusiastically on the phrase …

Indent longer quotes (more than two or three lines). No quotation marks are needed. Leave a line before and after the quoted passage. Use a slightly smaller font in printed text if you wish. Here is an example.

> It is not surprising that Shakespeare, a practical man of the theatre, should use an image drawn from the theatre when he wants to describe the stages of human life:
>
>> All the world's a stage,
>>
>> And all the men and women merely players;
>>
>> They have their exits and their entrances,
>>
>> And one man in his time plays many parts,
>>
>> His acts being seven ages.
>
> To assume, however, that the jaundiced view of humanity that follows is Shakespeare's own is to forget that Shakespeare is speaking through the voice of one of his created characters, in this case Jaques.

Leaving out part of a quote

When you want to leave out part of a quote, an ellipsis (three dots with a space on either side) is used (…), as in this example.

> As Brodie McKee (1999) says in his influential legal history of the 1930s: 'Many Australians suffered great hardship during the Depression … but the wealthy were unaffected'.

ISBN 9780170183048

Formatting your written work

Word processing has opened up huge and exciting prospects for formatting your work in interesting ways, including the use of templates. Remember, however, the importance of clarity of design. The following points are worth keeping in mind.

1   If you use headings and subheadings, use them consistently, with the same font size and type selected for headings of the same level of importance.

2   Limit your use of fonts: too much variety can give your page a cluttered appearance.

3   Choose fonts for their readability, rather than for their decorative appeal.

4   As a rule, follow the default margins provided by your word-processing program: narrowing of margins can make your text difficult to read.

5   Adjust your page layout to the nature of the medium you are using; for example, most printed documents are designed to be read from left to right and from top to bottom, but texts on screen are read differently, with the reader's eye drawn first to the central panel.

6   Keep paragraphs relatively short, usually from three to five sentences in length.

7   Single-sentence paragraphs can be a very effective way of drawing attention to a significant point, especially if used as an introductory or concluding paragraph.

8   Single-sentence paragraphs should be used sparingly as they can be a symptom of poor planning, indicating an inability to integrate main points or a lack of supporting evidence or detail.

9   Short sentences are clear and effective; however, a string of short sentences can seem abrupt or disjointed. Good writing has a variety of sentence lengths and patterns.

Paragraphing

Paragraphs are the building blocks used to create an organised, unified piece of writing such as an essay. When planning an essay, it is important to consider the points you will make in constructing your argument. Each paragraph should contain only one main idea or point. A helpful step in planning an essay is to determine how your argument can be 'broken down' into a series of different points, each of which helps to validate your case – in other words, work out the paragraph points you will make.

A good paragraph should have the following structure.

1   A topic sentence (sometimes called a paragraph opener): this introduces the point being made in the paragraph.

2   Supporting sentences: these develop the main point, providing explanation, elaboration and examples or evidence to support your point. Quotations may also be included to illustrate the point.

3   A summary sentence: this sums up your point, 'rounding off' the paragraph.
    Other features include:
    • variation in sentence structure (that is, a blend of simple, complex and compound sentences)
    • variation in the length of sentences
    • a varied vocabulary
    • linking words or text connectives to connect ideas. Ways of making connections include the following: adverbs such as 'furthermore', 'also', 'moreover' and 'similarly'; adverbs of time such as 'first' and 'finally'; pronouns used in place of nouns and noun phrases; repetition of words; and the use of related words such as synonyms and antonyms.

Constructing a paragraph

The sample paragraph on the next page is from an argument essay in response to the novel *Follow the Rabbit-Proof Fence*. Note how the paragraph is organised logically and sequentially to develop the point stated in the topic sentence.

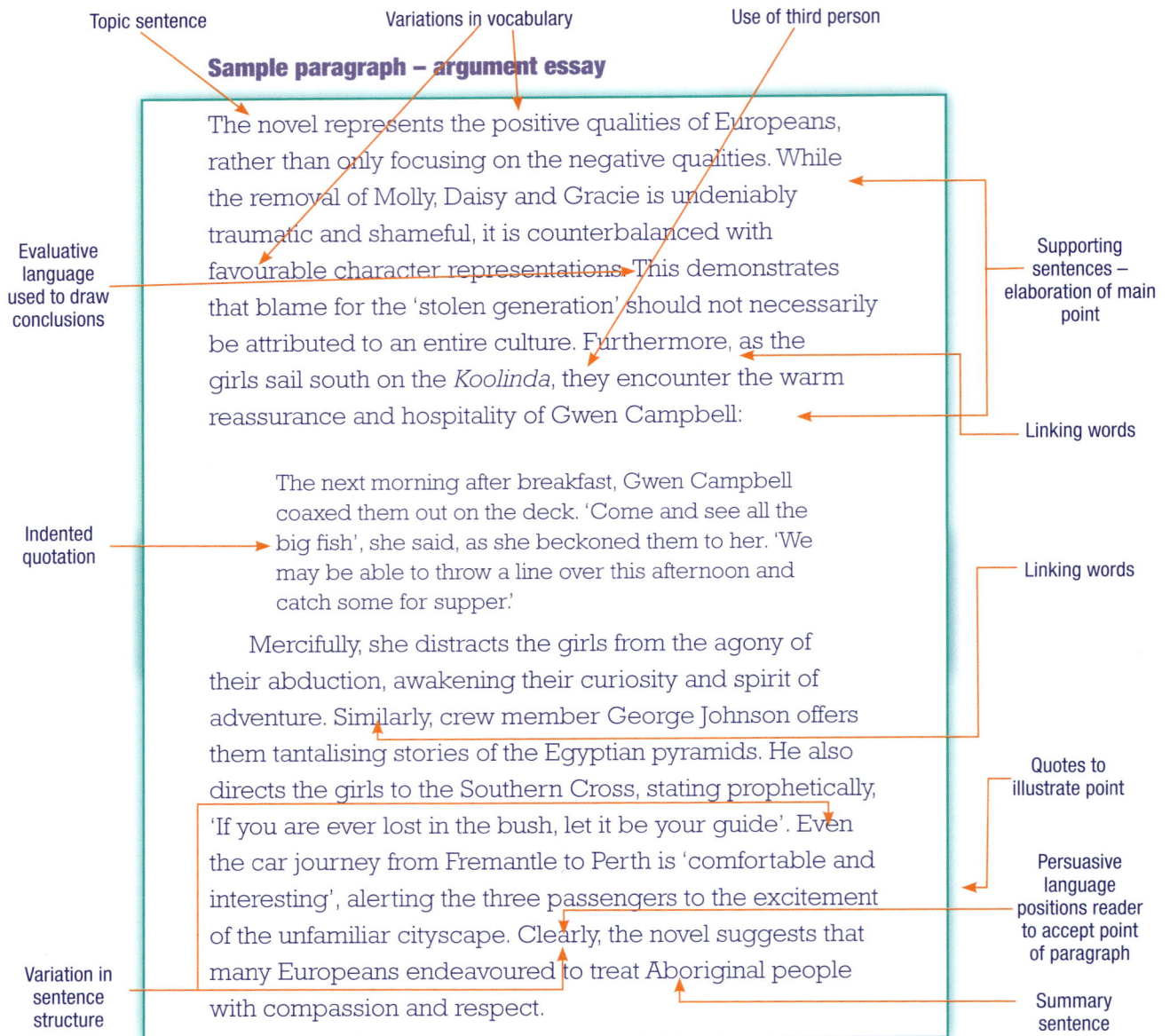

Topic sentence   Variations in vocabulary   Use of third person

Sample paragraph – argument essay

Evaluative language used to draw conclusions

Supporting sentences – elaboration of main point

The novel represents the positive qualities of Europeans, rather than only focusing on the negative qualities. While the removal of Molly, Daisy and Gracie is undeniably traumatic and shameful, it is counterbalanced with favourable character representations. This demonstrates that blame for the 'stolen generation' should not necessarily be attributed to an entire culture. Furthermore, as the girls sail south on the *Koolinda*, they encounter the warm reassurance and hospitality of Gwen Campbell:

Linking words

Indented quotation

The next morning after breakfast, Gwen Campbell coaxed them out on the deck. 'Come and see all the big fish', she said, as she beckoned them to her. 'We may be able to throw a line over this afternoon and catch some for supper.'

Linking words

Mercifully, she distracts the girls from the agony of their abduction, awakening their curiosity and spirit of adventure. Similarly, crew member George Johnson offers them tantalising stories of the Egyptian pyramids. He also directs the girls to the Southern Cross, stating prophetically, 'If you are ever lost in the bush, let it be your guide'. Even the car journey from Fremantle to Perth is 'comfortable and interesting', alerting the three passengers to the excitement of the unfamiliar cityscape. Clearly, the novel suggests that many Europeans endeavoured to treat Aboriginal people with compassion and respect.

Quotes to illustrate point

Persuasive language positions reader to accept point of paragraph

Variation in sentence structure

Summary sentence

ACTIVITY 43

Find a textbook for a subject other than English. Choose one that has sections of text that explain concepts or processes (such as a science textbook) or that narrates events, such as a history textbook. Select and photocopy three paragraphs at random from your chosen book. Working with a partner, see if you can annotate each paragraph, as in the example above. In particular, look for the topic sentence, supporting sentences and the summary sentence. You might like to mark these with different-coloured highlighters. Draw circles around linking words. If you have difficulty finding the different types of sentences, discuss whether it may be because the paragraph is poorly constructed.

ISBN 9780170183048

Good writing practice for any occasion

Drafting

Professional writers consider drafting essential. Drafting is the term that describes the process writers go through in revising their work until it says exactly what they want it to say. It involves a thinking process in which writers move from:

- exploration ('What do I want to say?')

  to

- celebration ('Look what I have said!').

When you begin to write, you may not be clear about what you want to say, but this doesn't matter. It is just important to get started. As you pour your ideas onto paper in a first draft, you begin to work out your ideas on the subject. Writing the first draft helps to clarify your thoughts.

In further drafts your emphasis should be on revising and therefore clarifying what you are saying. As you draft and redraft, you will find yourself:

- crossing out
- changing or adapting
- extending and adding
- cutting
- refining
- moving a sentence or paragraph to another place in your text.

As you work on your drafts, you will need to be more and more influenced by your audience, your purpose and the form of writing you have chosen.

You will develop your own techniques for drafting. Some writers like to work with a hard copy of their text and make changes by crossing out, adding text, even using different coloured pens to indicate different kinds of changes. However, most writers redraft by editing their work electronically. If you need to provide a portfolio that shows the stages of your work, you can use the 'track changes' feature of your word-processing program to keep a record of the editing process.

Editing your work

Professional editors distinguish between two different kinds of editing:

- substantive, or structural, editing
- copy editing.

Substantive editing involves looking at the text as a whole and evaluating its success in terms of audience, purpose and type of text. It might involve such changes as recommending the use of a different point of view in a narrative, or the reorganisation of chapters in a textbook. It might involve looking at the language register the author has chosen and its appropriateness to the intended audience.

When you are redrafting your own work, begin by taking on the role of a substantive editor. Look at the text as a whole and see what changes are needed to ensure its effectiveness.

A copy editor is responsible for accuracy and consistency in such matters as spelling, grammar, punctuation and style. It can be quite difficult copy editing your own work, as you often don't see your own mistakes. You need to read very closely; some writers find it helpful to read their work aloud. If you are editing on computer, run the language and spelling check programs as a guide to changes that may need to be made. These programs are very helpful, although you may not always accept their recommendations. Keep the following points in mind.

- Make sure that your program uses Australian spelling as a default.
- Keep in mind that the spell check feature cannot distinguish between most homophones.
- While the program will note repeated words, it cannot tell that sometimes the repetition may be deliberate.
- The program may not pick up a word that has been omitted accidentally.
- The program will usually highlight a use of the passive voice, but there are times when you will have deliberately chosen a passive construction.
- The program may pick up colloquial or non-standard language that you have deliberately chosen to use, for example in a passage of dialogue.

Professional writers have their work checked by professional editors before publication. Whenever possible, ask other people – fellow students, teachers, parents – to read and comment on your work.

Editing checklist: the final draft

- Have I said exactly what I wanted to say to my audience?
- Have I remained focused on my purpose in writing?
- Is my subject matter relevant?
- Have I included sufficient evidence, illustration and elaboration?
- Have I included any unnecessary or redundant material?
- Is my tone consistent and appropriate to the text type?
- Have I used a varied and interesting vocabulary, appropriate to my audience?
- Are my ideas well organised?
- Have I met any length requirements?

Proofreading your work

Professional proofreading is done just before a work is published. It involves locating and correcting errors and ensuring that everything is consistent. In the school situation you should proofread your own work just before handing it in. Check your final draft to pick up any careless mistakes or typing errors, especially inaccurate spelling or punctuation.

Proofreading is a specialised skill that needs to be learnt. When you read for meaning you skim the words quickly because it is possible to predict much of what you read. You read what you expect to read. When proofreading, you need to stop yourself from predicting the words; otherwise you will not see mistakes. Read slowly and try to look at each word individually. A ruler under the line helps. Many writers like to read aloud. It is also helpful to scan your text separately for errors in spelling, punctuation, grammar and consistency (for example, in tense).

Proofreading symbols

The following are some of the standard proofreading marks that are widely used as a way of indicating corrections to be made to a hard-copy draft. Marks placed in the text itself indicate the location of the error. These are accompanied by marks in the margin of the text, which identify the particular error. Further proofreading marks, accepted as conventional in Australian publishing, can be found in the *Style manual for authors, editors and printers*.

ISBN 9780170183048

Meaning	Mark in text	Mark in margin
Delete from text	Strike through characters to be deleted	◌
Add to text	∧	Material to be added followed by /
Change to italics	Underline characters to be altered	ital
Change to bold type	Squiggle under characters to be altered	bold
Close up space	Use ⌒ to link characters	⌒
Insert space	Use ∧ to show where space is needed	#
Begin a new paragraph	Put [before first word of new paragraph	n.p.
Insert apostrophe	∧	⌣
Insert question mark	∧	?/
Insert comma	∧	,/

Sample proofread text

The following text is an extract from a feature article on advertising written by a student. In the final draft, the expression is clearer, the vocabulary is more precise, and spelling and punctuation errors have been fixed.

The rough draft

Advertising ~~secretly~~ subtly plays on ~~man's~~ human weaknesses and insecurities by distorting and idealising everyday ~~scenes in idea~~ situations. ~~I ways.~~ When subjected to the idealistic realities depicted in ~~of advertising~~ advertisements, ~~the advertisements position us in such a~~ we are positioned to ~~way as we~~ feel inadequate~~, driving us~~ and are driven to surrender and An example of idealised representations of people occurs in food advertising. buy products in an effort to be `normal'. Commercial's targeting families usually include a mother or a father who ~~as a means of~~ help to construct an idealised representing ~~and thereby generating an~~ In particular, ~~idealistic~~ parent child relationship. The mothers we see on television are proud ~~of their homes~~ house-, always smiling and entirely devoted to their ~~greatful~~ grateful children however, on the other hand, father's are busy professionals who leave the groceries and cooking to their wives. ~~Mums~~ Mothers will choose Nutella when rushing through a supermarket, and Kellog's Nutri-Grain subconsciously basing their selection on the belief that they are being `proper mums' ~~if they do.~~

The improved version

Better vocabulary choices

Inclusive language

Advertising subtly plays on (human) weaknesses and insecurities by distorting and idealising everyday situations. When (subjected) to the idealised realities depicted in advertisements, (we are positioned) to feel inadequate and are driven to surrender and buy products in an effort to be 'normal'. An example of idealised representations of people occurs in food advertising. Commercials targeting families usually include a mother or a father who represent and help to construct an idealised parent–child relationship. In particular, the mothers we see on television are house-proud, always smiling and entirely devoted to their grateful children. Fathers, on the other hand, are busy professionals who leave the groceries and cooking to their wives. Mothers will choose Nutella and Kellogg's Nutri-Grain when rushing through a supermarket, subconsciously basing their selection on the belief that they are being 'proper mums'.

Subject–verb agreement

Tighter, more succinct expression

Additional sentence introduces example

Additional information for greater clarity

Additional phrase to connect ideas

Improved sentence construction

Additional phrase to connect ideas

Improved sentence construction

ACTIVITY 44

Select a piece of writing that you have done for school recently, for any subject. Work with a partner and swap your work. This can be either a handwritten or printed copy of your work, or an electronic copy.

Edit your partner's work carefully, annotating the changes you have made as in the improved version above or using your word processor's mark-up features. Check:

- spelling
- punctuation
- grammatical correctness, including sequence of tenses, subject–verb agreement and pronoun reference
- word choice
- appropriateness of register (formal, informal)
- paragraphing
- length and variety of sentences
- clarity of expression.

Then discuss the changes you have made to each other's work.

ISBN 9780170183048

INTRODUCING TYPES OF TEXTS 7

The word **text** is used to mean any communication involving language. Such communication can consist of:

- written text
- spoken text
- visual text
- electronic text
- a combination of some or all of these to make a multimodal text.

Texts can be classified in different ways. You will notice that they were classified above according to the medium used (writing, speech, images and so on). One common classification is to divide them into:

- literary texts
- information texts
- media texts
- everyday texts
- workplace texts.

However, you will notice that these can overlap: a workplace text is quite likely to be offering information, and a media text, such as a television drama, is at the same time a literary text. While it is convenient to categorise texts into different types, the very nature of language is so complex that neat categorisations are difficult.

The most useful classification – although here too the distinctions are not always clear-cut – is to see texts as:

- imaginative texts (also called literary texts)
- information texts (also called expository or factual texts)
- argument texts (including persuasive texts).

These are the categories that we have used for a closer look at text types in Chapters 8, 9 and 10.

Audience

Texts are created for different purposes and for different audiences. The language that we use and the way in which we organise a text depends on who it is intended for and why it is being produced.

For example, a reality television show might target a young audience and use contemporary language and lots of humour to appeal to its viewers. A horror film intends to frighten its audience, so the narrative unfolds gradually and the audience feels a growing sense of anticipation and dread, heightened by an appropriately spooky sound track and some gruesome special effects. In both cases, the text is shaped by its audience and purpose.

The audience for any text is the person or persons for whom it is intended: a reader, a listener or a viewer.

An important aspect when considering the audience for a text is the situation or context of the text.

For example, if you were to write letters to your best friend, the deputy principal of a school and someone you had never met, each letter would be quite different because of your different relationship with each reader and the situation that has led to you writing the letter. In fact, you would probably only write one draft of the letter to your best friend, but you might do more than one draft of the other letters.

ISBN 9780170183048

Checklist: audience

Whenever you begin to plan a text – written, spoken, visual or electronic – first ask yourself these questions about your audience.
- Is my language formal enough / too formal?
- Are the words I have used too difficult / not sophisticated enough?
- Is my writing too complex or not detailed enough?
- Will what I say and the way I say it have the desired effect on my audience?

Purpose

All composers have a reason behind their compositions. They have something they wish to express and they want a response from their audience.

For example, if you were to write to a local shopkeeper inviting her to speak to a class group, asking her for a job, or thanking her for a generous donation to the school production, each of these letters would be different because your purpose would be different.

Checklist: purpose

Whenever you begin to plan a text – written, spoken, visual or electronic – ask yourself these questions about your purpose:
- Is my purpose to inform or advise, predict or hypothesise, explore or maintain relationships, make comparisons, command or direct, persuade, entertain, record, describe, or clarify my thinking?
- Does the draft achieve my purpose?
- Could it be improved, for example, by selecting another text type, changing the layout, making the language more formal or more personal, adding a new section, deleting some of the text or changing the point of view?

Choosing a written text type

The text type you choose for your writing should be appropriate to your purpose and audience.

Imaginative text types (sometimes called literary text types)	Information text types (sometimes called factual or expository text types)	Argument text types (including persuasive text types)
description	explanation	argument or exposition
recount	procedure	discussion
narrative	report or information report	review or response
poetry	factual description	
	factual recount	

Within these categories, there are sub-categories. Drama, film and television scripts are forms of narrative, but each has its own particular conventions. A news report, with its emphasis on catching the eye of the reader, is set out quite differently from an information report that might be found, for example, as an entry in an encyclopedia. A news report might incorporate some text that is factual recount. A biography or an autobiography is primarily an information text, but it may incorporate many of the features of literary texts. An examination essay might need to be an information report, outlining factual material, or it may be an argument text, presenting a particular point of view on an issue.

Within these text types, you will find dozens of forms of writing, each with some of its own particular characteristics: novels, short stories, personal letters, business letters, CVs, feature articles, news reports, editorials, letters to the editor, display advertisements, classified advertisements, back-cover blurbs, posters, emails, text messages, play scripts, news bulletins, transcribed speeches, essays, hyperfiction, song lyrics, picture books, graphic novels, memoirs, biographies, autobiographies and memos.

In the real world, many texts will have more than one purpose and audience, and a consequent blend of text types. A newspaper editorial, for example, obviously has many of the characteristics of an expository essay, but it also has its own distinctive characteristics. A report might include interviews with people that are examples of recount. While you might rarely read or compose a text type that fits quite strictly into the definitions you will find in the next chapters, a knowledge of text types helps in reading a text and in composing your own.

Checklist: choosing a text type

- Is the text type appropriate to my audience and purpose?
- Can I rework my first draft to fit more closely with the text type I have chosen?
- Have I maintained the conventions (or rules) of the text? Have I structured the text properly? Have I chosen language that suits the text type? (The conventions of drama scripts, for example, are different from those of radio or television scripts; newspaper reports are different from feature articles.)

The next three chapters give you more information about:

- imaginative text types
- information text types (also called expository or information texts)
- argument text types (including persuasive texts).

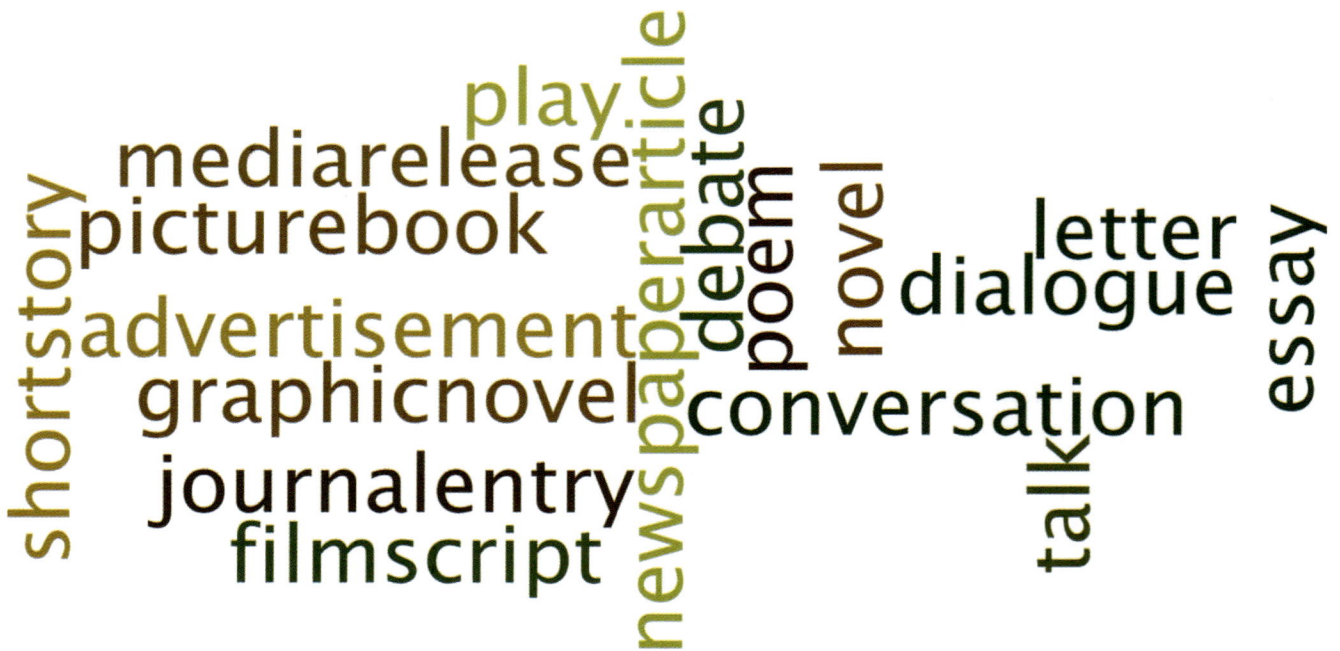

play article
mediarelease debate poem novel letter
shortstory picturebook dialogue essay
advertisement conversation
graphicnovel
journalentry newspaper talk
filmscript

ISBN 9780170183048

ACTIVITY 45

Audience

During the next week, keep a diary of the different types of communication that you are involved in and the audience for each type. For example:

Type of communication	Audience
casual conversation	friends family members
interview about late homework assignment	teacher
oral presentation in history class	teacher and fellow students
email	friends
phone call received	telemarketer

Purpose

Brainstorm as many verbs as you can think of that describe the purpose of communication. Begin with 'to inform', 'to persuade', 'to entertain' … See how many you can find.

Forms of writing

Brainstorm as many different types of written text as you can think of, beginning with the ones under the heading 'Choosing a written text type' on page 101: novels, short stories, personal letters …

Text types and essay writing

You will know without any doubt when an assignment requires you to produce an imaginative text type, but it is more difficult to know whether an information text type or an argument text type is appropriate to a particular task – partly because, in the real world, many pieces of writing borrow features from both types of text.

Examining the topic

The first step in writing an essay involves examining the topic so that you understand exactly what is required of you in researching and writing it. Most essay topics include a key word that indicates the approach you are asked to follow. The following explanation will help you to understand what approach each of these key words requires you to take.

Account for: Explain how something came about

Compare: Look for similarities and differences

Contrast: Set in opposition in order to bring out differences

Criticise: Give your judgement about the merit of theories or opinions or about the truth of facts, and back your judgement by a discussion of the evidence

Define: Set down the precise meaning of a word or phrase. Show that the distinctions implied in the definition are necessary

Describe: Give a detailed or graphic account

Discuss: Investigate or examine by argument, sift and debate, giving your reasons for and against

Evaluate: Make an appraisal of the worth of something, in the light of its truth or utility; include to a lesser degree your personal opinion

Explain: Make plain, interpret and account for

continued

Illustrate: Use a figure or diagram to explain or clarify, or make clear by the use of concrete examples

Interpret: Expound the meaning of, make clear and explicit, usually giving your own judgement also

Justify: Show adequate grounds for decisions or conclusions

Outline: Give the main features or general principles of a subject, omitting minor details and emphasising structure and arrangement

Relate: Do two things:

- narrate
- show how things are connected to each other, and to what extent they are alike or affect each other

Review: Make a survey of, examining the subject critically

State: Present in brief, clear form

Summarise: Give a concise account of the chief points or substance of a matter, omitting details and examples

Trace: Follow the development or history of a topic from some point of origin

From Harry Maddox 1980, *How to Study* (rev. edn), Pan Books, London.

The key words above may be placed into two major categories according to the difficulty of the task.

1   **Describing**: define, describe, illustrate, outline, review, state, summarise, trace. You are asked to find the main and supporting ideas and write them down in logical order, giving examples where necessary. These are examples of the information text type.

2   **Analysing**: compare, contrast, criticise, discuss, evaluate, explain, interpret, justify, review.

With essays which have these key words in their topics, you will be expected to do more than present information. You will need to look critically at the topic and present an argument of your own. This will involve using an argument text type.

ACTIVITY 46

Text types

1   Collect as many assignments as you can from the last 12 months or so and examine them to see which of the key words above are used. What kind of text type seems to be appropriate in each case?

2   Can you find examples where a blend of text types (sometimes called a **hybrid text**) would be appropriate?

ISBN 9780170183048

IMAGINATIVE TEXT TYPES

8

The imaginative, or literary, text types include:

- description
- recount
- narrative
- drama scripting
- film and television scripting
- poetry.

Descriptions

Descriptions may be literary or factual. The following applies to a literary description.

Literary description	
Purpose	• to present information about something specific – a person, a character in literature, a place, an event
Suggested audience	• general audience (a novel or short story with descriptive passages); a specific audience for a particular group of readers (teenagers; sci-fi fans)
Structural features	• introduction defining the subject to be described • series of points, each describing one feature of the subject • one paragraph for each major point • conclusion (optional)
Language features	• technical language if appropriate • choice of precise words to allow for clarity and accuracy of description • figurative language, including similes, metaphors and personification • adjectives and adverbs for precision • emotive language • use of the present or the past tense
Examples	• descriptive paragraph in a novel about setting or character • descriptive paragraph in a short story about setting or character

Passages of description are common in novels and short stories and are an important feature in developing the reader's understanding of setting and character. They are rarely pure description; almost always they incorporate some material to do with the action or plot of the novel or short story.

Sample script

Precision of
the description

Description is
through the eyes
of the character;
it is subjective

Reference
to what the
character is
doing and how
he is reacting to
what he sees

Use of descriptive
adjectives – in this
case including vivid
compound adjectives

> Chen turned to look down the ravine and was so terrified
> he nearly fell off his horse. There on a snow-covered slope
> not less than fifty yards away was a pack of golden-hued,
> murderous-looking Mongolian wolves, all watching him
> straight on or out of the corner of their eyes, their gazes
> boring into him like needles. The closest wolves were the
> biggest, easily the size of leopards and at least twice the
> size of the wolves he'd seen in the Beijing Zoo, half again
> as tall and as long, nose to tail. All dozen or so of the larger
> wolves had been sitting on the snowy ground, but they
> immediately stood up, their tails stretched out straight,
> like swords about to be unsheathed, or arrows on a taut
> bowstring. The alpha male, surrounded by the others, was
> a gray wolf whose nearly white neck, chest and abdomen
> shone like white gold. The pack consisted of thirty or forty
> animals.

Comparison
to the wolves
in the zoo – a
comparison to
something with
which readers
are likely to be
familiar, to give
them a point of
reference

Use of strong similes
that have emotional
overtones

Specific nouns to
describe the wolves'
bodies

Precision of
the description

ACTIVITY 47

Literary description

1 You are writing a short story set in either a science-fiction or fantasy world. Write a descriptive
paragraph in which your main character first sees something very unusual in that world.
2 Find a paragraph of description in a novel or a short story you have read. Type it up, with wide
margins on either side, and print it off. In small groups label and identify the main features of
the description.

Recounts

Recounts may be literary or factual. However, factual recounts have the same features as literary recounts, and
both show the writer or speaker shaping events to suit their purpose. Even the most factual recount does not
include every single event that occurs. The writer or speaker makes a selection.

ISBN 9780170183048

Recount	
Purpose	to retell past events in the order in which they occurred
Suggested audience	friends and relatives; readers of biography or historical recount; oneself (for example, diary)
Structural features	• orientation: who? what? where? when? • series of events, usually in chronological order • some personal comments on the events, either at the end of the retelling or interspersed throughout
Language features	• use of the past tense • possible use of first-person pronouns (I, we, my) • proper nouns to refer to specific people and places • descriptive words, especially adjectives and adverbs • connecting words to place events in time sequence (then, first, eventually)
Examples	• oral memoir • written autobiography • part of a newspaper article, probably quoting the words of an eyewitness or participant • part of a television or radio interview • personal conversation with a friend

Recounts tend to focus on specific people, places or events.

Sample recount

Proper nouns for specific places

Use of first-person pronoun

Use of past tense

There was a big school truck. We used to go in that truck in Ulumparru. We would play in the water there, and some girls would dig for katjutarri close by. We used to eat apuralyi there too. The older ones used to go a long way to get pura. They got ipalu as well. They used to get those foods there, in that bushy country.

When we finished playing in the water, we would eat dinner. The whitefeller teachers would provide meat and food and cool drinks there for us.

Then we would go again and play and swim in the water. We would stay all afternoon in that place. Then we would come back again to Papunya.

Elva Poulson

Chronological order – a new paragraph for each new period of time

Connecting words for time sequence

ACTIVITY 48

Recount

1 Record an eyewitness account of a current news item; you will probably find it easier to record from an Internet report rather than a television or radio report. Work with a group to identify the features of the spoken recount that are similar to those of a written recount.

2 Write a brief recount (approximately three paragraphs) of something very funny or embarrassing that happened to you. It can be literary (made up) or factual. You will select the events to emphasise either the humour or the embarrassment of the event. Make printed copies of your recount and work with a group to identify the features that are characteristic of this type of text.

Narratives

Narrative	
Purpose	• to tell a story
Suggested audience	• children; teenagers; members of a particular cultural group; fans of a fiction genre (romance or crime, for example)
Structural features	• orientation: who? where? when? • complication • sequence of events triggered by the complication, crisis or climax • resolution or denouement • optional coda (a comment or moral) • may be organised in a series of chapters
Language features	• usually past tense • time words to connect events to tell when they occur (previously, then, after) • proper nouns for specific people and places • verbs to show the actions that occur in the story • descriptive adjectives and adverbs to give information about the characters and setting • use of dialogue
Examples	• short story • novel • film that tells a story • cartoon strip • spoken bedtime story

The most important elements of a narrative are the orientation, the complication and the resolution. Make sure that you have a genuine complication, something that presents a problem that must be resolved. Sometimes the situation is just a disappointment, not a complication. For example, you might be telling a story about a girl who is in the city when someone steals her purse. If she is shopping with her mum, that's just a disappointment. But if she has run away from home and the only money she has is in that purse, it is a complication, and your story will need to show how she resolves that problem.

Establishment of character and setting are also important, but one may be more dominant than the other, depending on what kind of narrative you are writing.

ISBN 9780170183048

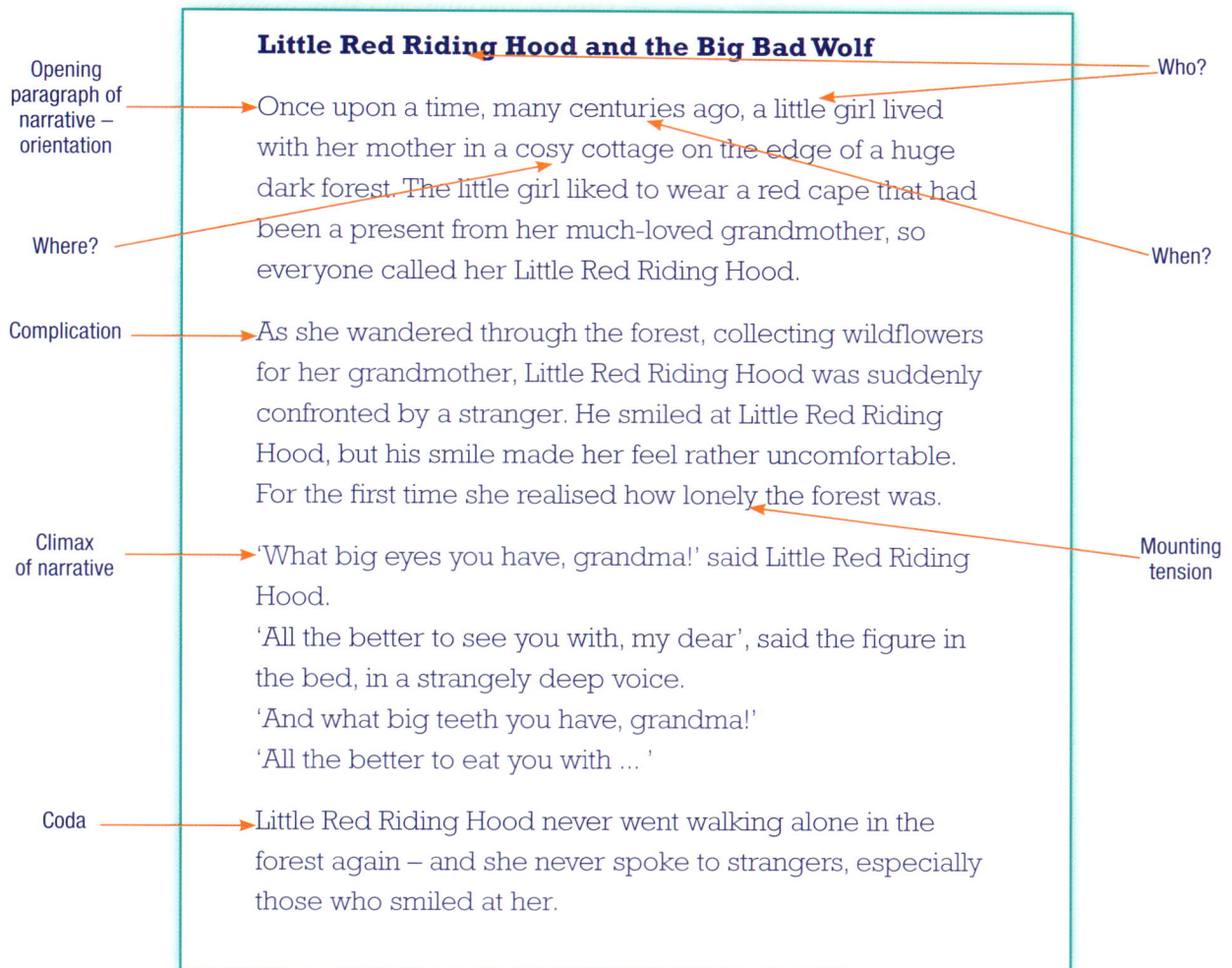

Little Red Riding Hood and the Big Bad Wolf

Opening paragraph of narrative – orientation

Where?

Who?

When?

Once upon a time, many centuries ago, a little girl lived with her mother in a cosy cottage on the edge of a huge dark forest. The little girl liked to wear a red cape that had been a present from her much-loved grandmother, so everyone called her Little Red Riding Hood.

Complication

As she wandered through the forest, collecting wildflowers for her grandmother, Little Red Riding Hood was suddenly confronted by a stranger. He smiled at Little Red Riding Hood, but his smile made her feel rather uncomfortable. For the first time she realised how lonely the forest was.

Mounting tension

Climax of narrative

'What big eyes you have, grandma!' said Little Red Riding Hood.
'All the better to see you with, my dear', said the figure in the bed, in a strangely deep voice.
'And what big teeth you have, grandma!'
'All the better to eat you with … '

Coda

Little Red Riding Hood never went walking alone in the forest again – and she never spoke to strangers, especially those who smiled at her.

ACTIVITY 49

Narrative

1 Look at the first couple of pages of a novel that you have read recently and identify the who? when? and where? of the orientation.
2 Find the last story you wrote and print off copies (with a good margin on either side) to give out to members of your group. Work together to annotate your story, looking for the characteristic features of narrative.

Drama scripting

A drama script has the features of a narrative – with orientation, complication, series of events and denouement – but it also has its own characteristic language and structural features.

Drama scripting	
Purpose	• to tell a story for performance on stage or on radio
Suggested audience	• general audience
Structural features	Narrative features: • orientation: who? where? when? • complication • sequence of events triggered by the complication, crisis or climax • resolution or denouement • optional coda (a comment or moral) • a series of scenes and possibly of acts Publishing conventions: • characters' names set apart from the dialogue, according to certain conventions • stage directions set apart from the dialogue, according to certain conventions • a list of characters' names at the beginning of the play, perhaps with brief character descriptions
Language features	• usually present tense • use of colloquial language representing actual speech • possible use of dialect representing the speech of a particular time or place • proper nouns for specific people and places • emotive language
Examples	• a play • a radio play

Playwrights have a lot to think about when writing drama scripts.

- They must write realistic dialogue to bring out the relationships between the characters and the concerns of the play.
- They must be able to imagine how the play will look on stage to be sure that what they suggest will work in practice.
- They may also need to provide background information about some of the characters and about the play's setting in time and place.
- They may need to give directions about set design (how the stage should look), stage lighting and costuming, how the characters should say significant lines and, where appropriate, what their stage movements should be.

ISBN 9780170183048

Setting out the script

There are a number of possible ways to present drama scripts. The following format, illustrated with the opening of Act One of Oscar Wilde's *The Importance of Being Ernest*, is straightforward and easy to follow.

Sample script

ACT ONE

Scene: *Morning room in* **Algernon's** *flat in Half-Moon Street. The room is luxuriously and artistically furnished. The sound of a piano is heard in the adjoining room.*

Lane *is arranging afternoon tea on the table, and after the music has ceased,* **Algernon** *enters.*

Algernon Did you hear what I was playing, Lane?

Lane I didn't think it polite to listen, sir.

Algernon I'm sorry for that, for your sake. I don't play accurately – anyone can play accurately – but I play with wonderful expression. As far as the piano is concerned, sentiment is my forte. I keep science for Life.

Lane Yes, sir.

Algernon And, speaking of the science of Life, have you got the cucumber sandwiches cut for Lady Bracknell?

Lane Yes, sir. (*Hands them on a salver*)

Algernon (*inspects them, takes two and sits down on the sofa*) Oh! … by the way, Lane, I see from your book that on Thursday night, when Lord Shoreman and Mr Worthing were dining with me, eight bottles of champagne are entered as having been consumed.

Lane Yes, sir; eight bottles and a pint.

Algernon Why is it that in a bachelor's establishment the servants invariably drink the champagne? I merely ask for information.

Stage directions are shown in italics. (If script is handwritten, show the stage directions in blue pen and write the script in black pen.)

Stage directions provide information about some or all of the following:

- set and costume design
- stage lighting
- sound effects
- stage props
- instructions about stage movements
- how significant lines are to be spoken
- the setting of the play (in time and place)
- background information about the characters.

Stage directions within a scene should be in brackets, starting with a capital letter but with no full stop at the end.

If the character's name precedes the stage direction, the first word inside the brackets does not begin with a capital letter.

Lane I attribute it to the superior quality of the wine, sir. I have often observed that in married households the champagne is rarely of a first-rate brand.

Algernon Good Heavens! Is marriage so demoralising as that?

Lane I believe it is a very pleasant state, sir. I have had very little experience of it myself up to the present. I have only been married once. That was a consequence of a misunderstanding between myself and a young woman.

Algernon (*languidly*) I don't know that I am much interested in your family life, Lane.

Lane No sir, it is not a very interesting subject. I never think of it myself.

Algernon Very natural, I am sure. That will do, Lane, thank you.

Lane Thank you, sir. (**Lane** *goes out*)

Place the character's name in the margin opposite her or his dialogue. In print, the character's name is written in bold, but this could be represented in handwriting by using a coloured (perhaps green) pen.

When characters' names appear in the stage directions, they are written in bold (or whatever colour you are using to represent bold).

ACTIVITY 50

Playscripts

Different publishers follow different conventions in setting out playscripts. Some playwrights also have firm ideas about how their plays should be set out.

Collect at least half a dozen plays from the library – preferably from different publishers – and compare the way they are set out.

1 Look at the list of characters at the beginning of the play. How detailed is the description of the characters? Is it just a list of names?
2 How detailed are the stage directions, in terms of information about set and costume design, stage lighting, sound effects and stage props? How detailed are the directions about stage movement and of how lines should be delivered?
3 Are the characters' names set out as in the sample script? Is bold print used for the characters' names? Is the name followed by a colon? Is the name perhaps centred above the piece of dialogue that the character will deliver?
4 Are the stage directions in round brackets? Are they in italics? What punctuation conventions are used?
5 Find an example of a radio play. How are the stage directions different?
6 Choose, from the examples that you have examined, the format that you will follow when writing your own scripts or dialogues. You can choose the features that you find easiest to follow, but remember that you must be consistent.

ISBN 9780170183048

Film and television scripting

This section applies to literary film and television scripts – those that tell a story. See page 124 for non-literary or documentary film and television scripts.

A literary script has the features of a narrative – orientation, complication, series of events and denouement – but it also has its own characteristic language and structural features.

Film and television scripting	
Purpose	• to tell a story for the screen
Suggested audience	• general audience; audience of a particular genre (chick flick; horror)
Structural features	Narrative features: • orientation: who? where? when? • complication • sequence of events triggered by the complication, crisis or climax • resolution or denouement • optional coda (a comment or moral) • a series of numbered scenes Publishing conventions for the printed or written script: • characters' names set apart from the dialogue, according to certain conventions • stage directions set apart from the dialogue, according to certain conventions • a list of characters' names at the beginning of the play, perhaps with brief character descriptions
Language features	• usually present tense • use of colloquial language representing actual speech • possible use of dialect representing the speech of a particular time or place • proper nouns for specific people and places • emotive language
Examples	• a film • a television drama • an episode in a television series

The important task of writers of screenplays is to make their scripts as interesting and as easy to read as possible. They also need to visualise each scene clearly and make the dialogue of their characters seem realistic and natural. They do not need to do the work of the director or camera crew.

There is a range of possible formats for any kind of script. The approach suggested here is appropriate for either film or television and emphasises dialogue and scene descriptions rather than camera directions.

Sample script

The following is an extract from the film script for *Looking for Alibrandi*.

Location of scene

Title line of scene

SCENE 65 INT./EXT. JOSIE'S HOUSE – THE LIVING ROOM. NIGHT.

The time when the scene takes place (DAY or NIGHT)

Flustered, Josie adjusts her clothing as she opens the door. She stands, stunned by what she sees.

Voice-overs indicated by square brackets

CHRISTINA: [*voice over*] Josie, invite him …

Christina reaches the door.

… In.

Jacob stands with his arms folded, exposing holes in the elbows of his jumper. He is dressed in old torn jeans and has a three-day growth. His hair hangs down over his face, stringy and uncombed.

Hello, Jacob.

Jacob grunts a hello which further stuns Josie.

JOSIE: I'll just go get my jacket.

Upper-case letters used for character names

SCENE 66 INT. JOSIE'S HOUSE – THE BEDROOM. NIGHT.

Josie stands defensively in the middle of the room, and when Christina bursts through Josie holds a finger to her mouth to silence her.

A line is left between scene directions and dialogue

JOSIE: [*whispering*] It is so sad. His mother's dead and he has nobody to sew for him.

Each scene is numbered

SCENE 67 EXT. A STREET NEAR JOSIE'S HOUSE. NIGHT.

Josie and Jacob walk down the street in silence until Josie stops, looks at him and then his clothes. Jacob looks at his clothes defensively.

Scene directions are placed in italics

JACOB: What?

The location of the scene is either EXT. (exterior) or INT. (interior)

SCENE 68 INT. THE VILLAGE CENTRE. NIGHT.

The atmosphere of the Village Cinema Centre is lively and friendly. Contrasting this atmosphere are the figures of Josie

ISBN 9780170183048

and Jacob standing side by side looking stonily ahead at the list of movies. Once in a while someone walks between them. Josie turns away from the list.

Scene directions and characters' names are left-justified

JOSIE: There's *La Dolce Vita* at the Dendy.

JACOB: *La* what? Man, I'm not watching a movie with subtitles.

JOSIE: So what do you want to see, Mr Bill Collins?

JACOB: A normal movie. Cops and robbers. Good guys and bad guys. People I can relate to.

JOSIE: Well, sorry. *Morons from Outer Space* is no longer showing.

JACOB: Look, this is the way I dress when I go to the movies and pardon my ignorance about the mother thing; I've never had to go out with an ethnic girl before.

JOSIE: Had to? Well, if we're slumming it, I've never had to go out with an *Anglo* before.

JACOB: What the hell's an 'Anglo'?

JOSIE: You people should go back to your own country if you're so confused.

Josie walks out.

ACTIVITY 51

Film and television scripting

1 Storyboard the scene from *Looking for Alibrandi* – that is, in a series of frames show each camera shot, indicating camera angle and closeness. Afterwards, get hold of a copy of the DVD and see how close your storyboard is to the choices the director made.
2 Different publishers follow different conventions when printing film and television scripts, just as they do with playscripts. Find half a dozen film or television scripts in the library, preferably from different publishers, and compare the way they are set out. In particular, see how much detail is given about camera movement, angle and closeness.

Poetry

Poetry	
Purpose	• to entertain • to arouse the emotions of the reader (laughter, sadness, pity, admiration, wonder) • sometimes to tell a story
Suggested audience	• general readers; young children (nursery rhymes); listeners of all ages to the lyrics of songs
Structural features	• a form on the page that is clearly not prose (not printed from left to right occupying the whole page) • possible pattern of line lengths • possible repetition of pattern in stanzas • rhythm, probably regular and patterned • possible rhyme scheme • heightened use of language for its sound values
Language features	• the grammar may not be the same as for prose – words can be omitted; the usual word order may be inverted • use of figurative language such as simile, metaphor and personification • emotive words • descriptive and evocative words, especially adjectives • possible use of motifs and symbols
Examples	• poems of all kinds – ballads, sonnets, odes, song lyrics, free verse, haiku, cinquain • verse of all kinds, including nonsense verse and limericks • the lyrics of songs

Poetry is a huge and varied field. It is almost impossible to define: for any definition, you will find an example that you want to call a poem but that does not fit. It is generally agreed that, in writing a poem, a writer chooses words as much for their sound qualities and for the images they bring to mind as for their meaning. It is also generally agreed that a poem has a shape on the page that is different from prose, although generalisations cannot be made about that shape.

Sample poem

This poem was written early in the twentieth century. It follows the tradition of centuries of English poems before it by using a regular stanza pattern, but it was also in its time very modern, because you will notice that the poet uses half-rhyme, rather than strict rhyme. The poet, Wilfred Owen, was fighting in World War I (he died just after this was written) and he is writing about one of the many young men who died in that war. This young man, like so many others, had been recruited from the farms of England.

ISBN 9780170183048

Recurring motif of the sun throughout the poem – contrast 'the kind old sun' of the first stanza with the 'fatuous sunbeams' of the second

Use of words to convey a heavy load of meaning – connections are implicit not explicit – e.g. the word 'Futility' in the title has no obvious connection to what follows but, in fact, sums up the whole theme of the poem

Futility

Move him into the sun –
Gently its touch awoke him once,
At home, whispering of fields unsown.
Always it woke him, even in France,
Until this morning and this snow.
If anything might rouse him now
The kind old sun will know.

Think how it wakes the seeds –
Woke, once, the clays of a cold star.
Are limbs so dear achieved, are sides
Full-nerved, – still warm, – too hard to stir?
Was it for this the clay grew tall?
– O what made fatuous sunbeams toil
To break earth's sleep at all?

Regular stanza patterns

Use of half-rhyme

Parallel structure

Use of eye-rhyme (words that look as if they rhyme because they have similar spelling patterns)

Use of the recurring motif of the seeds: symbol of new life

Words chosen for their sound value

ACTIVITY 52

Poetry

1 Do the lyrics of popular songs have any features in common with traditional poetry? Type up the words of a favourite song, print off some copies and bring it to class for your group to look at. Annotate the features that are common in traditional poetry.

2 Browse through the poetry shelves in your library. Find a poem that you have never heard or read before and practise reading it aloud. If it's a very long poem, you might choose an extract. Try learning it off by heart. Try reading it in different ways, varying your pace and volume. Read the poem aloud to your group.

9 INFORMATION TEXT TYPES

Information (or factual, or expository) text types include:

- explanations
- procedures
- factual descriptions
- factual recounts
- reports
- newspaper reports
- feature articles
- letters
- job applications
- résumés.

Explanations

Explanation	
Purpose	• to tell how and/or why things are, or how things work
Suggested audience	• school or university students; machinery operators; vehicle owners; consumers who have bought new equipment
Structural features	• introductory statement about the subject • what is to be explained • series of explanatory statements that tell the how's and why's • these may be in chronological order • optional summarising paragraph
Language features	• technical language specific to the subject • use of the present tense • use of impersonal, objective language • words that show cause and effect (as a result, due to, caused by) or time links (initially, following, finally) • written or spoken explanations are often accompanied by diagrams or charts

ISBN 9780170183048

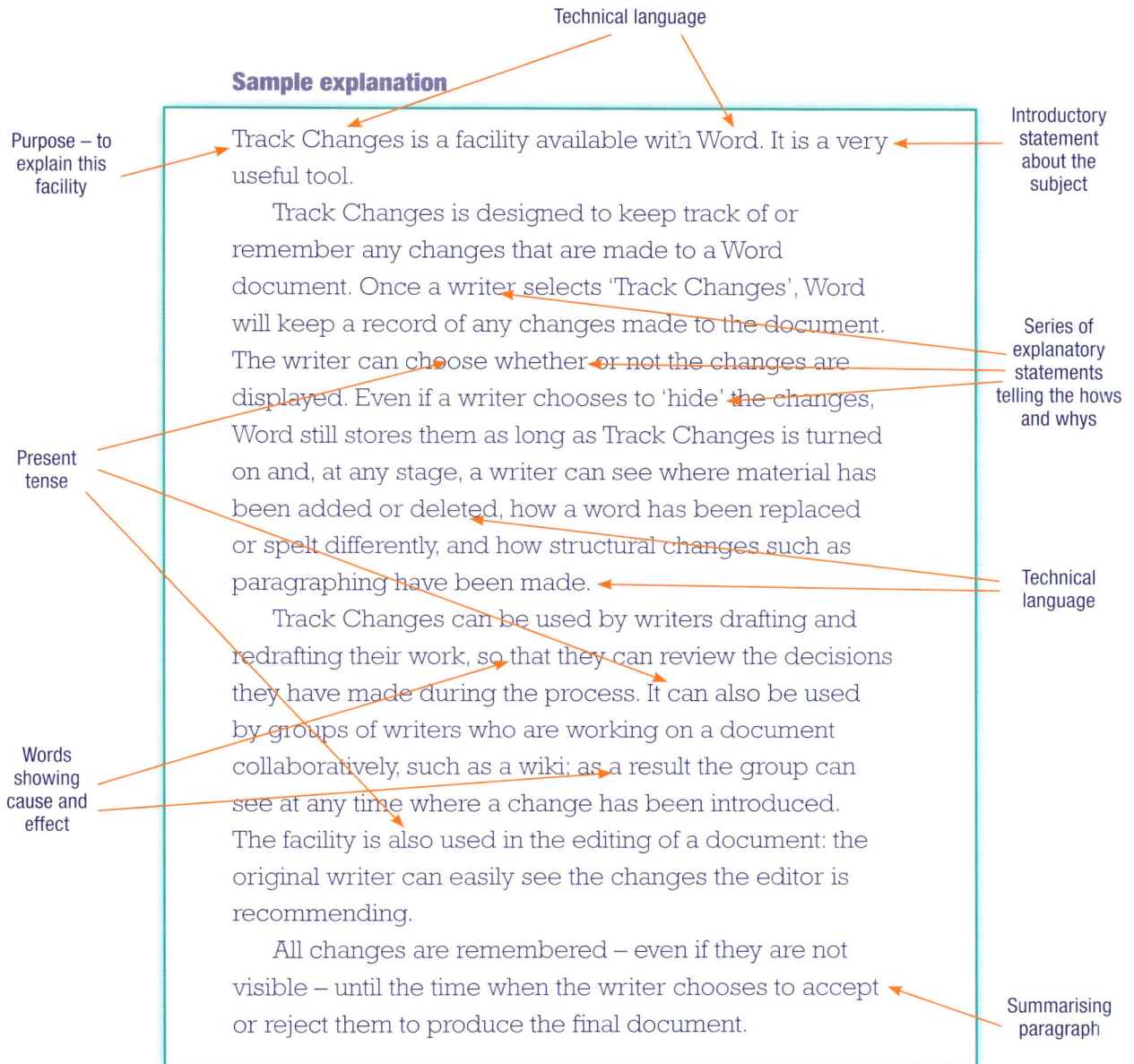

Technical language

Sample explanation

Purpose – to explain this facility

Introductory statement about the subject

Track Changes is a facility available with Word. It is a very useful tool.

Track Changes is designed to keep track of or remember any changes that are made to a Word document. Once a writer selects 'Track Changes', Word will keep a record of any changes made to the document. The writer can choose whether or not the changes are displayed. Even if a writer chooses to 'hide' the changes, Word still stores them as long as Track Changes is turned on and, at any stage, a writer can see where material has been added or deleted, how a word has been replaced or spelt differently, and how structural changes such as paragraphing have been made.

Track Changes can be used by writers drafting and redrafting their work, so that they can review the decisions they have made during the process. It can also be used by groups of writers who are working on a document collaboratively, such as a wiki; as a result the group can see at any time where a change has been introduced. The facility is also used in the editing of a document: the original writer can easily see the changes the editor is recommending.

All changes are remembered – even if they are not visible – until the time when the writer chooses to accept or reject them to produce the final document.

Present tense

Series of explanatory statements telling the hows and whys

Words showing cause and effect

Technical language

Summarising paragraph

ACTIVITY 53

Explanations

Find some examples of explanation texts in your school textbooks. Ideally, see if you can find the same concept explained in two different texts: for example, two different mathematics or science textbooks. Compare the two explanations, deciding which one is better at fulfilling its purpose and meeting the needs of its audience, and why.

Procedures

Procedure (also called 'instruction')	
Purpose	• to show how something can be done
Suggested audience	• appliance owners; school students; members of a cooking class
Structural features	• opening statement stating the aim or goal
	• list of materials, skills or ingredients needed to carry out the procedure
	• steps required to complete the task, listed in sequential order
Language features	• numbers to mark the steps of the procedure
	• impersonal, objective language
	• verbs as commands (mix, place, prepare)
	• adverbs to tell how the action should be done (shake vigorously, fold gently)
	• technical language
	• precise words (numbers for quantities)
Examples	• instruction manual for an electric appliance
	• recipe
	• itinerary
	• solution to a technical problem
	• instruction booklet for a board game

Sample procedural text

Numbered and sequential steps

Opening statement specifying the task

Track changes while you edit

1 Open the document that you want to revise.

2 On the **Review** tab, in the **Tracking** group, click the **Track Changes** image.

To add a Track Changes indicator to the status bar, right-click the status bar and click **Track Changes**. Click the **Track Changes** indicator on the status bar to turn Track Changes on or off.

3 Make the changes that you want by inserting, deleting, moving, or formatting text or graphics. You can also add comments.

Technical language

Precise terms

Verbs as commands

ISBN 9780170183048

ACTIVITY 54

Procedures

The instruction manuals for household products, including electronic equipment, can be very poorly written. Collect some that you have at home and consider how well each one fulfils its purpose and caters for its intended audience. Look at the structural and language features used.

Descriptions

Descriptions may be factual or literary. The following information applies to a **factual description**. A factual description is different from a report because it presents a specific subject rather than a general group. For example, you might write a description of the tiger you saw at Western Plains Zoo or a report on tigers generally.

Factual description	
Purpose	• to present information about something specific – a person, a character in literature, a place, an event
Suggested audience	• friends (a description of a holiday destination); science teacher (a report on tigers)
Structural features	• introduction defining the subject to be described • series of points, each describing one feature of the subject • one paragraph for each major point • conclusion (optional)
Language features	• technical language if appropriate • choice of precise words to allow for clarity and accuracy of description • figurative language, including similes, metaphors and personification • adjectives and adverbs for precision • use of the present or the past tense
Examples	• article in an information book • English essay about a character in a novel you are studying • conversation with a friend about a specific person, place or event • television nature program

Passages of description are a very important way of conveying information. Good descriptive passages are clear and precise.

Sample factual description

Use of adjectives for precision

Precise details, including measurements

Reference to specific body parts

The wolf was a little over a metre long, with a bushy tail that was almost another half a metre in length. He had a grizzled coat, with gray, black and light brown fur covering his head and upper body, and yellowish white fur on his legs and belly. His paws seemed too big for him and his legs were much longer than you would expect on a dog of similar size. He was standing quite still and staring malevolently at the zoo visitors.

Use of comparison – in this case a literal comparison rather than a figurative one – to give the reader a point of reference

Use of adverb, showing subjectivity, although the rest of the description is objective

ACTIVITY 55

Descriptions

1 Write a short, factual description of something that you are actually looking at: your classroom, your bedroom, a friend, a bookcase.
2 Write a description of a character in a novel, play or film that you have studied recently.

Recounts

Factual recounts show the same features as literary recounts. See the section on literary recounts on page 106.

Reports

Report (also called 'information report')	
Purpose	• to present information about a particular subject
Suggested audience	• teacher; members of finance industry; adult viewers of a documentary
Structural features	• introductory statement, which may include a short description and a definition • series of points about the subject, each one describing a new feature • summary (optional)
Language features	• use of the present tense, although past tense is used when dealing with historical material • technical language specific to the subject • generalised nouns (tigers, not the tiger lying under the tree; basketball players, not my friend Anna who loves playing basketball) • often accompanied by visual texts such as photographs, diagrams, sketches
Examples	• lecture • article in an information book • research assignment • business journal • film or television documentary presenting information on a general subject

ISBN 9780170183048

Sample report

Wolves and human fear

Introductory statement

While sharks, snakes and spiders are the stuff of Australian nightmares, in much of the world the creatures most feared throughout human history have been wolves. Wolves have been seen as a threat to humanity and an embodiment of evil. A recent North American bumper sticker declared: 'Wolves – nature's terrorists'.

Inclusion of visual text

Present tense

Wolves are familiar characters in European storytelling, almost universally depicted as creatures to be feared and hunted. Generations of children have shuddered at the evil wolves depicted in 'Little Red Riding Hood' and 'The Three Little Pigs'. In adult storytelling, wolves morphed into one of the most terrifying monsters of all: werewolves whose human form became that of the predatory and uncontrollable beast.

Past tense for historical material

Series of points – new paragraph for each new point

Wolves were once very common in Great Britain and continental Europe, in Central Asia and in North America, but human dread of wolves led to persistent persecution of the creatures, including government-sanctioned bounty hunting. The campaign in Great Britain was the most successful, with wolves extinct in England by the end of the fifteenth century. In recent years wolf populations have been so low in some parts of the world, such as western Europe, that some types of wolves have been listed as endangered species.

Generalised nouns

In many parts of the world in recent years, laws have been enacted to protect wolves, although farmers fearing for their livestock are usually exempt. There are even calls in Great Britain to reintroduce wolves, especially in the Highlands where the deer population is unsustainably high. Conservationists argue that human deaths caused by wolves are statistically almost insignificant, while horses, undoubtedly one of our favourite animals, kill quite a lot of people – mostly in falls – each year. Yet statistical information has little power over the longstanding paranoia about wolves.

Generalised nouns

The long-term survival of wolves depends on the ability of human beings to overcome their primitive fears and to acknowledge the importance of all creatures in the ecological balance of our environment.

Summary

Film and television documentaries

Most film and television documentaries are information reports, although they may incorporate some of the features of argumentative or persuasive texts, depending on the purposes of the documentary maker. Some even include imaginative elements, such as the use of re-enactments of events. Almost all documentaries use sound as well as visual images to convey their message. This can include the voice of a narrator who is seen on camera, a voiceover narrator, or interviews with experts with passers-by or with eyewitnesses. Music and **diagetic sound** (sound recorded during the filming, such as traffic noise) are also commonly used.

Documentaries have many of the features of fictional films but they cannot be scripted beforehand in quite the same way, as documentary makers do not always know exactly what will happen. Documentary makers do not direct their subjects in the way film directors direct actors. However, documentary makers must have a clear plan of what is to be filmed. Most documentary makers will produce a short overview (sometimes called a **treatment**), which outlines the film's purpose and intended audience, as well as its likely content. The script is developed progressively throughout the shooting. Many documentary makers use a two-column format, with all audio material listed in one column and all visual material listed in the second column.

ACTIVITY 56

Reports

1 Find a report that you have written recently for a subject other than English. Working with a partner, look through your reports and see whether you can identify the characteristic features of this text type.

Documentaries

2 Watch a television documentary that aims to provide information on a particular subject. Make notes as you watch, identifying structural features such as the introductory statement (which may be visual and/or spoken) and the use of a series of points about the subject (again presented visually as well as in the spoken text). Decide whether there is a summary statement.

ISBN 9780170183048

Newspaper reports

Newspaper reports are a specific example of the information report text type. A newspaper report gives information about recent events. It usually answers the following questions about the event: who? what? when? where? why? and how?

News reports usually have the following features.

- They do not comment on the news.
- They may include a by-line (the name of the journalist responsible for the story) under the headline. This is more likely to happen if the story is a scoop, or if the journalist is well known.
- The stories are printed in columns. Sometimes the introduction is printed across two or three columns.
- Stories from overseas or interstate may begin with the name of the city in which they took place or from which the report was sent. This might be printed in block capitals or bold type and be followed by a colon. Alternatively, the city might be mentioned with the journalist's by-line (for example, William Hollosy in Budapest).

US forces deliver food, aid

WASHINGTON: US armed forces yesterday successfully delivered food and aid supplies to regions devastated by recent natural disasters.

- The headline aims to catch the reader's eye and sum up the story. Headlines usually appear in bold type. They vary in size depending on their position in the paper and on the page. The larger the headline, the more important the news report.
- Headlines do not necessarily follow normal grammatical conventions. For example, it is acceptable to use abbreviations and to write a headline in the present tense even if the story is written in the past tense.
- Subheadings appear in bold in the more important reports. They break up columns of type and highlight different sections of the news item.

Structure of a news report

Reporters do not know how much space will be available in the paper so their news stories need to be easy to cut. Therefore, they begin with the most important information and finish with the least significant details.

Some people think of news stories as having the shape of an inverted pyramid, as shown below.

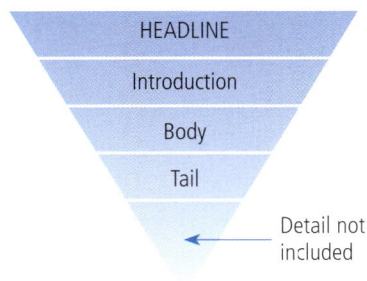

HEADLINE

Introduction

Body

Tail

Detail not included

Headline

The first thing to catch our eye when we see a newspaper is usually the main headline. A headline explains in a few words the main idea or event in the report. Headlines usually appear in bold type. The paper's view of the importance of the story is reflected in the size of the headline: the larger the type, the more important the news report.

Introduction

A newspaper report begins with one or two sentences answering some or all of the questions who? what? when? where? why? and how?

The introduction of an important news item is set either in bold or in a larger type than the rest of the report.

Body

The body of the report tells the news story in detail using short, simple sentences, short paragraphs and unemotive language. It starts with the most important and most interesting aspects of the story. Any subheadings should be set in bold type. When writing or typing in columns, try not to break words at the end of lines. If this is unavoidable, break words according to syllables (in/spectors, con/cerned, environ/mental, con/sumption, yester/day) and sound.

Tail

The tail of the story contains the less important detail. It may sometimes be cut by subeditors to fit the available space.

Sample newspaper report

Fish of the day hooks the gourmets

by Richard North

Catchy headline

By-line

Block capitals for first word of report (first two words when first word is 'A')

Indent beginning of all paragraphs

A MYSTERIOUS fish, not previously identified by inspectors at Billingsgate, has been making an appearance in the regular consignments flown to the markets from the Seychelles in the Indian Ocean.

'It turned up in one of our weekly loads,' Jim Moran, of R.W. Larkins, the Billingsgate fishmongers, said yesterday. 'We were surprised at first, and, frankly, a little concerned. It has bright blue and yellow fins. Its head is a little like that of the *Vara Vara*, which we do quite often see.'

Chris Leftwich, an environmental health officer at the market and chief inspector for the Worshipful Company of Fishmongers, was called in to check on the arrival, and pronounced it fit for human consumption, having first run a trial on his domestic cat. 'She seemed to like it', Mr Leftwich said. 'At first she was worried by the distinctive blue and yellow fins.'

The fish is provisionally being known as the Moran, and is being sold – so far in small quantities – to the Café Fish in Panton Street, London, where it was honoured by being stewed as the *Plat du jour*.

Customers say that the fish is delicious, and the chef compared its cooking quality with that of sea bass.

ISBN 9780170183048

'At first we thought it might be wise to use it in a *bouillabaisse*, or perhaps a *fruits de mer*, where its presence would not be so obvious. But people like it so much that we haven't bothered.'

It will be on the menu today. The restaurant recommends a 1985 Mersault Charmes as the ideal wine to accompany it, or for those wishing to be more economical, a simple Muscadet 1986.

The fish has so far defied precise classification. A spokesman [*sic*] for the Natural History Museum said yesterday that it was unusual for a new fish to come through the fish market. However, the new fish was never likely to have been poisonous, he said.

'A lot of fish which would never have sold twenty-five years ago now goes like lightning. The red mullet is a classic case of fish which occurs in our waters, in small catches, but now merchants bring it from all over the world.

'The only fish which are really dicey are the Puffer fish; they are very toxic, but very rarely imported. Providing they've got their heads on, they're obvious enough. Otherwise, nine times out of ten, fish are wholesome.

'Sometimes dinoflagellates, which contain toxins, do get eaten by smaller fish, which are eaten by bigger ones. But this doesn't happen in the Seychelles.'

It is being suggested that the new fish should provisionally be given the Latin name, *Stulta sprilia*.

North, R, 'Fish of the day hooks the gourmets', *Independent*, 1 April 1987

Column format →

ACTIVITY 57

Newspaper reports

1 **a** Cut out a news report and paste it in the centre of a page, leaving space on either side.
   b On the left side, under the heading 'Style', identify who, what, when, where, why and how. Use a ruler and red pen to draw arrows to the word(s) that show these features.
   c On the right side under the heading 'Structure', identify the following:
   - headline
   - introduction
   - body
   - tail.
   Use arrows or brackets to identify the sections.
2 Write a 200-word news story of your own. Use arrows or brackets to identify the sections of structure and style.

Feature articles

A feature article is another specific type of information report found in newspapers and magazines. Feature articles are more than just reports of what happened. They aim to provide background or add human interest to current news stories, or to explore and comment on an issue or subject of interest. These articles often appear to take a particular viewpoint, incorporating some of the features of an argument text type (see Chapter 10).

While news reports are concerned with what happened yesterday or today, features focus on topical or newsworthy subjects but do not go out of date after one day. Feature articles include:

- human-interest stories
- in-depth accounts of world trouble spots or major international issues
- profiles of important national or international personalities or interviews with them
- background stories to local, national and international events
- regular columns and reviews of plays, films, television programs, books and concerts.

Conventions of feature articles

Feature articles usually:

- have an interesting, eye-catching headline
- have an opening paragraph designed to catch the reader's attention
- are written in short paragraphs
- use colourful and imaginative but simple language
- include subheadings to break up the article
- have a column format similar to that used in news reports
- include a by-line; that is, the writer's name.

All daily papers contain regular and special features and some have magazine sections consisting exclusively of features.

Feature articles tend to reflect in style and substance the paper in which they appear. One important reason for this is the target audience of the paper. You might look at the difference between the *Herald Sun* and *The Age* in Victoria or the *Daily Telegraph* and the *Sydney Morning Herald* in New South Wales for examples of this.

Sample feature article

Interesting headline

A grim tale of humourless narks

Writer's viewpoint established

Children will always pursue dark stories, however much oldies huff and puff.

Block capitals for first word

Attention-grabbing opening

Column format

PURSED-lipped teachers, librarians and booksellers are trying to ban the latest book by Andy Griffiths, one of the few authors who writes specifically and spectacularly successfully for reading-averse little boys. *The Bad Book*'s bum-joke-laden black humour has caused such outrage that some booksellers have refused to stock it and have been rendered sleepless by the horror of it. Schools have cancelled appearances by Griffiths, complaining the book is too violent.

An Angus & Robertson shop has locked 50 copies of *The Bad Book* in its storeroom, slamming it as the 'South Park for five-year-olds', although few five-year-olds would have the reading skills to tackle it.

Shops which stock the book are doing so without the usual fanfare that greeted previous Griffiths hits such as *The Day My Bum Went Psycho* and *Zombie Bums from Uranus*, which this year debuted at No. 6 on the *New York Times* bestseller list.

Griffiths, a former Melbourne schoolteacher, in Brisbane yesterday on a book tour, said the fuss was about 'over-parenting and political correctness'.

'Children need space to dream and do kid things away from the adult agenda,' he said in his hotel room. 'It's easy to say "Be nice" and suppress children.

ISBN 9780170183048

'But with repression, it doesn't mean it goes away. Just because you're told not to pick your nose and not to hit people doesn't mean the urge has gone – it is quite primal. Children's literature is a safe place to explore that darker side of our natures.'

One of the characters in the book, Bad Daddy, always says 'no' to his son until finally the child asks for permission to breathe. The exasperated father shouts 'NO!' and the boy keels over dead.

In his hotel room yesterday, Griffiths said Bad Daddy represented the parent 'who is repressing the child, giving them no space to be a child'.

When he was an English teacher, Griffiths found that boys had 'no relationship to books' because well-meaning parents and teachers have tried to 'soften literature, get rid of the horrible stories'. But 'no self-respecting boy', said Griffiths, wanted to read about kittens, puppies and ponies.

The Bad Book is full of vulgar poems, jokes, cartoons and riddles about such things as 'severed heads, severed limbs and gross cranial disfiguration caused by excessive nose-picking, death by gluttony, cannibalism, bum-lighting' and so on.

Examples to support viewpoint

Among the favourites of a nine-year-old guinea pig, Tom, whom I asked this week to read the book, was 'The Old Lady Who Swallowed a Poo'. Another was Humpty Dumpty, a graffiti-thug who spray paints a wall until all the king's horses and all the king's men 'smash his head in'.

Another was 'Bad Mummy and the Very Busy Six-Lane Highway'. A boy says: 'Mummy, can I run across this very busy six-lane highway with my eyes shut?' The mother says: 'Well, I don't know.' The child nags and the mother relents. 'All right but be careful', and then the child is, of course, run over. 'Oops,' says the mother.

Tom found *The Bad Book* 'funny and interesting and involving. Kids love funny poems.' He pointed out there are no more deaths in *The Bad Book* than in Harry Potter books, which were feted by custodians of children's literary virtue.

'In *Harry Potter and the Order of the Phoenix* they are scary fatal deaths that happen really slowly.' But in *The Bad Book*, 'they're just fake deaths. As if anyone who reads this will think it's fun to run across a road and kill yourself.'

Children also have a fascination with death, which explains the dark themes in nursery rhymes and even lullabies. Take, for instance, *Oranges and Lemons*, whose last sinister lines are said to have been added before 1783 by children.

'Oranges and lemons, say the bells of St Clement's. Here comes a candle to light you to bed. Here comes a chopper to chop off your head. Chip, chop, chip, chop – the last man's dead.'

And few mothers would have missed the incongruity of rocking a precious newborn to sleep while crooning: 'Rock a bye baby on the tree top, When the wind blows the cradle will rock, When the bough breaks the cradle will fall, Down will come baby, cradle and all.'

Jack and Jill is similarly bleak: 'Jack and Jill went up the hill to fetch a pail of water, Jack fell down and broke his crown, And Jill came tumbling after.'

The old woman who lived in the shoe needed a visit from DOCS. 'There was an old woman who lived in a shoe, She had so many children, she didn't know what to do, She gave them some broth without any bread, She whipped them all soundly and put them to bed.'

The farmer's wife should be reported to the RSPCA: 'Three blind mice, three blind mice. See how they run! See how they run! They all ran after the farmer's wife, Who cut off their tails with a carving knife.'

Griffiths, 43 'going on eight', with two daughters aged three and 11, also points to 100 years of children's literature as precedent from *Hansel and Gretel*, with its fears of parental abandonment, murder and cannibalism, to cautionary literature of the late 19th century.

When he was five, Griffiths was given a classic German children's book, *Struwwelpeter*, full of stories about children who disobey their parents and get hurt. 'It fired me with a love of literature.'

In an over-parented world, in which children are at risk of being suffocated by cotton wool, Griffiths' books strike a dark, subversive chord, in the same way as *The Simpsons*, the longest-running sitcom in TV history, has done for the past 15 years.

On Tuesday night's repeat episode, for instance, death makes an absurd appearance when Ned Flanders' wife is killed at a speedway after being hit by promotional T-shirts fired out of a cannon at Homer.

The Simpsons succeeds because, unlike most pop culture, it owes allegiance to no rules. Homer, Bart's beer-swilling father, unexpectedly has become the favourite of young fans, perhaps because he is the most daringly, refreshingly bad.

In one episode his daughter, Lisa, berates him for plugging in a dancing Santa. 'Dad, no. We're trying to conserve energy.'

Homer replies: 'Lisa, if we start conserving, the environmentalists win.'

Summarised argument

Children will always find a way of thinking for themselves. So the humourless narks who ban *The Bad Book* are fighting a losing battle.

Devine, Miranda, 'A grim tale of humourless narks', *Sydney Morning Herald*, 30 September 2004

ACTIVITY 58

Feature articles

1 List the major differences between a feature article and a news report.
2 Explain why feature articles in *The Age* or the *Sydney Morning Herald* have a different content and style from those you would find in local newspapers.
3 Find some interesting examples of feature articles and make a wall display of them.
4 Write eye-catching headlines for the following stories.
   a A cleaner wins the 10-million-dollar lottery
   b The first cloning of a human being
   c A business person wrapped only in a towel is locked outside a hotel room
   d A young royal becomes engaged to a notorious celebrity
   e Your favourite team wins the premiership for the first time in years

Letters

Most letters are information texts, although they may include persuasive or argumentative elements as well. A letter to the editor is an example of a text that is primarily persuasive or argumentative. You will find information on writing letters to the editor in Chapter 10.

You know that emails have a set format, where you need to enter, for example, the email address of the person to whom you are writing and you have provision for copying (and blind-copying) others, for filling in a subject line and for supplying attachments. Similarly, there are set formats for letters. The format – and the strictness of the rules – vary, depending on how formal the letter is.

Personal letters

Here are two formats for setting out personal letters. One uses closed punctuation (there is punctuation in the layout of the letter); the other uses open punctuation (there is no punctuation in the layout).

The traditional personal-letter format is semi-blocked. This means that not everything starts on the left-hand margin. The address and date are on the right-hand margin with the complimentary close and the signature directly underneath them at the end of the letter.

Closed punctuation, semi-blocked

Sample personal letter – handwritten

Start address in the middle of the page

Write 'Street', 'Avenue', 'Road' etc. in full

Block capitals, no punctuation for last line of address

17 Biram Street

BALLIEVEY NSW 2999

Note: No comma or full stop in the date

15 March 2011

Leave a line

Salutation is followed by a comma

Dear Elaine,

Start each paragraph on a new line, 2.5 cm from the margin

How's life? I hope you are enjoying yourself.

I'm well and school's great.

ISBN 9780170183048

We've just been working out what excursions we're going on for <u>Come Out</u>. I'm going to <u>Carmen Miranda</u> and <u>All That Jazz</u> for music and <u>Changing Face</u> and <u>Call Me Jo</u> for drama, all in the space of three days. So we should have a ball.

I have to play a flute solo for an assessment in a week and a half. I should go all right but I'm not looking forward to it.

We've got a really great history textbook this year called <u>Their Ghosts May Be Heard: Australia till 1900</u>, by Sheena Coupe and Mary Andrews. It's interesting, easy to read and has great questions, even though it weighs a ton!

Well, I've got another letter to write, so it's goodbye.

Lots of love,

Kath.

Other complimentary closes are: Yours truly, Best wishes, Regards, Yours sincerely

Address, date, complimentary close and signature should begin directly in line

Complimentary close is followed by a comma. Only the first word has a capital letter

There is a full stop after your signature

Open punctuation, fully blocked

Most people who use computers to write personal letters will find this format easier to use, as it is fully blocked. This means that every item begins at the left-hand margin.

Open punctuation is used because it saves time when you are writing with a computer or typewriter.

Sample personal letter – typed

Every line begins on the left-hand margin; there is no indentation

Capital letters for the first letter of each word

Write 'Street', 'Avenue', 'Road', 'Crescent' etc. in full

Note: Block capitals, no punctuation

Leave a line

17 Biram Street

BALLIEVEY NSW 2999

15 March 2011

Dear Elaine

Salutation

How's life? I hope you are enjoying yourself. I'm well and school's great.

We've just been working out what excursions we're going on for *Come Out.* I'm going to *Carmen Miranda* and *All That Jazz* for music and *Changing Face* and *Call Me Jo* for drama, all in the space of three days. So we should have a ball.

There is a gap of one line between paragraphs

I have to play a flute solo for an assessment in a week and a half. I should go all right but I'm not looking forward to it.

We've got a really great history textbook this year called *Their Ghosts May Be Heard: Australia till 1900,* by Sheena Coupe and Mary Andrews. It's interesting, easy to read and has great questions, even though it weighs a ton!

Leave a line

Well, I've got another letter to write, so it's goodbye.

Only the first word of the complimentary close has a capital letter

Lots of love

Kath

Other complimentary closes are:
Yours truly, Best wishes, Regards,
Kind regards, Yours sincerely

Business letters

Business letters are written using open punctuation, which means that no punctuation is used in the layout. They are fully blocked; that is, every item begins on the left-hand margin.

The format suggested here is favoured by many business people as it saves time.

Sample business letter

Magpies
Talking About Books for Children

25 February 2011

Leave at least one line

Mr PF and Mrs L Raja

13 Cooloola Drive

Block capitals

TOOWOOMBA QLD 4350

The date is written:
- day of the month first, in figures
- then the month
- then the year, in full

Include the name and address of the person(s) to whom you are writing. When appropriate include:
- the person's title
- the person's position in the company
- the name and the address of the company

ISBN 9780170183048

Leave at least
one line

Dear Mr and Mrs Raja

Thank you for your support of our children's literature magazine, *Magpies*, in the past year. We hope you have found it interesting and useful. If you have any comments or suggestions, we would like to hear from you.

Your subscription for the next five issues is now due. Would you be kind enough to return the lower portion of this letter with a $39.50 cheque or credit card notification.

Leave at least
one line

Yours sincerely

Traditionally, business letters were signed 'Yours faithfully'. Generally, today, letters that are addressed 'Dear Sir or Madam' are signed 'Yours faithfully' and those addressed to a person by name are signed 'Yours sincerely'

Leave enough
room to sign
the letter

Rayma Turton
Editor

If you are not using letterhead, put your own company name and address below your signature and title at the foot of the letter, as shown below.

Your subscription for the next five issues is now due. Would you be kind enough to return the lower portion of this letter with a $39.50 cheque or credit card notification.

Leave a line

Yours sincerely

Leave enough
room to sign
the letter

Rayma Turton
Editor

Your name and
address

Magpies
PO Box 563
HAMILTON QLD 4007

A typical machine-addressed envelope

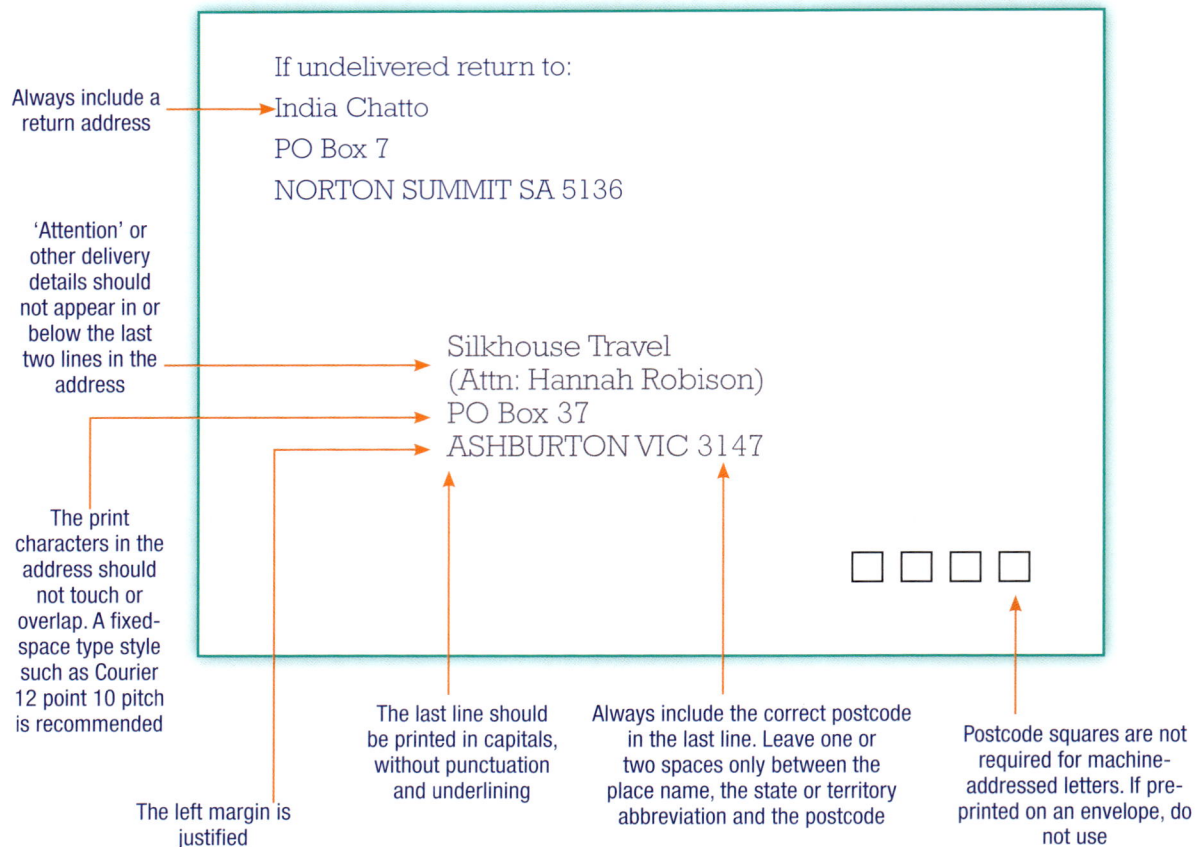

Always include a return address →

If undelivered return to:

India Chatto

PO Box 7

NORTON SUMMIT SA 5136

'Attention' or other delivery details should not appear in or below the last two lines in the address →

Silkhouse Travel
(Attn: Hannah Robison)
PO Box 37
ASHBURTON VIC 3147

The print characters in the address should not touch or overlap. A fixed-space type style such as Courier 12 point 10 pitch is recommended

The left margin is justified

The last line should be printed in capitals, without punctuation and underlining

Always include the correct postcode in the last line. Leave one or two spaces only between the place name, the state or territory abbreviation and the postcode

Postcode squares are not required for machine-addressed letters. If pre-printed on an envelope, do not use

Job applications

Reading the advertisement

To prepare a job application in answer to an advertisement, you need to note several details from the advertisement.

- The title of the advertised job
- The essential requirements
- Duties that would be required of the successful applicant

Explain in your application how you meet all of the advertised requirements. If you do not, show that you are willing to learn. It can also be to your advantage to show that you already know something about the firm.

Ways of applying for a job

There are two ways of applying for a job.

1   Send a letter of application by post or email

Write a letter, making sure you include:

- reference to the job that was advertised and how it came to your attention
- your full name, address and telephone number
- your date of birth (optional)
- your educational and other qualifications

ISBN 9780170183048

- all details of relevant employment experience
- copies of suitable references or the telephone numbers of referees
- a brief statement of the reasons you are interested in the position
- a request for a personal interview.

2   Send a résumé and a covering letter

Alternatively, you could send a copy of your résumé (see format on page 138), with a covering letter that should include:

- reference to the job that was advertised and how it came to your attention
- a brief statement of the reasons you are interested in the position
- a request for a personal interview.

Writing your job application

1   A letter of application is an information text but it will have some of the qualities of a persuasive text as well, as you will want to influence the recipient to think favourably of you.

2   The appropriate format for the letter of application or the covering letter is the same as that used for any other business letter: a fully blocked letter with open punctuation (see page 131).

3   Remember that the quality of your application is likely to influence the decision of whether or not to grant you an interview. Your application should be either typed or written in neat handwriting on good-quality paper (if posting by mail). Careful expression and accurate spelling are vital.

4   If possible, address your letter to the person who will make the decision about recruitment. If the advertisement does not mention this person's name, it may be possible to find out by making a phone call.

5   For future reference, keep a copy of each job application you write.

Sample job application

18 November 2011

Ms Hannah Bonato
Personnel Manager
Myer
Innaloo Shopping Centre
INNALOO WA 6018

Dear Ms Bonato

Mention the job that was advertised and how it came to your attention →

I am writing to apply for the position of temporary junior salesperson for the Christmas holidays, which was advertised in last week's *Stirling Times*.

Educational and other qualifications →

I have successfully completed Year 9 at Mt Lawley Senior High School, passing all subjects that I studied. As well as this, I have a bronze medal in lifesaving and have played basketball for the school team. I won a Citizenship Award in my last year at primary school.

Relevant employment experience →

I delivered papers for the Ocean Glimpses Newsagency from 2008 to 2010. Then I worked part-time for the Red Rooster store in Dog's Swamp from January 2011 until the present time.

Copies of suitable references →

I enclose copies of references from the owner of the newsagency, Mr Brodie McKee, the manager of the Red Rooster store, Ms Emilia Galatis, and my Year 9 form teacher, Ms Katherine Bennetts.

Explain why you are interested in the position →

I am applying for this temporary position as I enjoy serving the public and I would like to know more about the retail trade and future employment possibilities in this area. Therefore, I believe this job would be useful work experience for me. If you were looking for temporary staff next year, I would be willing to work on Thursday evenings and Saturdays.

Request a personal interview →

As I am particularly interested in this position, I would very much appreciate it if I could have an interview with you so that I can discuss it in greater detail.

Yours sincerely

Andrew Patterson

Andrew Patterson
42 Woodsome Street
MT LAWLEY 6050

Telephone: 08 9271 0890

Include your full name, address and telephone number

enc.

Applications for work experience

Most initial arrangements for work experience are made by phone. You will, however, need to write to the person employing you to give them some background information and to explain why you would like to do work experience with them. You could write a letter, giving all of the relevant details.

ISBN 9780170183048

Sample letter confirming acceptance of work experience

20 May 2011

Dr B Mellor
Director
Chalkface Press Pty Ltd
8 Graham Court
COTTESLOE WA 6011

Dear Dr Mellor

Introduction →

Thank you for offering me a work experience placement at Chalkface Press from 20 to 24 June 2011.

Explain why you are interested in the position. →

I am keen to work at Chalkface Press because I am interested in a career in the publishing industry. By working for you for a week, I feel that I could gain some insight into how a publishing company operates. I also would like to work at Chalkface Press because it is a small company and I would learn something about most aspects of the publishing process. If I went to a larger company, I would be working in only one section, whereas with you I would be able to try a wider variety of tasks.

Explain how and when you will make contact. →

I will ring you on 31 May to make final arrangements for work experience. In the meantime, if you have any enquiries, please feel free to ring our Youth Education Officer, Mr Nicholas Bennetts, on (08) 9734 2675 during school hours.

Yours sincerely

Kate Hopkins

Include your full name, address and telephone number. →

Kate Hopkins
RMB 234 Preston Road
COLLIE WA 6225

Telephone: (08) 9732 1321 (home)
　　　　　　 04000 99009 (mobile)

Résumés

A résumé (pronounced 'rez/u/may') is a summary of information that might be useful to an employer. You should vary it to suit the job for which you are applying. Here is a sample résumé.

NAME:	Kate Hopkins
DATE OF BIRTH*:	14 May 1994
ADDRESS:	RMB 234, Preston Road, COLLIE WA 6225
EMAIL:	katehopkins@gmail.com
TELEPHONE:	(08) 9732 1321 or 04000 99009

EDUCATION:

1999–2005	Amaroo Primary School
2006–2011	Collie Senior High School

SUBJECTS STUDIED:

English	Indonesian	Society and Environment
Japanese	Mathematics	Design and Technology
Science	Information Technology	

AWARDS:

Education Department of WA, Country Week Speech Awards, Gold Medal in Storytelling, 2010
Esso Science Competition, Credit, 2004
Westpac Mathematics Competition, Credit, 2008
Suzuki Association of Australia, Piano, Levels 1 & 2 (2005 and 2006)

WORK HISTORY

2010:	Cashier, part-time, Coles, Collie
2004:	Work experience with Collie Veterinary Clinic

ACTIVITIES:

Participant in Model United Nations General Assemblies organised by Rotary Clubs at Harvey and Rockingham, 2010
Member Wellington Pony Club, 2005–2010

INTERESTS:

Reading science fiction and fantasy novels
Writing
Horse riding

SKILLS:

Typing (35 words per minute)
Confident public speaker
Piano
Basic knowledge of Indonesian and Japanese

REFEREES:

Jenny Eastman	Huw Mugford
Veterinary Surgeon	Manager
21 Doonan Road	Coles
NEDLANDS 6009	PO Box 64
Business (08) 9386 0000	COLLIE 6225
Home (08) 9712 3123	(08) 9712 3123

* Note that supplying your date of birth is optional. However, an employer may require proof of age if they doubt whether you are legally old enough to take the position.

ISBN 9780170183048

ACTIVITY 59

Letters

1. Explain the difference between open and closed letters.
2. Write a letter of complaint to a business from which you have purchased a faulty product. Refer to page 132 for help with the format of a business letter.
3. Find an email that you have written lately. Rewrite it as a letter.
4. What are the differences between personal and business letters? In your answer include information on audience, purpose, format and punctuation.

Résumés

5. Prepare your own résumé and a covering letter on a computer. Refer to pages 134–8 for help.

10 ARGUMENT TEXT TYPES

Argument text types include:

- the persuasion or point of view text type
- the discussion text type
- the editorial
- the letter to the editor
- the review or response text type.

Presenting an argument

There are four main ways of developing an argument on a particular issue.

1   Putting forward only your own case, or point of view
2   Arguing for one point of view, while also revealing the opposing viewpoint
3   Presenting an overview of both sides
4   Reflecting on the issue without taking a personal stance

Approaches to developing an argument

If you are asked to develop an argument, you would need to consider which of these approaches is most appropriate, given your knowledge of the issue and your views about it. Your approach might vary according to the topic. Arguments about the Australian flag, wearing the school uniform, the killing of kangaroos or duck shooting might each be tackled differently. If you feel very strongly about the issue, you might just want to put one side of the case. On the other hand, if you are not sure what viewpoint you should take, you might be happy to present an overview of both sides.

In each case, you need to clarify your knowledge of the topic and decide if you need to do further research before developing your argument.

1 Putting forward only your own case or point of view

Using this approach, you would present only your views on the topic. Sometimes you would do this in the strongest manner possible. You might choose to write in the first person ('This is what I believe').

Before writing, you would need to decide on:

- the main points you could make to support your case.
- the evidence you could summon to support your views.

Ever since Federation there has been strong debate in Australia about our national flag. One deeply felt and passionately argued point of view was expressed by Dr Lowitja O'Donoghue:

ISBN 9780170183048

Our national flag should be a symbol of our national ideals and of the people we want to be. We regard ourselves as independent, individual and inclusive – but our existing flag, our national symbol, says none of this.

Instead, it symbolises a narrow slice of our history including a significant period when the rights of Australia's indigenous peoples were overlooked. For this reason, most of Australia's indigenous people cannot relate to the existing flag. For us, it symbolises dispossession and oppression. And it just doesn't reflect the reality of Australian life in the late 1990s.

We are a country that prides itself on diversity and tolerance, yet some of us cling to the flag that represents a monoculture and intolerance. We are a country that has debated important national issues such as justice, rights and identity, yet the current flag symbolises quite the opposite – complacency, dependency and subordination

I reject the proposal that we are risking our sense of historical place by seeking a new flag.

2 Arguing for one point of view while also revealing the opposing viewpoint

This kind of argument involves developing your own viewpoint while taking account of opposing views. These should be either countered or conceded in a rational way.

The Australian National Flag Association website (www.australianflag.org.au) examines the points made by those who argue for a new Australian flag. It has a page of debating points where it lists some of the arguments that people make for a new Australian flag and then counters them. For example:

It is a colonial flag that signifies our subordination to Britain.

Although Australia was once a collection of six separate British colonies, this is no longer the case. The creation of the Australian Federation on 1 January 1901, the Statute of Westminster Act in 1942, and the proclamation of the Australia Act in 1986 make it quite clear that the British Parliament no longer has authority over our independent and sovereign nation. The Australian National Flag is unambiguously democratic in its origins as it is the product of an open public competition. The Union Jack represents the principles on which Australia's unique style of liberal democracy is based.

The Australian National Flag stands for freedom of speech, parliamentary democracy, rule of law, egalitarianism and the courage and sacrifice of the ANZACS. It also represents our geographic position in the southern hemisphere with the Southern Cross while the Commonwealth Star represents Australia's federation of States and Territories.

The Australian National Flag is a positive reflection of the values and ideals that have been the bedrock of a society and a system of Government that are among the most envied in the world.

3 Presenting an overview of both sides

Since Federation, there has been debate in the Australian community about our national flag. As early as September 1901 the *Bulletin* magazine was condemning the choice for the new flag as 'a stale rechauffe of the British flag, a symbol of Australian subordination to Britain', while others argued just as strongly that the flag symbolised the best Australian values, including freedom of speech, participatory democracy and egalitarianism.

4 Reflecting on the issue without taking a personal stance

Reflection enables you to explore the possibilities of a topic as you think and write about it. It clarifies your thinking and develops your understanding without you having to make any final decision about the issue.

In looking at the issue of the Australian flag, you might reflect on how important the issue is for you and what experiences you have had that might explain your reaction. You might then do some reading about the topic and consider the views of others by conducting a survey.

These activities might help you to put your own thinking into a wider context, to understand the complexity of the issue and to see how feelings and attitudes often play a more significant part in people's views than rational argument.

Using the essay form to reflect could help you to determine what you think about an issue.

ACTIVITY 60

Arguments

When you read or listen to an argument, consider which of the four approaches presented above is being used. Below you will find four different approaches to the question of cloning. Which one puts forward one case only? Which argues for one point of view, while also revealing the opposing viewpoint? Which presents an overview of both sides? And which reflects on the issue without taking a personal stance?

1 Cloning is an insult to God. There is no ethical basis for the experiments and further work should be stopped.
2 Cloning is an important issue. At this moment I can't see how it affects society, although a survey of the thoughts of the scientific and religious communities should clarify matters in my mind.
3 Experimentation without moral dilemma is the hallmark of science. At times this experimentation crosses the ethical boundaries of some people and this must be recognised. However, we must push ahead.
4 On the one hand, cloning can be seen as a breakthrough for medical science; on the other, it characterises the worst fears of science fiction. We need to consider these views carefully.

ISBN 9780170183048

Persuasion text types

Persuasion text types present one point of view. They are a good text type to use when you have to present an argument such as an essay in which you present your point of view on a topic.

Here is a summary of the features of persuasion text types.

Persuasion or point of view	
Purpose	• to persuade, by arguing one point of view
Suggested audience	• members of a jury; voters; newspaper readers; school examiners
Structural features	• introductory statement presenting the author's point of view • series of arguments to support the point of view • concluding summary of the author's position
Language features	• words with a high level of modality (will, must, definitely) • emotive words, especially adjectives and adverbs, that reflect the author's bias • technical language if appropriate • use of the present tense • use of conjunctions to link the flow of argument
Examples	• advertisement • editorial • legal defence • political pamphlet • letter to the editor • essay in which you are asked for your opinion

Use of alliteration

Use of exaggeration

Sample persuasive text

Introductory statement

Use of strong emotive adjectives

Barbaric behaviour in Yellowstone Park

In May 2009 the gray wolves of the Northern Rocky Mountains region of the United States were removed from the federal Endangered Species List. Legal challenges continue to protect wolves in some states but the famous wolves of Yellowstone Park – loved by television viewers around the world – have been decimated by reckless and barbaric hunters looking for trophies. Among the slaughtered are Wolf 527 and her daughter, Wolf 716, two radio-collared females who have been carefully studied by researchers. The mindless killing has shattered years of scientific study.

Use of personalised example

Are we to see next an extension to the area of the horrendous Alaskan practice of allowing wolves to be gunned down from planes and helicopters? We must challenge now the idea that we have a God-given right to gun ownership. Write to your Congressman today.

Use of rhetorical question

Use of strong verbs with emotional connotations

Call to action

High modality

ACTIVITY 61

Essays

Write an essay designed to persuade your readers of one of these points of view.
1 That the school leaving age should be raised
2 That the school leaving age should be reduced
3 That all school students should have longer periods of compulsory physical education
4 That all school students should learn a language other than English
5 That maths should not be compulsory

Discussion text types

Discussion text types present both sides of an issue with a conclusion as to which is the stronger argument. They are a good text type to use when you have to analyse two sides of an issue.

Here is a summary of the features of discussion text types.

Discussion (an argument, like the 'argument' or 'point of view' text type, but both sides of an issue are examined)	
Purpose	• to examine something from more than one point of view
Suggested audience	• members of the local community; a committee
Structural features	• introductory statement presenting the subject to be examined • series of paragraphs giving arguments for different points of view, with supporting evidence • conclusion that probably contains a recommendation or opinion
Language features	• technical language if appropriate • use of the present tense • generalised nouns (politicians rather than my local member of parliament; students rather than my brother Bruno) • words that introduce different viewpoints (however, on the other hand, although)
Examples	• segment on talkback radio • television panel show • debate • letter to the editor • school essay

ISBN 9780170183048

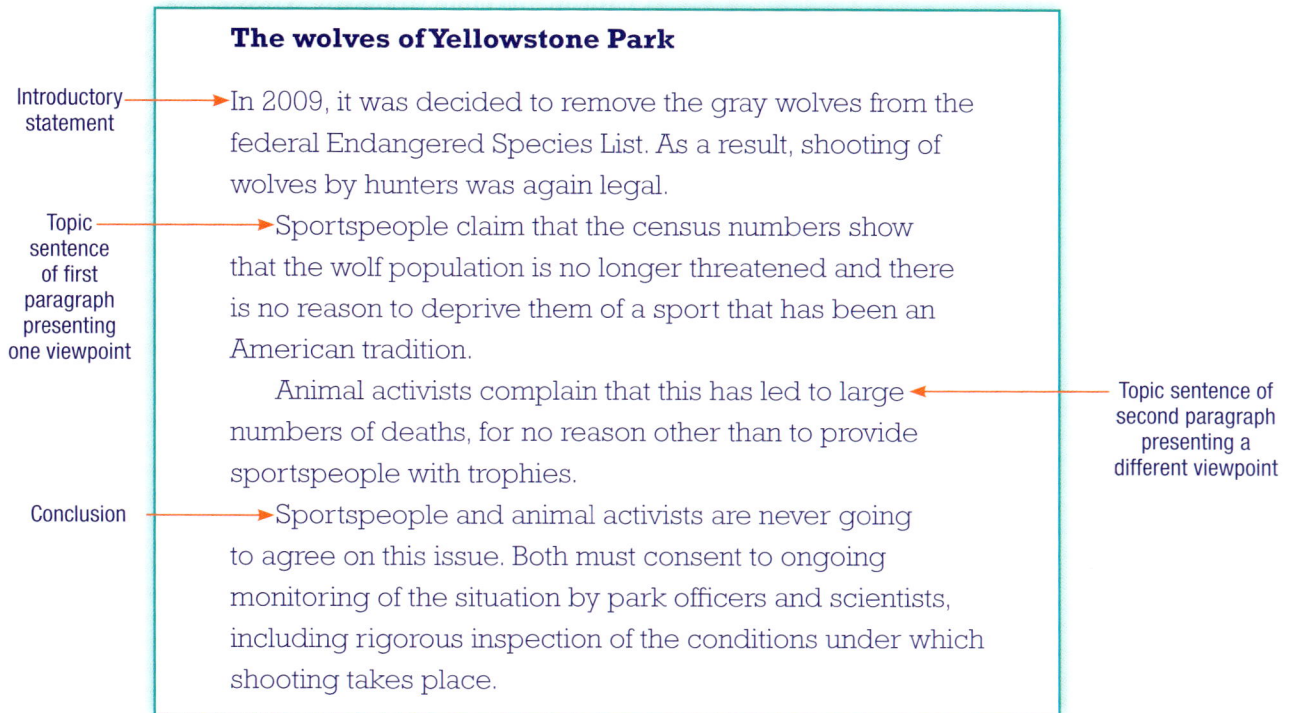

The wolves of Yellowstone Park

Introductory statement → In 2009, it was decided to remove the gray wolves from the federal Endangered Species List. As a result, shooting of wolves by hunters was again legal.

Topic sentence of first paragraph presenting one viewpoint → Sportspeople claim that the census numbers show that the wolf population is no longer threatened and there is no reason to deprive them of a sport that has been an American tradition.

Animal activists complain that this has led to large numbers of deaths, for no reason other than to provide sportspeople with trophies. ← Topic sentence of second paragraph presenting a different viewpoint

Conclusion → Sportspeople and animal activists are never going to agree on this issue. Both must consent to ongoing monitoring of the situation by park officers and scientists, including rigorous inspection of the conditions under which shooting takes place.

Editorials

Newspaper editorials are opinion-based texts that respond to a current issue or recent news event. The purpose of an editorial is to represent the editor's or publisher's stance on a particular issue, to convince readers that this stance is the right one and to argue for action. Unlike lengthy feature articles, editorials are generally shorter and focus on persuading readers to adopt an opinion rather than exploring an issue in great detail. They are published as a regular column, often alongside letters to the editor.

Structure of an editorial

Headline

Like newspaper reports and feature articles, the headline is attention-grabbing and should provide a clue as to the issue addressed in the editorial. You can create a headline that appeals to your audience by using:

- a pun or 'play on words' (Undertaker Makes Grave Decision)
- alliteration (Potter Pandemonium at Palace Cinema!)
- a rhetorical question (How can anyone dislike 'Australian Idol'?).

Introduction

Also called the 'lead' paragraph, your introduction needs to assert an opinion or a thesis in relation to a current event or issue. You need to secure your reader's interest by confidently stating your view.

Body

Elaborate on the view stated in your introduction, giving persuasive evidence and examples to convince your reader. Keep your paragraphs short and make sure that each one deals with a separate point.

1   Connect your ideas using linking words (such as furthermore or similarly) and emphasise the validity of your view by choosing persuasive language. Useful phrases include:
   - 'clearly'
   - 'therefore'
   - 'It is obvious that ...'
   - 'without a doubt'.

2   Use a range of persuasive strategies such as:
   - emotive language that encourages the reader to react emotionally

     Such an abysmal state of affairs is utterly heartbreaking and soul-destroying.

   - hyperbole or exaggeration

     The entire universe would agree with me!

   - rhetorical questions that encourage readers simply to consider the issue rather than actually to respond

     How can we sit back and do nothing?

   - alliteration; that is, a series of words starting with the same letter or sound

     This shocking shark attack has shaken the community.

   - figurative or metaphorical language such as personification, simile or metaphor

     The new bridge will be an ugly sore on the face of our beautiful city.

     The drought has devoured the countryside, leaving the land barren and thirsty.

   - references to authority figures and experts that are intended to impress readers

     As the Prime Minister stated in her recent press conference …

   - inversion or switching the usual order of words in a phrase for dramatic effect

     Ask not what your country can do for you, but what you can do for your country. (John F Kennedy)

   - cumulation; that is, a series of words with a similar meaning

     The behaviour of the rugby fans was abominable, unforgivable, outrageous and shameful!

   - use of the first person to express opinion
     - 'I believe that …'
     - 'We cannot simply accept this nonsense!'
     - 'It is my firm belief that we need to protect our rainforests'.

Conclusion

Leave your reader feeling convinced that your view and interpretation of the issue is worthy. In concluding your argument, you might call upon the reader to take action or you might issue a warning about likely outcomes if your views are not heeded. A powerful way to demand a response or action from your reader is to use an imperative or a command. In an editorial focusing on the issue of water shortages, you might finish with the imperative: 'Be responsible. Conserve water wherever possible'.

ISBN 9780170183048

Sample editorial

Title: use of alliteration; sarcastic tone is established

Such sincere, sensitive exploitation

Media focus on the 'anniversary' smacks of prurient commercialism and blurs reality, writes John Huxley.

Cumulation: grabs our attention and establishes focus

Reference to recent news event provides a context for editorial

Imperative used to involve readers

Use of a range of supportive evidence and illustrations to validate argument

Note tone: sarcasm

Linking words to show sequencing of ideas

Clear statements of viewpoint

Sentence fragments used to capture the dramatic scene

Vivid imagery appeals to readers' emotions

Repetition to emphasise point

Emotive language to persuade readers

INCREDIBLE. Unbelievable. Extraordinary. Exclusive pictures. Panorama graphics. Victims' stories. Provocative essays. Memorial editions. Commemorative issues. Lift-out tributes. Four pages. Eight pages. Sixteen pages. Today. Tomorrow. On Wednesday. Every day this week.

That's just a selection from the Sydney newspapers. Not to be outdone, never concerned that the whole thing may be overdone, most of the television channels, many claiming to use 'previously unseen footage', are staging their own September 11 'specials'.

So many 'specials', in fact, that the tragedy becomes commonplace; the dead, the bereaved, the rescuers, the rebuilders mere players in a sordid media event, a prurient re-screening of a worn-out movie.

Worst by far are the images. The double-page spreads. The cut-out-and-keep pictures. Of tilting, tangled buildings. Of billowing clouds of smoke. Of tiny bodies twisting, falling from the skies. Of fleeing crowds. Of faces covered in dust, contorted in shock.

Black-edged, framed with white space, artfully cropped, flung across double-page spreads, these pictures have generated a perverted 'aesthetic' quality of their very own. See, for example, how neatly the headlines can be made to fit into those bits of sky not filled with clouds of dust, collapsing buildings and falling bodies.

Or, a sensitive, self-consciously moving portrait of a little girl clutching a picture of a father who will never return.

Then there are those self-indulgent celebrity 'where I was when I heard the news' stories. Swimmer Sam Riley, for example, was in a Sydney hotel on a promotional tour.

The Victorian Premier, Steve Bracks, had just arrived home from a function. And so on. Fascinating!

And the 'think' pieces on how the world has changed forever; or not, as the almost-mandatory contrarian columnist, will argue. Well, there are four, eight or 12 pages to fill.

Little wonder Laura Bush, the President's wife, urged parents not to let their children watch television on September 11. Or, she might have added, read the newspapers, or pose for pictures. As she said, they were too young to understand.

And what of us adults? How much better will we understand the events of September 11 after being exposed to this saturation coverage, this orgy of horror, this overkill for which some people somewhere clearly

Opinionative vocabulary →

believe there is insatiable public demand?

Of course, it is a big 'story' (what an event becomes once deemed significant by the media), possibly the biggest in our lives, given that it is still being played out. It was always going to be retold, reinterpreted, given the preoccupation with 'anniversary' journalism.

Note that writer makes a small concession to show fairness and balance →

It would be foolish to deny that, amid the massive accumulation of tumbling words and pictures, there have been many intelligent, well-intentioned pieces.

But with so much video footage, still photography,

mobile-phone transcript and personal recollection available after all, this is America, not Bangladesh or Ethiopia where thousands die in anonymity it is not surprising, perhaps, that perspective has lost out to hyperbole, explanation to gratuitous excitement, inspiration to intrusion.

← Summary of editorial

Far from helping us better to understand the real-life events of last September, this year's commemoration will merely have reinforced clichéd perceptions that they look like something out of a bad movie.

← Analogy (comparison) to help reader accept writer's viewpoint

Huxley, J, 'Such sincere, sensitive exploitation', *Sydney Morning Herald*, 9 September 2002.

ACTIVITY 62

1 The following topics are often examined in newspaper and magazine editorials. Imagine you are writing a series of editorials. Create a catchy headline for each topic. Your headline should give an indication of your stance on the issue.
   - The need to conserve water
   - The level of violence on television
   - Overprotective parents
   - Refugees seeking asylum in Australia
   - Reality television

2 Respond to one of the following headlines by writing an editorial that addresses the issue suggested by the headline.
   a Virtual Reality More Real than Reality
   b Harry Potter: the Reading Wizard
   c Why Write When You Can 'Text'?
   d Adolescence: the Fast and the Furious

Letters to the editor

People write letters to the editor because they have something to say. It may be to comment on something that has been said or done recently, to share their point of view with others or to get something done. They might tell a story to make a point or just to share it with the wider world.

If you intend to send a letter to a newspaper via post or email, you should use the following format for your final draft. It is the same as that used for business letters.

If you intend to publish your letter in a class newspaper, it should be set out in the same way as letters printed in newspapers.

ISBN 9780170183048

Before you begin

Use the following steps to plan your letter.

1 Discuss what you want to say with a friend or other members of your group.
2 Make notes on the most important points you want to make.
3 Think about:
   • what your main paragraphs will contain
   • the order of the paragraphs
   • how you will open and close your letter.

Opening your letter

Finding suitable opening sentences or paragraphs for a letter to the editor is quite difficult. The following sample introductions show different ways of writing in reply to statements made by others.

> Your correspondent Lucy Milan ('Planning for the Twenty-First Century', Letters 6/3) warns of the dangers of pollution. Her concern for our fragile environment deserves the careful attention of all our politicians.
>
> Sir – I was surprised to read Niland Stuart's letter (1/4) proposing a new way to celebrate the first day of this month. His proposition defies belief.
>
> I support the views expressed in your editorial 'Much too tall' (August 31). The time has come for governments at all levels to oppose any further development of our beach fronts.
>
> Eliza Chalmers (Letters, June 12) reminds us of the joys of exploring the outback. It may be appropriate to balance her story with a warning about the dangers of travel in remote areas without prior preparation.

You could also look at the 'Letters to the editor' section of a range of newspapers to read other letter opening sentences.

The date is written:
• day of the month first, in figures
• then the month
• then the year, in full

The letter is addressed to 'the editor'. Include the name and address of the newspaper

Block capitals

Sample letter to the editor

5 June 2009

Leave at least one line

The Editor
The Australian
GPO Box 4162
SYDNEY NSW 2001

Leave a line →

Every line
begins on
the left-hand
margin

Leave a line
between
paragraphs

Dear Sir/Madam

Stan Wright's railway letter (31/5) reminded me of the story about the commuter who always occupied the same seat, year in, year out, and promptly fell asleep to be awakened by his fellow commuters on reaching his destination.

One day the train stopped short of the station. The commuter awoke with a start, opened the door and fell onto the track.

Sheepishly, he clambered back, shaking his head at his grinning colleagues, muttering, 'I knew I would do that one day'.

Then he stomped to the other side of the carriage, opened the door and fell out again!

Yours faithfully

Mark Byrne

Mark Byrne
20 Station Street
DEE WHY NSW 2022

Generally, today, business letters that are addressed 'Dear Sir/Madam' are signed 'Yours faithfully' and those addressed to a person by name are signed 'Yours sincerely'. *Note:* The second word does not have a capital letter

Leave enough room to sign the letter

Revising your letter

Most newspapers prefer brief letters to the editor, so it is important to revise your first draft to keep it as short and to the point as possible. Use the following questions to help you improve your first draft.

1   Does my introduction grab the reader's attention?
    Is it immediately clear what my subject matter is?
    Does the opening make my viewpoint clear?
2   Will my ending have an impact on the reader?
    Does the conclusion sum up my argument or draw the threads of my case together?
3   Are there any sections of the letter that could be left out?
4   Would my argument be strengthened by using better examples?
5   Is the letter divided into appropriate paragraphs?
    Could any of the paragraphs be placed in a different order to develop my case more logically?
6   Are there any sentences, phrases or words that don't sound exactly right and could be replaced?
7   Have I checked the punctuation to see that it is correct?
8   Have I proofread for spelling errors?
    Ask your writing partner or a friend to read your letter carefully to make any suggestions for improvement. If possible, ask your teacher for advice.

    Before writing a final draft, make sure that your letter says exactly what you want it to say, as clearly and as briefly as possible.

ISBN 9780170183048

Producing your final draft

Produce your final draft, following the recommended format for setting out letters to the editor.

Readers complete the writing process. Enjoy the satisfaction that comes from having others read your letter.

ACTIVITY 63

Letters to the editor

You feel strongly about an issue and want to express your views to the public through a letter to the editor. Use a computer to create a letter. Refer to the format on page 149 to help. You could choose your own topic or one of the following: euthanasia, abortion, women priests, school discipline, attitudes to young people, driving age.

Responses (or reviews)

Response (also called 'review' or 'personal response')	
Purpose	• to comment on an artistic work, such as a book, a film, a concert, an art exhibition
Suggested audience	• readers of lifestyle magazines; members of a book club or online forum; newspaper subscribers
Structural features	• introduction giving the context of the artistic work: the title, the author or artist, appropriate dates, the venue if appropriate • description of the artistic work detailing key features • summarising evaluation, perhaps including a recommendation
Language features	• use of the present tense • descriptive adjectives and adverbs • emotive words reflecting the author's judgement
Examples	• book review • television critic's newspaper column • review of a website • restaurant review

A review is an opinionative text. Its purpose is to express an opinion or to evaluate an event, a place, an experience or a product. Reviews are powerful texts as they can influence people's perceptions and decisions. In the case of a restaurant, for example, a bad review can lead to empty tables. We often choose to see a film or to read a particular book on the basis of a review in a newspaper or magazine.

Whether a review targets a film, a television program, a book, a restaurant, a CD, a holiday resort or the latest model car, it aims to:

- evaluate
- persuade
- inform.

A good review not only asserts an opinion, but also justifies this opinion so that an audience can make an informed judgement about the subject of the review. In the case of a film review, the reviewer must have an understanding of film language and cinematography.

Writing a film review

Targeting your audience

First of all, it is important to consider both your audience and the type of publication in which your review is to appear. What kind of relationship will you as reviewer have with your readers? If you are writing for a specialist film magazine, you can assume that your readers have a reasonable knowledge of and interest in film. Therefore, you could include plenty of film jargon or cinematographic terminology in your review, confident that your readers will understand. A film review that targets the general viewing public may take a simpler approach, focusing more on the plot of the film rather than on the finer points of film-making.

Consider, also, the tone you will adopt as reviewer. Whether you choose to be light-hearted, sarcastic, controversial, scathing or enthusiastic in your praise, you must be consistent if you wish to be convincing.

Content

A film review usually addresses the following:

1   **Plot:** Give a brief outline of the film's storyline. Be careful not to reveal too much!
2   **Cast and characterisation:** Describe the cast and characterisation. Are the actors well-chosen and credible in their roles? Do the characters represent recognisable social types – for example, the villain or the hero? How might audiences respond to these characters?
3   **Setting/location:** Describe the time and place in which the film is set. How is the authenticity of the film's setting created through the use of colour, props and set design? Where did filming take place? Did the filming location pose any challenges to the director and actors?
4   **Cinematography:** Examine the film techniques. This includes the use of the camera (shot types, camera angles and movement), colour, lighting, special effects (for example, animated sequences or computer-generated images), editing (for example, the sequencing of shots) and symbolism.
5   **Music and sound:** Evaluate the film score or sound track. Are particular sounds used for symbolic effect?
6   **Purpose of the film:** Does the film have a message? What emotional impact does the film have? How does it relate to other films of a similar type? You might also give some details about the director's other work. What genre or style of movie is it: romantic comedy, thriller or action?

Structure of a film review

The structure of a film review is similar to the structure of an essay. Like an essay, a review consists of an introduction, a body and a conclusion. Unlike an essay, a review usually also has a title, a by-line to identify the reviewer and perhaps a short synopsis or description of the film separate from the body of the review.

1   **Title:** The title must be attention-grabbing, like a newspaper headline. The title often indicates whether the review is a favourable one or not.
2   **By-line:** The name of the reviewer is given.
3   **Introduction:** This includes the film's title, date of release, name of the director and genre. Other points to consider might be the director's earlier work, the cost of the film or any controversial aspects of the story or the filming process. Your opinion of the film needs to be established clearly here.
4   **Body:** Develop your views of the film in a series of well-constructed paragraphs. You might choose to devote each paragraph to a particular aspect of the film. Remember that your aim is to persuade and to evaluate, so make careful language choices. A convincing film review will persuade through emotive appeals and other forms of persuasive language outlined in the Editorials section on page 145.
5   **Conclusion:** Sum up your assessment of the film. Perhaps indicate the audience most likely to appreciate the film's merits. Some reviewers end by giving the film a rating out of 10. Leave your readers in no doubt as to what you think of the film.

ISBN 9780170183048

Sample film review

There is no one way to approach a film review. Take a look at the following example, an online review of *The Lord of the Rings: The Fellowship of the Ring*.

The Lord of the Rings Part 1

Rating: ★★★★

Classification: M

Director: Peter Jackson

Cast: Elijah Wood, Cate Blanchett, Sean Astin, Liv Tyler, Ian Holm, Sir Ian McKellen, Viggo Mortensen, Christopher Lee

Nominated for four Golden Globe Awards including Best Picture, The Fellowship of the Ring introduces to movie audiences the enchanted world of Middle Earth and its memorable inhabitants – men, hobbits, elves, dwarves, wizards, trolls and orcs.

Review:

The Lord of the Rings has an extraordinary place in popular culture. Released in the early '50s, this trilogy, set in a mythical place called Middle Earth, was perhaps the single most influential literary work of the past century. If you believe readers' polls, you would be led to believe it was also the best.

Consider, then, the incredible responsibility New Zealand director Peter Jackson assumed when taking on the trilogy. This is more than a piece of literature; it is the template for every work of fantasy in the past five decades. This is more than a passing fad; it is an enduring phenomenon. This is more than a simple story; to some, it is a religion.

The first edition, *The Fellowship of the Ring*, was an epic piece of film-making in every respect, quite mythic in itself. In fact, Jackson shot all three films in the series in a single two-year shoot. His labours have been brilliantly realised and rewarded. Jackson has delivered an awesome adaptation of a modern classic. It's a shame it's been out-hyped by *Harry Potter and the Philosopher's Stone*, because comparing *Harry Potter to Lord of the Rings* is like comparing the Bible to a Sunday school book. One is the source, the other merely a sample.

Annotations (margin notes):
- Establishes film's quality
- Synopsis given to identify film
- Stresses cultural importance of film and book
- Use of imperative to involve reader
- Film's enduring significance is emphasised
- Director is introduced
- Clear indication of reviewer's opinion
- Analogy used to highlight film's superiority
- Comparisons with other texts to place film in context

Humour used to appeal to reader

For those who think a hobbit is a quaint piece of furniture, *Lord of the Rings* is the story of a ring that has irresistible powers. In the wrong hands, it can be an extraordinary instrument of evil and is capable of controlling the weak-hearted. It falls into the hands of a hobbit, an elf-like creature called Frodo Baggins who, realising its nefarious nature, sets out on a brave quest to finally destroy it. He is accompanied on his mission by a rag-tag team of hobbits, dwarves and handsome he-men, not to mention Gandalf, a white wizard with a pointy blue hat who was Obi Wan Kenobi before George Lucas was even born.

Summary of plot

Details of setting

New Zealand makes a marvellous Middle Earth, given that its wilderness looks so otherworldly, and the filmmakers so expertly mesh the digital with the real life that it actually looks like an entirely plausible universe. Jackson succeeds in making this not only visually opulent but exhilarating entertainment by realising that this needs to be more than just a quest story … it's a chase movie as well. Frodo and his friends seem inches away from evil at any moment and this makes the tale surprisingly suspenseful. Their pursuit is relentless, and the pacing is impeccable. What makes the film truly mythic is some classic casting. Elijah Wood is perfect as Frodo, the hobbit that comes into possession of the ring. His childlike countenance and his earnest eyes make him a perfectly unassuming hero. Equally, Sir Ian McKellen is superb. He must have one of the most expressive faces in the business, a truly great screen actor who makes a potentially pulpy part into a splendid archetype. He manifests not only the film's magic but also its soul.

Use of director's surname

'Genre' or classification of film

Atmosphere of film

Evaluation of actors

Clear linking of ideas

And this is a story with great soul. One of Tolkien's remarkable achievements in creating the ring as a central symbol is that this thing reveals the evil in men's hearts. This is quite extraordinary in storytelling because the story has the audacity to suggest that evil is relative and that we are all capable of it, whether we are a malevolent overlord or a humble hobbit.

Symbolism

First person ('we') involves reader and connects film to readers' world

Conclusion sums up central message or theme of film

Kerry Bashford, *Lord of the Rings Part 1*, NineMSN Movie Guide, viewed 14 January 2005, <http://movieguide.ninemsm.com.au/movieguide/4asp>.

ISBN 9780170183048

ACTIVITY 64

Persuasive language

Provide an example for each of the following types of persuasive language.

1 alliteration
2 rhetorical question
3 cumulation
4 inversion
5 metaphor
6 hyperbole

ISBN 9780170183048

Types of oral texts

Like written texts, oral forms of communication have particular conventions and formats. Just as we do when writing, we also need to consider our purpose and our intended audience when we speak. This helps us to make effective choices regarding the most appropriate language and tone to use. We generally think of formal speeches (for example, a persuasive or a reflective speech to a class) when we consider oral texts. Below are some other types of oral texts, each of which involves a particular relationship between speaker and audience.

- Debate
- Lecture
- Eulogy
- Dramatic performance (group or monologue)
- Electronic or multimedia presentation
- Interview
- Working group discussion
- Panel discussion

Giving a talk

The key to presenting an effective talk is being prepared. This involves knowing who the audience is, what you are going to say and how you will say it.

Six signals every audience wants to hear

In his excellent book, *The Overnight Guide to Public Speaking*, Ed Wohlmuth lists six signals that all audiences want to hear.

1   I will not waste your time.
2   I know who you are.
3   I am well organised.
4   I know my subject.
5   Here is my most important point.
6   I am finished.

Wohlmuth makes it clear that you don't have to say these words, but you do have to give these signals in what you say and do in your talk. This means that you should do the following.

1   Get down to business quickly, and make sure that everything you say is relevant to your subject.
2   Make your audience aware that you know them and their interests and/or problems.
3   Tell the audience how your talk is organised. (This is like the introduction of a written essay.)
4   Let your audience know that you understand your topic. Give them credit for what they already know.

ISBN 9780170183048

5   Present your most important point with a two-part signal: the first, to warn the audience that you are about to make your key point; and the second, to let them know that this is the vital point.

6   Signal that your talk is about to finish. Always end on a positive note.

Preparing your talk

1   Make sure you know what is expected of you.
    • The precise topic
    • The purpose of the talk
    • The length of the talk

2   Think about what you are going to say. Research your topic by reading and collecting information from all available sources.

3   Gather your notes and think about the ideas, information and arguments you will use.

4   Write out some notes in point form to help you think about:
    • how you will begin
    • how you will organise the body of your talk
    • what your main point will be
    • how you will finish.

Opening

Your opening should attempt to capture the audience's interest. You could do this by:
• telling a story that is relevant to your topic
• using a quotation that illustrates a point you wish to make
• asking a question that challenges the audience to think about your topic
• mentioning some information which shows the audience that your talk is important to them.

Body of the talk

The way you organise your talk will vary with the material you use and your purpose in giving the talk, but you will always need an introduction and a conclusion.
    Here are some suggested ways to organise the body of your talk.
• If you are giving a talk about a trip you have made, you might relate three incidents that give a good idea of what the trip was like.
• If you are explaining how to do something, you might divide it into five essential steps and talk about each of these.
• If you want to put one side of a case – for example, opposing the logging of rainforests – you might discuss four main reasons for holding your views. You need to give some examples to support your position.
• If you want to examine both sides of one issue, you might choose three main points and discuss these one at a time. Discuss both sides of each point before moving on to the next point.

Conclusion

The conclusion might involve:
• summing up what you have said in your talk
• asking the audience to take some action or to accept your viewpoint.

5   Now use these notes to help you to write a first draft of your talk.

6   Are there any sections of your talk that need to be filled out with more detail or examples? Is there anything that is not strictly relevant and could be left out?

7   Look at your first draft and think about Wohlmuth's six signals. If these are not already part of your talk, add them now.

ISBN 9780170183048

8 Read your speech aloud.
  • How close are you to the time allocated for your talk?
  • How could you improve the talk?
  • Are there any charts, diagrams or pictures that you could use in PowerPoint to reinforce a point you wish to make?

9 When you are satisfied with your draft, write a final version of the talk.

10 Go through your final draft, looking for places to pause (mark these) and words or phrases that need to be emphasised (underline these). You should also underline your versions of the six signals that all audiences want to hear.

11 Summarise your talk on small, numbered, palm-sized cards (called 'palm cards' or 'cue cards'). Use only key headings and subheadings to help you remember what you want to say.

Presenting your talk

Once you are clear about what you want to say, you are free to concentrate on how to deliver your talk.

It is important that you rehearse your talk. Some people use a tape recorder to practise with, while others rehearse in front of a mirror, or with a small audience of friends, or in front of parents.

1 You need to speak loudly, clearly and at a reasonable pace.

2 It is important to keep eye contact with the audience. You don't need to focus on individuals, but people in the audience will have trouble listening to you unless you seem to be looking at them. Try moving your eyes around the entire audience.

3 Having to keep eye contact with the audience means that you can only look briefly at your notes. Pause when you need to look at your palm cards. Wait until you've checked your next point, then re-establish eye contact with the audience before continuing your talk. Know what's on the palm cards, so that you only need to glance at them.

4 Know your opening and conclusion really well. It is worth learning these by heart and practising them many times.

5 Emphasise any important points you are making.

6 Pause to give the audience time to think after each section of your talk.

7 Appropriate gestures can help you emphasise the important points you want to make, but don't overdo them. The best gestures are those that appear natural, usually because they have been carefully rehearsed. If you are not at ease with gestures, don't use them.

8 The correct way to begin is by addressing the chairperson who introduced you, and then the audience: 'Chairperson, ladies and gentlemen'.

9 Do not begin by saying, 'My topic today is …'. The chairperson who introduces you should tell the audience your topic. Check beforehand to make sure that you and your topic will be introduced. You can then get into your talk immediately.

10 Do not finish by thanking the audience. They will thank you by applauding.

ACTIVITY 65

Giving a talk

1 Choose one of the following topics and prepare a talk about it.
  a Whaling should be banned.
  b If only …
  c Tomorrow?
  d Rescue your skin
  e Beat the end-of-year rush: fail your exams now!
  f All students should be made to work part-time.

ISBN 9780170183048

2 Prepare your talk by following these steps.
  a Analyse the topic by underlining the key words. These aspects must be addressed in your talk.
  b Write down the purpose of your talk.
  c Identify your audience.
  d Estimate the length of your talk.
  e Write out the opening line of your talk – something that will capture your audience.
  f In point form, outline the body of your talk, including the conclusion.
3 Summarise the first 10 key points about preparing a talk (these are listed on pages 157 and 158).
4 Read the extract below, which is part of a talk by Jacob Coote, a student in *Looking for Alibrandi* by Melina Marchetta. Answer the questions that follow.

> He shook his head and gave a little laugh.
>
> 'And I felt lucky. Because we have a choice, and I think that we vote, not to get the best party in, but to keep the worst party out. Because we can stand here and protest. We can get all riled up about the Premier's ideas. We can say he's a dickhead even. We can call the Prime Minister and the Leader of the Opposition one as well.
>
> 'We can scream and shout and protest and even burn our flag if we want to. Because we're free to do whatever we want to do and if we break the law we get a fair trial.
>
> 'But in some countries, people can't do that. They can't go out into places like Martin Place and protest. In some countries people our age can't concentrate on their schoolwork or their lives because of the sound of gun-fire.
>
> 'In some countries they have one-party systems and they have things called the People's Army and when people come out and have a say like we're doing today – scream and shout and voice their opinion – the People's Army shoots the people. Young people like us,' he added in almost a whisper.

  a What do you think the topic is?
  b Explain the purpose of his talk and identify his audience.
  c What part of his talk is presented in this extract? Explain.
  d In the first line he 'gave a little laugh'. Do you think he was trying to be humorous? Explain.
  e Read this part of his talk aloud using the 10 points on page 158.

Making an electronic presentation

The invention of software such as PowerPoint made electronic presentations simple – so simple that it was assumed that the addition of slides to an oral presentation would make that presentation more interesting. Most of us have sat through enough boring electronic presentations to know that this is not necessarily the case.

An electronic presentation must be planned with the same care as you bring to other kinds of oral presentations. Well-chosen and well-designed slides will enhance your presentation. The ability to incorporate audio and/or video clips and links to Internet sites can enrich your talk, but the material selected must fit into your planned structure. It is important to remember these points.

1   This is a visual medium. Where possible, use images, rather than words, to convey your message.

2   The slide templates encourage you to use bullet points. Keep these brief. You will be talking around these points; you do not need to put on the screen everything you intend to say.

3   Limit the amount of text on each slide and ensure the font size is large enough to be read comfortably in the back row of the room in which you will be presenting.

4   Never read your slides aloud; the audience can read silently much more quickly than you can read aloud.

5   There are many clever features available – such as flashy transitions – but keep them to a minimum. You do not want to distract from what you have to say.

6   Too many font types and too many different colours will distract your audience.

7   A good electronic slide show is an aid to your oral presentation, not a replacement for it.

Key words

The **background** or template is the overall design of the slide. You can choose a design from the program or create your own.

The **font** is the style of printing or writing.

Transition is the feature you choose to move from one slide to the next. Sound effects can be used during transitions to add interest or impact.

Build is the way to bring individual parts of a slide such as headings and dot points onto the screen. This allows the audience to stay focused on the point under discussion.

Graphics are the cartoons, pictures, diagrams and photographs you want to use. Recolouring allows you to change the colour of a graphic so that it matches your background colour scheme. You can also insert sound effects, music and film clips.

Creating an electronic slide presentation

Before creating a slide presentation, it is best to plan exactly which slides you will need – the content, format, style, number and sequence. You can do this on paper first, or edit your work on screen. Ideally, you should use the slide sequence to supplement and enhance your presentation, rather than making it your primary means of communication. The best way to do this is to have only an outline or a summary of your material on screen. You can then elaborate and explain your points to your audience, ensuring that your presentation has a lively, 'human' dimension.

A good PowerPoint presentation …

- programs transitions to move from left to right and top to bottom
- uses no more than two or three transition styles per presentation
- matches the speed of transitions with the subject of the presentation
- uses relevant graphics and sounds that are interesting but not distracting
- presents information in summary form, set out as points; text building is not overdone
- uses appropriate colour and background design to engage the audience
- is consistent with font style and size, heading size and use of capitals

ISBN 9780170183048

Working in small groups

Every time you work in groups, you need to have a specific goal to achieve or a task to perform. Your task is likely to vary at different stages of the learning process.

- You might be attempting to clarify new information.
- Your group might be completing a task. Often you will be expected to present the results to another audience, possibly a sharing group or the whole class.
- Your task might be to reflect on what you have learnt. You may also be asked to discuss how effectively you have worked and how you can improve.

The following points should help your group to operate more effectively.

- Develop a set of rules to guide you. Do you need to assign specific roles (a group leader, a recorder, a spokesperson) or is this not necessary for the kind of work you will be doing?
- Gain experience. The more you work in groups, the better at it you will become.
- Reflect on what you do. It is useful to think about and discuss how well your group has worked and how it can improve.

Characteristics of effective and ineffective groups

Effective groups		Ineffective groups	
1	The atmosphere tends to be informal, comfortable. People are involved and interested.	1	The atmosphere reflects either indifference or boredom.
2	There is a lot of discussion in which everyone takes part. Everyone keeps to the point.	2	Only one or two people talk. Little effort is made to keep to the point of the discussion.
3	Everybody understands their individual task.	3	It is difficult to understand what the group task is.
4	The group members listen to each other. Every idea is given a hearing.	4	People do not really listen to each other. Some ideas are not put forward to the group.
5	There is disagreement. The group is comfortable with this and works towards sorting it out. Nobody feels unhappy with the decisions made.	5	Disagreements are not dealt with effectively. They are put to the vote without being discussed. Some people are unhappy with the decisions.
6	People feel free to criticise and say honestly what they think.	6	People are not open about what they are thinking. They grumble about decisions afterwards.
7	Everybody knows how everybody else feels about what is being discussed.	7	One or two people are dominant. What they say goes.
8	When action needs to be taken, everyone is clear about what has to be done, and they help each other.	8	Nobody takes any interest in what has to be done, and nobody offers to help others.
9	Different people informally assume a leadership role from time to time.	9	Only one or two people make the decisions.
10	The group is conscious of how well it is working and of what is interfering with its progress. It can look after itself.	10	The group does not talk about how it is working or about the problems it is facing. It needs someone to look after it.

Adapted from Douglas McGregor 1960, *The Human Side of Enterprise*, McGraw-Hill, New York.

Debating

A debate is a verbal contest between two opposing teams. There are different kinds of debates, but the format discussed here is that used in most school and university debating competitions.

The topic of the debate is expressed as a hypothesis such as 'That Australians take sport too seriously' or 'That rabbits should be green and two metres tall'.

The Affirmative team must affirm or prove the hypothesis being debated.

The role of the Negative team is to negate or disprove the hypothesis or to prevent the other team from proving it.

Each team consists of three speakers. The debate is controlled by a chairperson who works with a timekeeper to make sure that each team has the same amount of time in which to argue its case. The winning team is decided by an adjudicator or a panel of adjudicators.

Order of speakers

First speaker, Affirmative
First speaker, Negative
Second speaker, Affirmative
Second speaker, Negative
Third speaker, Affirmative
Third speaker, Negative

Times

Both sides are allocated the same amount of time. Speakers are penalised for going under or over time. Usually, the first two speakers are given the same amount of time and the third speakers have longer (for example: 3, 3 and 4 minutes; 4, 4 and 6 minutes; 5, 5 and 7 minutes; 6, 6 and 8 minutes; 8, 8 and 10 minutes). The times must be agreed upon before preparation for the debate begins.

Debating duties

Affirmative team

First speaker, Affirmative

1 Introduces the Affirmative team and outlines the aspects of the topic to be tackled by each speaker.
2 Explains the Affirmative's definition of the topic, using dictionary definitions of individual words, and the team's interpretation of the topic as a whole.
3 Explains the team's central argument.
4 Begins the argument for the Affirmative team. Covers at least one major aspect of the topic.

Second speaker, Affirmative

1 Rebuts the points made by the first speaker, Negative.
2 Presents the major part of the Affirmative team's argument, covering at least two major aspects of the topic.
3 Emphasises the team's central argument.

Third speaker, Affirmative

1 Rebuts the arguments of the second (and, where possible, the first) speaker, Negative.
2 Attacks the opposition's central argument.
3 Concludes the argument for the Affirmative, covering at least one major aspect of the topic.
4 Summarises the Affirmative team's argument, explaining how each speaker contributed to the case developed by the team.

ISBN 9780170183048

Negative team

First speaker, Negative

1   Introduces the Negative team and outlines the aspects of the topic to be tackled by each speaker.
2   Has a definition of the topic to suit the Negative team. Agrees or disagrees with the Affirmative definition.
3   Rebuts the arguments of the first speaker, Affirmative.
4   Explains the team's central argument.
5   Begins the argument for the Negative team. Covers at least one major aspect of the topic.

Second speaker, Negative

1   Rebuts the points made by the second speaker, Affirmative.
2   Presents the major part of the Negative team's argument, covering at least two major aspects of the topic.
3   Emphasises the team's central argument.

Third speaker, Negative

1   Rebuts the arguments of the third speaker, Affirmative, and then of the other members of the opposition.
2   Attacks the opposition's central argument.
3   Summarises the Negative team's argument, explaining how each speaker contributed to the case developed by the team. Pays particular attention to the team's central argument. May not introduce any new material.

Instructions to chairperson

1   Introduce the topic to be debated.
2   Introduce the two teams, the Affirmative and then the Negative.
3   Check that the adjudicators are ready and then introduce each speaker before they speak.
4   Thank each speaker after they finish.
5   Request that the timekeeper pass on the speakers' times to the adjudicators.
6   Call for questions from the audience after the debate has finished (while the adjudicators are preparing to announce the result).
7   Call on the chief adjudicator to announce the result and comment on the debate.
8   Call on the leader of the winning and then the losing team to thank the adjudicators, the opposition and the audience.
9   Thank the adjudicators, the teams and the audience and close the debate.

Instructions to debaters

1   The correct way to begin your speech is by addressing the chairperson and the audience: 'Chairperson, ladies and gentlemen'. Do not start by saying 'Today's debate is …' as the chairperson has already informed the audience of the topic.
2   Your opening is vital if you hope to capture the audience's attention. Work hard on preparing an interesting opening and try to memorise it.
3   A forceful conclusion is also an important element of a successful debating speech. It is worth memorising this too.
4   Do not thank the audience. They will thank you with a round of applause.

Instructions to timekeeper

1   Start timing from the moment the speaker begins to talk.
2   Ring a warning bell for each speaker when there is one minute to go.
3   Ring a final bell for each speaker when time is up.
4   Note the exact time taken by each speaker.

Instructions to the adjudicators

1   Use an adjudication sheet (such as the one on page 165) to make sure that all speakers are assessed on the same terms.
2   Indicate to the chairperson when you have finished assessing each speaker and are ready for the debate to continue.
3   After giving your verdict, explain the reasons behind your decision.

Preparing for the debate

Working out a team case

1   Make sure you know:
    • the duties of each speaker
    • what the adjudicators are looking for.
    Check, first, the section on 'Debating duties' and the 'Instructions to debaters' and, second, the sample adjudication sheet.
2   Brainstorm the topic. Jot down in point form as many different ideas about it as you can think of. Discuss the topic and organise your thoughts into a number of major issues or arguments.
3   Define the topic. Look up the meaning of each key word in more than one dictionary. Decide on a reasonable definition, preferably one that will suit your side of the argument.
4   Write in order to clarify your thoughts on the topic and especially on your side of the debate.
5   Decide on a central argument to provide the cornerstone of your case. In considering the topic, 'That Australians take sport too seriously', the Affirmative side might build its case around the idea that Australians take sport seriously, but problems arise because they take it too seriously. On the other hand, the Negative team might take as its central argument that sport needs to be taken seriously and Australians take it just seriously enough.

Writing your speeches

1   After deciding on your central argument, decide on the order in which you will speak. The third speaker needs to do most rebuttal of the opposition's arguments and so needs to be able to think on their feet. Choose your final speaker with this in mind.
2   Allocate different aspects of the topic to each speaker.
3   Each speaker will need to do some research to find evidence to support the arguments you wish to make. Examples that prove your point are an essential ingredient of a debate. Before writing your speeches, discuss your examples with the rest of the team to make sure there is no overlap.
4   Refer to the 'Debating duties' section on pages 162–3 to make sure that you know all your tasks and how to organise the various sections of your speech.

Rehearsing your speeches

1   After writing a first draft of your speech, go through this with other members of your team. Make sure that the team's central argument is clearly outlined in each speech. Check that each speech covers some major aspects of the topic. Help each other to make your examples as interesting and persuasive as possible.
2   Check each speech against the 'Debating duties' section. Make sure that all the necessary duties have been carried out effectively.
3   Practise rehearsing your speeches by presenting them to each other. Offer each other critical comments to help sharpen up your arguments.
4   Think of some of the arguments that the opposition will use against you. Rehearse ways of answering these arguments. Attempt to find evidence to back up your rebuttal.

ISBN 9780170183048

5   When you are confident that your speech is ready, make a summary of it in point form. Write this on palm-sized cards small enough to conceal in your hands while you are speaking. These should be all you need to remind you of the points you want to make. Do not attempt to read your speech word for word from notes as this will not allow you to make eye contact with the audience.

6   As palm cards can be difficult to use, rehearse your speech a few times to get used to handling them. Make up a few blank cards so that you can write down points to rebut while you are listening to the opposition's speeches.

7   You will probably feel nervous as you stand up to talk. This is quite normal. As long as you are thoroughly prepared, you should be able to stand up to the ordeal – and even enjoy it.

Sample adjudication sheet

(Place ticks in the appropriate columns.)

	Affirmative						Negative					
	1st		2nd		3rd		1st		2nd		3rd	
	Yes	No	Yes	No	Yes	No	Yes	No	Yes	No	Yes	No
Matter (what was said)												
1 Were the arguments interesting and logical?												
2 Was there evidence of research and accurate information?												
3 Was the subject understood and explained clearly?												
Method (how the speech was set out)												
1 Was the speech well put together?												
2 Was the speaker's time used to good effect?												
3 Did the speaker demonstrate evidence of good teamwork?												
4 Did the speaker refute the opposition's arguments accurately?												
Manner (the speaker's style)												
1 Could the speaker be heard easily?												
2 Did the speaker use their voice to advantage?												
3 Was the speaker's choice of language appropriate?												
4 Were the speaker's notes unobtrusive?												
5 Did the speaker's general appearance suggest confidence?												
6 Did the speaker seem to believe in what was being said?												
7 Was the speaker persuasive?												
Total for each speaker	**Affirmative total** ____ ticks						**Negative total** ____ ticks					

ACTIVITY 66

Debating

Debate one of the following topics.
1 That university entry should be open to anyone over 17
2 That the only true democracy is one in which 50 per cent of those in parliament are women
3 That academic excellence is more important than excellence in sport
4 That music should be compulsory in secondary schools

Interviews

Interviews enable us to get inside people's heads: to hear their personal feelings, ideas and opinions. The success of an interview depends on how prepared and skilful the interviewer is. It also depends on how the interviewer relates to the interviewee. There are 11 steps to conducting a good interview.

1 Decide who to interview and the topic you want to cover – issues, personal achievements, beliefs. Write down the topics you wish to cover and create a list of possible questions.

2 Contact the interviewee by phone, letter or email saying why you want to do the interview, the topics you wish to cover and suggesting a suitable time and place.

3 Research some background details on the interviewee: achievements, opinions, experiences.

4 Prepare your questions. Ten to 15 main questions is usually enough, with a few offshoot questions on each one. Learn your questions off by heart, but be prepared to alter and add new questions during the interview.

5 Collect your equipment: pen and notebook, spare batteries and digital voice recorder. Check that your recorder is working.

6 Choose clothing and appearance that are appropriate for your interviewee and the topic. Your appearance will affect how your interviewee responds to you.

7 Organise your transport so that you arrive at the interview on time. It is better to be a little early than late.

8 Introduce yourself and thank the interviewee for their participation. Ask for permission to use the recorder and ensure that it is as close as possible to the interviewee without being intrusive.

9 Control the interview. Make sure you:
- are respectful of the person's ideas and feelings
- are confident
- let the person speak freely without interruption
- don't talk about yourself unless asked, and then only briefly
- are ready to ask questions that you have not prepared
- check your question sheet to ensure you have not forgotten any important points.

10 Thank the person at the end of the interview and explain that you will be sending them a copy of your report.

11 Complete your report after the interview. Have the interviewee check your report before you publish or broadcast it.

ISBN 9780170183048

Interview checklist

Use a checklist such as this to organise your interview.

Step	Action	Date completed
1 Decide	Brainstorm to choose a topic and an interviewee.	
2 Contact	Ring, write or email the interviewee.	
3 Research	Find out background information.	
4 Prepare	Create questions.	
5 Collect	Organise equipment.	
6 Choose	Select clothing.	
7 Organise	Sort out transport.	
8 Introduce	Prepare introduction.	
9 Control	Follow the 11 rules.	
10 Report	Prepare report, check with interviewee, publish	

12 VIEWING IMAGES: THE CONVENTIONS OF VISUAL GRAMMAR

Studying visual images is important because, in the digital age:

- we are surrounded by visual images and icons that are central to communication in everyday life
- many texts in our society are multimodal, involving images as well as print – and often other modes as well, such as sound and lighting
- our ability to read visual texts depends on a knowledge of the conventions, in the same way as the reading of print texts does.

This chapter focuses on the conventions used to read an image. The next chapter looks at visual text types, where images interact with other modes, such as written text, sound and lighting.

Balance

An image maker makes constant choices about such elements as colour, line, shape and texture. One or more elements may be dominant. The term 'balance' is used to discuss the choices that have been made: the image maker may, for example, have made colour the dominant element because a particular emotion needed to be created, or angular shapes may have been selected to depict a cold, mechanistic world.

The term 'balance' is also used to refer to the way the objects within an image are arranged or composed. We tend to prefer images that are composed in an harmonious way: if objects are out of balance, we may be a little uneasy. Of course, an image maker may deliberately set out to cause uncomfortable or even shocking feelings.

Colour

Colour, which is technically referred to as 'hue', is an important contributor to the meaning of a visual text. The meanings attached to colours are different in different cultures and are learnt in childhood. For example, in Western culture, red frequently symbolises danger, whereas in Chinese culture it represents good luck. The term 'saturation' is used to describe the amount of grey present in a particular colour. A black-and-white image, which will probably have shades of grey, is completely unsaturated, whereas a brightly coloured display advertisement is highly saturated, with very little grey in any of the colours. Image makers make choices about their use of colour – depending on their purpose – and about the degree of saturation. Codes of colour and degrees of saturation matter because colours affect our emotional response to images; for example, colours with low saturation – such as black, white and grey – may be seen as uninteresting, or even depressing, but they can also have the effect of seeming peaceful. In contrast, in some images highly saturated colours can seem bright and cheerful, while in others they might suggest an unappealing gaudiness. Your role as the reader of the image is to interpret the particular meanings the image maker wants to convey.

ISBN 9780170183048

Always Adam is a story about a boy who migrated from the old world in the nineteenth century to the promised land of America. The first half of the book, the part of the story set in the old world, is in black and white. The second half is in bright – almost garish – colours.

Ziba Came on a Boat is the story of a little girl from Afghanistan whose family has been forced to leave their home. She makes the perilous journey to Australia on a small boat. The scenes of the journey are painted in a bleak grey/blue. The scenes of the home she remembers are in warm ochre.

Contextualised and decontextualised

'Contextualised' and 'decontextualised' are terms used to explain whether or not a visual image has a detailed setting. A contextualised image contains enough information to make the setting of the image obvious to the viewer. If an image is decontextualised, there is little or no information about the setting.

Foreground and background

The elements in an image which are closest to the viewer are part of the foreground, whereas those elements that are most distant from the viewer are part of the background.

Gorilla is the story of a little girl whose father is always too busy to spend time with her. A picture of her trying to get his attention is tightly framed, with lots of other frames within the main frame. The final happy image as they walk off together hand in hand has no frame as they are no longer restricted.

Framing, frame breaking and bleeding

Visual images may be framed or unframed. Frames are used to set limits to what the reader is viewing and to make an image feel contained. Frames can even be used within an image: for example, a character may be presented framed by a doorway. Sometimes the framing of an image is interrupted at some time; we use the term 'frame breaking' to describe this. The term 'bleeding' is used to describe an image that appears to have no bounds. For example, in many picture books the reader has a sense of continuity of the story and setting because pictures not only bleed outside the double-page spread but into the next spread.

Intertextuality

Image makers, like all artists and writers, draw on and remake the traditions of their culture. While each new text might seem unique, we understand it because it uses codes and conventions with which we are already familiar. This is true even of texts that deliberately subvert or break away from the traditions of the past. The term 'intertextuality' refers, in a sense, to the fact that all texts are interconnected and the meanings we make from a text are a result of our knowledge of what has gone before. A simple example is the old-fashioned Western: we know that the goodie is the guy wearing the white hat. A modern film maker, wanting to show that judgements about good and evil are rarely as clear-cut as in these old films, might play with this convention in some way, but our knowledge of the convention helps us understand the new meaning.

ISBN 9780170183048

Layout

Layout is the placement of elements in a text. The way in which the elements are composed determines the order in which we read them and, to some extent, what sense we make of them.

The issues to do with layout vary, depending on the genre and the medium. The layout considerations, for example, for a print-based report are different from the layout consideration for a web page. Most of a print-based report will be read in a traditional linear manner, reading from left to right, while a web page is usually read in a circular fashion.

Layout is particularly important with multimodal texts, where components from different modes must be interrelated in an engaging and accessible way. The elements to consider in the layout of a multimodal text include:

- visual text, such as images, diagrams and charts, tables and moving images
- audio text, such as voice, music and sound effects
- navigational devices, such as logos, symbols and icons
- print material, such as headings and labels, body text, captions and links.

Line and shape

The term 'line' is important when talking about visual images because lines are the means by which recognisable shapes are represented. By using different kinds of lines, image makers can achieve different moods or emotions in an image. Lines can also be used to indicate movement in an image. In cartoons and animation, motion lines are used to show actions and direction of movement across panels or frames.

Lines can differ in:

- thickness
- texture
- density.

They can be:

- solid
- shaded
- cross-hatched.

Lines are used to form shapes. The term 'shape' refers to the outline or contour of an object. All shapes have relationships to geometrical patterns, even abstract shapes. The viewer recognises an object by comparing its shape to shapes previously experienced. There are four basic shapes that underlie all others.

- The circle
- The square
- The triangle
- The rectangle

For example, a circle can become an oval and a rectangle may not have equal sides. Many objects are made up of several shapes. The extent to which a shape is rounded or angular can affect the way in which we read an image: rounded shapes, for example, tend to suggest comfort and security.

Offers and demands

When the subject of a visual text looks directly at you, making eye contact, there is a high degree of personal involvement invited by the image. The term used to describe this type of gaze is 'demand', as the subject of the image seems to be demanding that we respond in some way.

The effect is very different when the subject of an image is looking away from you. The viewer is not invited to have any social interaction with the subject. The term used to describe this type of gaze is 'offer' because the subject of the image is offered to the viewer for study.

These World War I propaganda posters are a great example of the use of the direct gaze.

Perspective

The term 'perspective' refers to a technique common in Western art where space and lines are used to indicate depth in a visual image.

Portrait and landscape

The terms 'portrait' and 'landscape' are used to describe the orientation of an image. An image that is in portrait view is longer than it is wide; the vertical axis is more important. In contrast, an image that is in landscape view is one which is wider than it is long; the horizontal axis is more important. You are probably familiar with choosing portrait or landscape when printing from a word-processing program.

The reading path

In Western culture our reading of visual texts tends to be circular: that is, our eyes travel around the image. The term for the movement of the viewer's gaze around the visual image is 'the reading path'. Reading paths are not exactly the same for everyone. Because we read in a circular way, viewers may enter the reading path at different points of the circle, depending on which element first attracts the eye.

ISBN 9780170183048

Salience

The term 'salience' refers to the prominent element of a visual text: that is, the item in the image (the element) that first attracts the viewer's gaze. What is most salient in a visual image is affected by a number of possible combinations of factors, including:

- size
- shape
- colour
- contrast of colours
- distance from the camera or viewer
- sharpness of focus.

Social distance

The term 'social distance' refers to the way we read and interact with objects in an image depending on how close or far away the image makes them seem. You are probably most familiar with this idea from film, where the camera zooms in and out from people or objects, changing their social distance from us. The extreme close up or detail shot focuses on a part of an object or person; that part fills the whole image. In contrast, an extreme long shot shows scenery or characters far in the distance.

The terms that are most commonly used are:

- extreme close up
- close up
- medium shot
- long shot
- extreme long shot.

Texture

Some book covers have embossed or raised lettering or images that invite us to touch. The term used to describe this raised surface is 'texture'. Many images, however, simulate texture: they are made to look the way we imagine they would feel. Jagged lines and cross-hatchings might indicate, for example, the roughness of rocks. Thick black lines might indicate an animal's matted fur.

Typography

The term 'typography' refers to the layout of printed text on the page. It covers font styles, sizes and spacing, as well as the positioning or formatting of the text on the page. A well-known traditional example of using non-linear typography is the shape poem, where the layout of the text is actually integral to the meaning of the poem.

In the digital age, poets have experimented with moving type. Film makers frequently use text that scrolls across the screen – or that zooms in or out. Even in PowerPoint presentations we can use typography that moves in various ways.

Picture-book composers have long made use of the possibilities.

Vanishing point

Lines or vectors in an image seem to converge and disappear, usually on a horizon. The spot where they disappear is called the 'vanishing point'.

Vectors

The term 'vector' is used to describe the elements of a visual text that function almost like pointers to direct our eyes around the image. The vectors determine our reading path around an image. Sometimes a vector is implied – for example, when the subject of an image is looking at an object within the image, our eyes tend to follow the line of gaze.

Vertical and horizontal axes

The term 'axes' refers to the powerful vectors in the layout of an image that lead our eye to read from left to right (the horizontal axis) and from top to bottom (the vertical axis). In reading some images, recognising the axes is very important. A portrait is an easy example of an image in which the vertical axis dominates. In a photograph or painting of a landscape, the horizontal axis is usually more significant.

Viewing angle

The angle from which we view an image affects the way we read that image and relate to the objects or people in it. When the elements of an image are viewed from above, the term used is 'high-angle view'; the viewer looks down on the image. A high-angle image may make the elements of the image seem smaller and less important. In contrast, a 'low-angle view' involves the viewer looking up at the image. This may make the image seem larger and more important, even overpowering. It is also possible to have an 'eye-level view', where the viewer and the subject of the image are roughly on the same level. This again affects the way we relate to the image. It gives us a sense of equality and involvement. The term 'bird's-eye view' refers to an image where the elements are presented as if seen from directly overhead.

ISBN 9780170183048

Visual texts are pictures – still, moving or electronic. Like written and spoken texts, visual texts or images follow conventions which allow us to make sense of what we are seeing. We 'decode' visual texts almost without thinking. We rely on images to tell stories, convey warnings, sell products, create an impression, represent organisations, and to make people laugh and cry. Street signs, company logos, greeting cards, cartoons, films, advertisements, graffiti, photographs, sculpture, websites and book covers are all examples of visual texts.

Cartoons

Cartoons are drawings that comment on the amusing, quirky or controversial aspects of everyday life. Cartoons are frequently satirical; that is, they ridicule people, situations and events, prompting us to reflect on important social issues. Political or editorial cartoons can be quite savage in their attacks on public figures and current social issues. Other cartoons may intend simply to entertain and to highlight human weaknesses and peculiarities.

Cartoons combine written and visual language to provoke their audience into feeling amused, angry, ashamed or even saddened. Cartoonists also rely on their audience's knowledge of current events and concerns. In order to get the joke, we need to be able to recognise the references the cartoon makes to the society and culture to which we belong.

In order to create memorable and engaging cartoons, consider the following conventions.

Visuals

- **Caricature**: the exaggeration of particular bodily features so that a cartoon character is recognisable and ridiculous.
- **Body language and facial expression**: humour can be created through gestures; a sense of movement can also be conveyed.
- **Clothing**: this can help to identify characters.
- **Size**: the relative size of characters and objects can signify particular relationships or status.
- **Setting**: this enables readers to understand the social context and the relevance of the cartoon.
- **Symbolism**: colours and objects can be used to represent ideas, people, places, attitudes or events.

Written text

- **Caption**: the 'punch line' of the cartoon. Many cartoons have no caption and rely on the impact of visual images.
- **Speech bubbles**: bring characters to life by giving them a voice.
- **Pun**: a 'play on words' or a word with a double meaning.
- **Irony**: occurs when words or images are intended to mean the opposite.
- **Hyperbole**: exaggeration.
- **Understatement**: when something is 'downplayed' for comic effect.

Note how some of these conventions are used in this cartoon.

Advertisements

The purpose of advertisements is to sell products. Successful print, television and Internet advertisements generally target a specific audience or consumer through appealing or striking visuals, written text or a combination of these. The most powerful advertising technique is an appeal to people's emotions so that they feel compelled to buy the product.

Advertisers frequently rely on stereotypes to appeal to their audience.

ISBN 9780170183048

What age group is the audience for this advertisement? Why do you think so?

What is the reading path here? What do you notice first? Where do your eyes travel next?

The focal character is using a direct gaze. What is the effect of this?

What is the point of using a celebrity as the focus of the advertisement?

This is a direct appeal to the reader. Is the pointing finger an example of intertextuality, reminding us of previous appeals such as the World War I posters on page 172?

JUSTIN BIEBER
FOR PeTA

ANIMALS CAN MAKE
U SMILE
ADOPT FROM YOUR LOCAL SHELTER.

What is the effect of the 'U' for 'you'?

How is colour used to make the words 'U SMILE' so prominent?

What is the purpose of the advertisement? How can you tell?

Websites

Websites are multimedia texts, as they combine a variety of media – visuals, sound and print – and consist of a range of text types. They are also interactive, non-linear texts: you can manipulate what you see on the computer screen and you can choose the order in which you read or view material. Websites are 'unstable' texts because they can be updated and altered. They may also consist of several 'pages', including a 'home page', which provides a guide to the contents of the whole site. Some of the many types of texts which can be found on websites include:

- film clips
- reviews
- diagrams
- graphics
- articles
- maps
- advertisements
- songs
- diary entries
- online forums.

Websites can have many different purposes: to entertain, to educate, to sell a product, to inform, to advertise or to provide a forum for sharing opinions.

Conventions of a website

For a website to be user-friendly and appealing to its audience, it needs to have some standard features. Most importantly, it must be easily accessible and quick to download.

A good website should be:	This is achieved through:
attention grabbing	• colour
	• graphics, including animation and rotating graphics
	• moving written text
	• sound effects
	• font style and size
well-organised	• clear headings and subheadings
	• information presented in columns or frames
	• bullet points
easy to navigate	• a 'search' function to help the viewer locate material and interact with the website
	• a home page with a site map of contents or navigational icons
	• prominent menu bars for navigating the website
	• quickly loaded graphics
up-to-date and relevant	• hyperlinks to external Internet sites or other information on the website

If you don't already know who Shaun Tan is (and you should), what can you tell about him from his home page?

Welcome page

Note the reading path, characteristic of a webpage: the eye is drawn first to the centre of the page and then moves around the page rather than from left to right, as in a print text.

Hyperlinks

Consistency of font and style

All the usual website features presented a bit differently

ISBN 9780170183048

The language of the Internet

Here are some useful website terms.

Banner: the headline at the top of a webpage

Bookmark: a hyperlink to a specific page of an Internet text

Breadcrumb trail: a navigation tool that enables the user to keep track of the location within a website. It usually looks like this: Home page>Section page>Subsection page. For example, Home>Televisions> Plasma screens

Domain name: the Internet address of a computer. A domain name indicates the origin of the site (e.g. au = Australia) and the type of organisation offering the site (e.g. edu = educational)

Download: to transfer material from a server or host computer to your own computer

Flash: a multimedia device that allows you to view animations

Frames: sections of text on a webpage

Freeware: copyright-free material that can be downloaded

Home page: the first page of a website

HTML: a language used to make webpages (Hypertext Markup Language)

Hyperlink: an instant link to another page or another site

Icon: a symbol representing a computer function or command

Menu bar: a list of contents on a website or window

Plug-in: an electronic device that enables access to video and sound

Podcast: an audio file that can be downloaded

Site map: a page that lists all the pages on a website, usually represented in a hierarchical form

Streaming media: live video and sound placed on a website

Toolbar: a group of icons representing frequently used computer functions

URL: a web address (Universal Resource Locator)

Vodcast: a video file that can be downloaded

Weblog (or **blog**): a webpage containing a regularly updated diary and space for a public forum. It may also include a gallery of images and hyperlinks.

Films

Films are narrative texts; that is, they tell a story. Whether the story is fictional, loosely based on reality or a documentary of 'real life', it follows the conventional narrative structure of an orientation, complication, climax and resolution. Films can be classified according to their 'genre' or style, including such popular film categories as:

- romantic comedy
- historical drama
- thriller
- science fiction
- action/adventure
- documentary.

As any list of credits will show, many individuals are required in the making of a film. The director – the person responsible for the overall appearance of a film – must enlist the expertise of people with a variety of skills (for example, screenwriters, actors, cinematographers, sound and lighting technicians, costume designers, special effects teams, set designers and editors).

The story of a film is told through a sequence of shots and through various symbolic codes that can be 'read' or interpreted by the audience. The director must make decisions about the following cinematographic (or film-making) codes.

Film codes

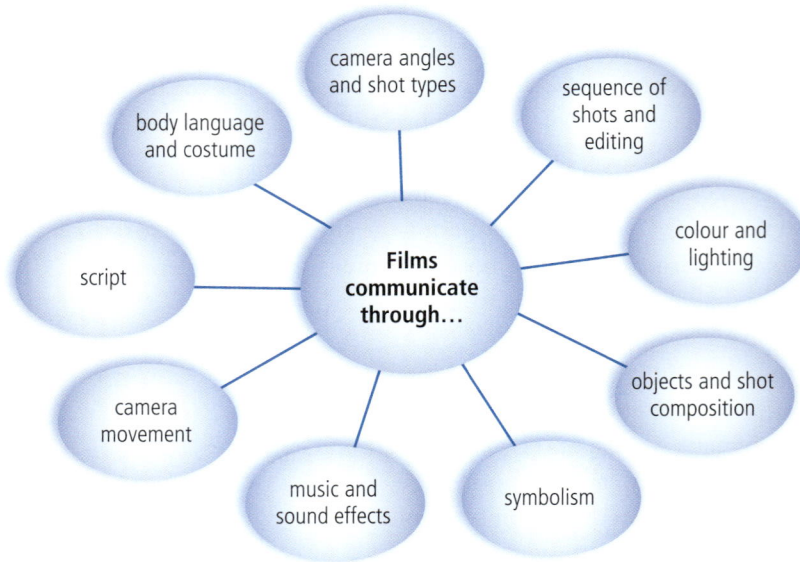

Understanding shots

With the help of a crew, a director determines the size, angle and movement of each shot or image filmed by the camera. Following is a list of camera terminology to help you appreciate the way films communicate to audiences.

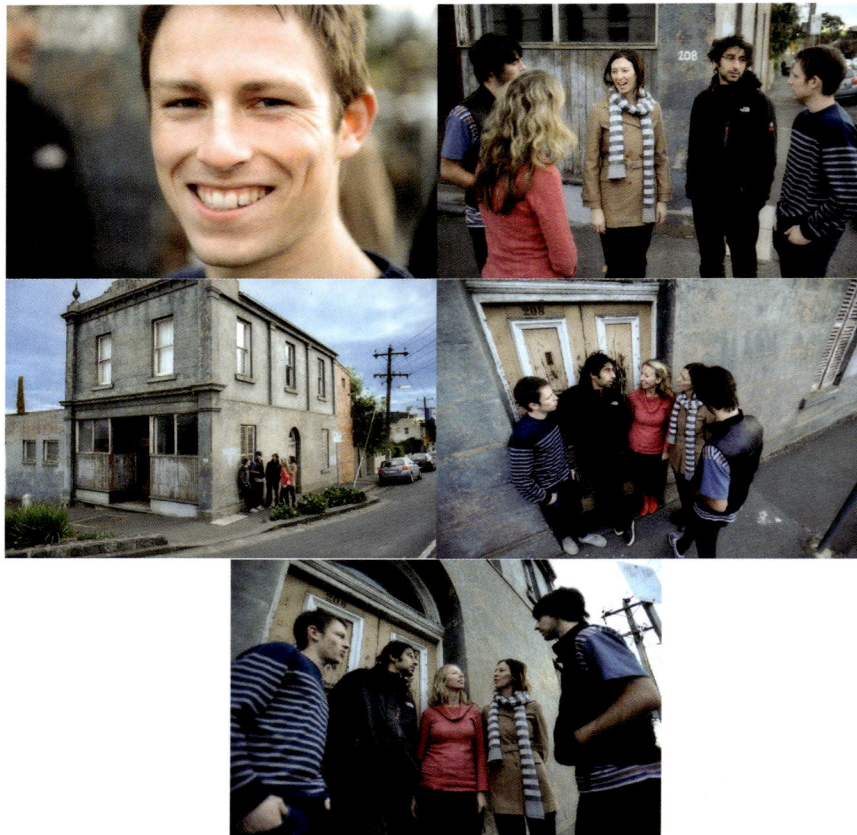

ISBN 9780170183048

Shot sizes

- Extreme close up (ECU)
- Close up (CU)
- Medium shot (MS)
- Long shot (LS)
- Extreme long shot (ELS)

Camera angles

- High-angle shot: the subject is filmed from above
- Eye-level shot: the subject is filmed at normal level
- Low-angle shot: the subject is filmed from below
- Overshot: the subject is filmed from directly overhead
- Undershot: the subject is filmed from directly underneath

Camera movement

- Panning: the camera moves horizontally, left to right or right to left
- Zoom: the camera moves from a distance to a close up
- Dolly shot: the camera moves on a trolley to follow the action
- Tilt shot: the camera moves vertically, up and down

Shot composition

The following still shots are from the film *Rabbit-Proof Fence*, directed by Phillip Noyce. Notice the shot composition – the way in which images are arranged in each shot. Another term for the placement of objects and figures in a shot is *mise en scène*, a French phrase meaning 'place in scene'.

Sample still shots

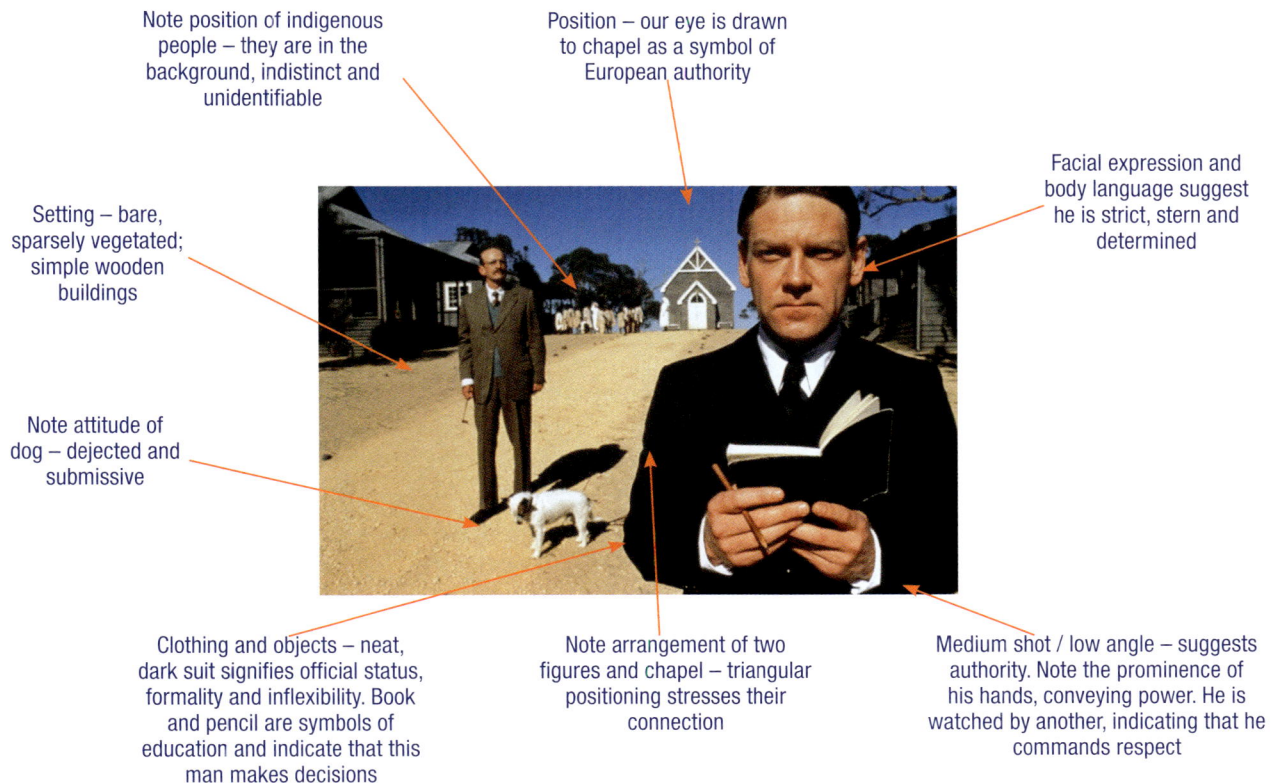

Note position of indigenous people – they are in the background, indistinct and unidentifiable

Position – our eye is drawn to chapel as a symbol of European authority

Facial expression and body language suggest he is strict, stern and determined

Setting – bare, sparsely vegetated; simple wooden buildings

Note attitude of dog – dejected and submissive

Clothing and objects – neat, dark suit signifies official status, formality and inflexibility. Book and pencil are symbols of education and indicate that this man makes decisions

Note arrangement of two figures and chapel – triangular positioning stresses their connection

Medium shot / low angle – suggests authority. Note the prominence of his hands, conveying power. He is watched by another, indicating that he commands respect

Body language – younger girl is cradled like a baby, her face hidden, which conveys her exhaustion and anxiety

Clothing – represents girls' poverty, suffering and intimacy (i.e. their clothes are identical)

Symbolism – fence signifies the European/Aboriginal cultural divide and the means of reaching home

Background – churning clouds convey feelings of trepidation and anxiety; the vastness of the landscape is also clear

Symbolism – eagle signifies freedom and strength

Lighting – symbolises girls' hope

Facial expression – fear? determination? confusion? confidence?

Position – figures placed in centre of frame to highlight the intensity of their experience

Low angle shot – suggests girls' power; our eye is drawn to the hand and face of the older girl

ACTIVITY 67

Cartoons

1 Design a cartoon that responds to a topical issue. Incorporate the features of a cartoon. You might choose one of the following issues to address.
- The environment (for example, global warming, recycling, land clearing)
- Technology (for example, the Internet, mobile phones, surveillance technology)
- Politics (for example, a federal campaign, international relations, political role-models)
- Sport (for example, sports celebrities, good or bad sporting conduct, drugs in sport)

Advertisements

2 Collect a range of print advertisements from such sources as newspapers, magazines, shopping catalogues, pamphlets or food packaging. For each advertisement, note:
- the product being advertised
- the target audience or consumer
- the advertising techniques used to sell the product.

Websites

3 Design a website for your school, using the conventions of websites listed on page 178. Incorporate your school's logo or symbol and motto, if it has one. Consider who would be most likely to use this site and the information that would be most useful to them. Consider the image of your school that you wish to promote. For example, you might emphasise the sporting program, the multicultural student body or the friendly, supportive atmosphere. Choose language and graphics that best suit your purpose. Think about some helpful hyperlinks you could include.

Films

4 Design a series of images to illustrate each type of camera shot and angle. Your illustrations should be suitable for publication in an education journal or textbook.

5 Imagine you are the director of *Rabbit-Proof Fence*. Write a short paragraph in which you discuss the use of cinematographic techniques in your film. Referring to the film stills provided, reflect on the visual impact you wished to create.

ISBN 9780170183048

INDEX

'a' (indefinite article)
   a or *an* 60
abbreviations 20, 28
absolute adjectives 50
abstract nouns 42
acronyms 28
action verbs 44
adjectives 49–50
   forms 50
   suffixes 18
adjudication sheet 165
adverbs 50, 51–2
   of manner 52
   of place 52
   recognising 52
   suffixes 18
   of time 52
advertisements 176–7
advice or *advise* 60–1
affect or *effect* 61
affirmative team (debating), duties 162
although or *though* 61
altogether or *all together* 61
American spelling 11
among or *amongst* 61
among or *between* 61–2
'an' (indefinite article) 56
and (as sentence opener) 57
apostrophes 21–2
applications
   job 134–8
   for work experience 136–7
argument text types 101, 104, 140–54
around or *round* 62
as or *like* 67
audience (for texts) 99, 152
auxiliary verbs 44–6

background (images) 169
balance (images) 168
better or *best* 62
between or *among* 61–2
between you and I 57
bleeding (images) 170
body (editorial) 146
body (news report) 126
body of the talk 157
bought or *brought* 62
brackets 23
British spelling 11
business letters 132–3
but
   at the end of a sentence 62
   as sentence opener 57
but, however or *yet* 62

camera angles 181
camera movement 181
can or *may* 62–3
cannot, can't or *can not* 63

can't hardly or *couldn't hardly* 63
capital letters 23–4
cartoons 175
   visuals 175
   written text 175–6
centre around or *centre on* 63
clauses 36
collective nouns 41
colons 25
colour (images) 168–9
commas 25–6
common nouns 41
comparative adjectives 50
complex sentence 37
compound sentence 37
compound-complex sentence 37
comprise 63
computer spell checks 12–13
conclusion (editorial) 146
conclusion (talk) 157
conjunctions 55
content words 41–52
contextualised 169
continual or *continuous* 64
contractions 21
contrast 64
coordinating conjunctions 55
could or *might* 64
could of or *could have* 64
couldn't hardly or *can't hardly* 63
criteria 64

dangling phrases 57
dashes 27
debating 162
   adjudicator's instructions 164
   affirmative and negative team
   duties 162–3
   chairperson's instructions 163
   debaters' instructions 163
   order of speakers 162
   preparing for the debate 164
   rehearsing your speeches 164–5
   timekeeper's instructions 163
   times 162
   writing your speeches 164
decontextualised 169
definite article 56
demands and offers (gaze) 171–2
demonstrative pronouns 53
descriptions (text types) 105–6, 121–2
determiners 56
developing an argument, approaches 140
   arguing for one point of view while also
     revealing the opposing viewpoint 141–2
   presenting an overview of both sides 142
   putting forward only your case or point
     of view 140–1
   reflecting on the issue without taking a
     personal stance 142

diagetic sound 124
dictionaries 19–20
different from, different to or *different than* 64
direct speech 32
discussion text types 144–5
disinterested or *uninterested* 65
documentaries, film and television 124
drama scripting 110–12

editorials 145–8
   structure 145–6
effect or *affect* 61
effective/ineffective groups 161
e.g. (for example) 65
ei or *ie* (spelling) 3
electronic presentation, making an 159–60
electronic slide presentation, creating 160
ellipsis points 27
enquiry or *inquiry* 65
envelopes, machine-addressed 134
essay writing
   and text types 103–4
   topic key words 103–4
etc. 65
everybody 58
everyone 58
everything 58
exclamation marks 28
explanations (text type) 118–19
expository text types 101

factual description 121
factual text types 101
feature articles 128–9
fewer or *less* 65
film reviews 152–4
   audience 152
   content 152
   structure 152
film and television documentaries 124
film and television scripting 113–15
films 179–82
   codes 180
   shots 180–2
first or *firstly* 65
foreground (images) 169
former and *latter* 66
frame breaking 170
frames (images) 170
full stops 28

gaze 171–2
got or *gotten* 66
grammar 35–59
   and usage 57–9
Greek roots 15
groups, effective and ineffective 161

hanging participles 57
headline (editorial) 145
headline (news report) 125

homophones 13
horizontal axis 174
however, but or *yet* 62
hue (images) 168
hyphens 29–30

i.e. (that is) 66
ie or *ei* (spelling) 3
imaginative text types 101, 105–17
imperative mood 45
imply or *infer* 66
indefinite article 56
indicative mood 45
infer or *imply* 66
infinitives 43
    split 59
inflection 40, 46
information reports 122–4
information text types 101, 104, 118–38
inquiry or *enquiry* 65
intensifiers 49
Internet terminology 179
interrogative pronouns 53
intertextuality 170
interviews 166–7
intransitive verbs 44
introduction (editorial) 145
introduction (news report) 126
inverted commas 31–3
italics 30–1
it's or *its* 66

job applications 134
    letter of application 134–5
    reading the advertisement 134
    résumés 135, 138–9
    ways of applying for a job 134–5
    work experience applications 136–7
    writing your application 135–6

landscape 172
Latin roots 15
latter and *former* 66
layout 171
'lead' paragraph 145
lend or *loan* 66
less or *fewer* 65
letter of application 134–5
letters 130
    business 132–3
    personal 130–2
letters to the editor 148
    before you begin 149
    opening your letter 149–50
    producing your final draft 151
    revising your letter 150
lexical words 41
like or *as* 67
lines (images) 171
linking verbs 44
literally 67

literary description 105–6
literary text types 101
loan or *lend* 66
loose or *lose* 67

machine-addressed envelopes 134
may or *can* 62–3
meaning of words 2, 20
media 67
might or *could* 64
modal auxiliary verbs 45
morphology 35

narratives (text types) 108–9, 179–82
negative team (debating), duties 163
newspaper reports 125
    structure 125–7
nice 68–9
none … is or *none … are* 58
noun–verb agreement 47–8
nouns 41–2
    categories of 41–2
    irregular plurals 4–5
    recognising 41
    suffixes 17–18

offers and demands (gaze) 171–2
one (pronoun) 69
opening (talk) 157
oral text types 156–67
origin of words 2–3

paragraphs 35
parentheses 23
participles
    hanging 57
    past 43
    present 43
passed or *past* 69
past participle 43
past tense 43–5
patterns in words 1, 3
personal letters 130
    closed punctuation,
        semi-blocked 130–1
    open punctuation, fully blocked 131–2
personal pronouns 53
personal spelling lists 9–10
perspective 172
persuasive text types 101
phenomena 69
phrases 36–7
    dangling 57
plurals, irregular 4
poetry 116–17
point of view 140–2
portrait 172
possession 21–2
PowerPoint presentations 159–60
practice or *practise* 69
predicate 36, 37

prefixes 7, 16, 46
preparing your talk 157–8
prepositions 55–6
    at the end of sentences 58
present participle 43
present tense 43, 44, 45
presenting an argument 140–3
presenting your talk 158
procedures (text types) 120
pronouns 53
proper nouns 41
prophecy or *prophesy* 70
punctuation 21–34
purpose (of text) 101

question marks 31
quiet or *quite* 70
quotation marks 31–3
quotes, short 32

reading paths 172
recounts (text types) 106–7, 122
recurrence 70
reflection 142
reflexive pronouns 53
relating verbs 44
relative pronouns 53
reports 122–4
responses 151–4
résumés 138–9
    and covering letter 135
reviews 151–4
round or *around* 62
run-on sentences 58–9

salience 173
scripts
    drama 110–12
    film and television 113–15
semicolons 33–4
sentences 36
    run-on 58–9
    types of 37
    verbless 59
    word order 39, 46
shall or *will* 70–1
shapes (images) 171
shots (films) 180–2
    composition 181
    sizes 181
should or *would* 71
should of or *should have* 71
simple sentence 37
small group work 161
social distance 173
speech marks 31–3
spelling 1–18
    American and British 11
    computer spell checks 12–13
    dictionaries 20
    memorising 8–9

personal spelling lists 9–10
   reform of 12
split infinitives 59
structural words 52–6
subject (sentence) 36, 37
subjunctive mood 46
subordinating conjunctions 55
suffixes 6, 17–18, 46
superlative adjectives 50
syntax 35

tail (news report) 126
talk, giving a 156
   making an electronic
      presentation 159–60
   preparing your talk 157–8
   presenting your talk 158
   six signals every audience wants
      to hear 156–7
television and film documentaries 124
television and film scripting 113–15
text types 99–104
   argument 101, 104, 140–54
   discussion 144–5
   and essay writing 103–4
   imaginative 101, 105–17
   information 101, 104, 118–38
   oral 156–67
   visual 175–82
texture (images) 173
that, *who* or *which* 72–3
'the' (definite article) 56

the reason is because, the reason why 71
there's or *theirs* 72
they're, their or *there* 71
though or *although* 61
till or *until* 72
to, too and *two* 72
'to be' 44–5
'to do' 45
'to have' 45
transitive verbs 43–4
treatment (documentary
   overview) 124
try and or *try to* 72
two, too and *to* 72
typography 173

uninterested or *disinterested* 65
unique 72
until or *till* 72
upper case letters 23
usage conventions 60–74

vanishing point 174
vectors 174
verb–noun agreement 47–8
verbless sentences 59
verbs 43–6
   forms 43
   moods 45–6
   prefixes 46
   recognising 46
   suffixes 18, 46

transitive and intransitive 43–4
   types of 44–5
vertical axis 174
viewing angle 174
visual images 168–74
visual text types 175–82

websites 177
   conventions 178
   terminology 179
which, who or *that* 72–3
while or *whilst* 72
who, which or *that* 72–3
who or *whom* 73–4
who's or *whose* 74
will or *shall* 70–1
word order (sentences) 39, 46
words
   content 41–52
   meaning 2, 20
   origin 2–3, 15–18
   patterns in 1, 3
   structural 52–6
   usage of 60–74
work experience applications 136–7
would or *should* 71
would of or *would have* 74
written text types 101–2

yet, however or *but* 62
you're or *your* 74